Python for Tweens and Teens

Learn Computational and Algorithmic Thinking

By
Aristides S. Bouras
Loukia V. Ainarozidou

Full Color Edition

Python for Tweens and Teens
Full Color Edition

Copyright © by Aristides S. Bouras and Loukia V. Ainarozidou
http://www.bouraspage.com

ISBN-13: 978-1543127942
ISBN-10: 1543127940

Python and PyCon are trademarks or registered trademarks of the Python Software Foundation.

Eclipse™ is a trademark of Eclipse Foundation, Inc.

PyDev is a trademark of Appcelerator.

Oracle and Java are registered trademarks of Oracle and/or its affiliates.

PHP is a copyright of the PHP Group.

The following are either registered trademarks or trademarks of Microsoft Corporation in the United States and/or other countries: Microsoft, Windows, Visual Basic, and Visual C#.

Mazda and Mazda 6 are trademarks of the Mazda Motor Corporation or its affiliated companies.

Ford and Ford Focus are trademarks of the Ford Motor Company.

Other names may be trademarks of their respective owners.

All rights reserved. No part of this book may be reproduced or transmitted in any form or by any means, mechanical or electronic, including photocopying, recording, or by any information storage and retrieval system, without written permission from the authors.

Warning and Disclaimer

This book is designed to provide information about learning "Algorithmic Thinking," mainly through the use of Python programming language. Every effort has been taken to make this book compatible with all releases of Python 3.x, and it is almost certain to be compatible with any future releases of Python.

The information is provided on an "as is" basis. The authors shall have neither liability nor responsibility to any person or entity with respect to any loss or damages arising from the information contained in this book or from the use of the files that may accompany it.

This book is dedicated to all the kids who believe they can change the world for the better.

Table of Contents

Preface 15
    About the Authors 15
    Acknowledgments 16
    Who Should Buy This Book? 16
    Where to Find Answers to Review Questions and Exercises 16
    How to Report Errata 16
    Conventions Used in This Book 17

Chapter 1 How a Computer Works 19
    1.1   Introduction 19
    1.2   What is Hardware? 19
    1.3   What is Software? 20
    1.4   How a Computer Executes (Runs) a Program 20
    1.5   Compilers and Interpreters 21
    1.6   What is Source Code? 22
    1.7   Review Questions: True/False 22
    1.8   Review Questions: Multiple Choice 23
    1.9   Review Questions 24

Chapter 2 Python and Integrated Development Environments (IDEs) 25
    2.1   What is Python? 25
    2.2   How Python Works 25
    2.3   How to Set Up Python 25
    2.4   Integrated Development Environments 26
    2.5   IDLE 26
    2.6   How to Set Up IDLE 26
    2.7   Eclipse 27
    2.8   How to Set up Eclipse 27
    2.9   Review Questions 31

Chapter 3 Basic Algorithmic Concepts 33
    3.1   What is an Algorithm? 33
    3.2   The Algorithm for Making a Cup of Tea 33
    3.3   Okay about Algorithms. But what is a Computer Program Anyway? 34
    3.4   The Three Parties! 34
    3.5   The Three Main Stages Involved in Creating an Algorithm 34
    3.6   What are "Reserved Words"? 35
    3.7   Your First Python Program 35
    3.8   What is the Difference between a Syntax Error, a Logic Error, and a Runtime Error? 36

3.9 What Does "Debugging" Mean? 37
3.10 Commenting Your Code 37
3.11 Review Questions: True/False 38
3.12 Review Questions: Multiple Choice 38
3.13 Review Questions 39

Chapter 4 Variables and Constants 41

4.1 What is a Variable? 41
4.2 How Many Types of Variables Exist? 43
4.3 Rules for Naming Variables in Python 43
4.4 What Does the Phrase "Declare a Variable" Mean? 44
4.5 Review Questions: True/False 44
4.6 Review Questions: Multiple Choice 45
4.7 Review Exercises 46
4.8 Review Questions 46

Chapter 5 Handling Input and Output 47

5.1 Which Statement Outputs Messages and Results to a User's Screen? 47
5.2 How to Alter the Default Behavior of a `print` Statement 48
5.3 Which Statement Lets the User Enter Data? Which Statement Prompts the User to Enter Data? 51
5.4 Review Questions: True/False 53
5.5 Review Questions: Multiple Choice 53
5.6 Review Questions 53

Chapter 6 Operators 55

6.1 The Value Assignment Operator 55
6.2 Arithmetic Operators 56
6.3 What is the Precedence of Arithmetic Operators? 57
6.4 Compound Assignment Operators 58
    Exercise 6.4.1 — Which Python Statements are Syntactically Correct? 59
    Exercise 6.4.2 — Finding Variable Types 59
6.5 String Operators 60
    Exercise 6.5.1 — Concatenating Names 60
6.6 Review Questions: True/False 61
6.7 Review Questions: Multiple Choice 61
6.8 Review Exercises 63
6.9 Review Questions 64

Chapter 7 Using IDLE 65

7.1 Introduction 65
7.2 IDLE - Creating a New Python Module 65
7.3 IDLE - Writing and Executing a Python Program 67

| 7.4 | IDLE - Finding Runtime and Syntax Errors | 69 |

Chapter 8 Using Eclipse ... 71

8.1	Introduction	71
8.2	Eclipse - Creating a New Python Project	71
8.3	Eclipse - Writing and Executing a Python Program	76
8.4	Eclipse - Finding Runtime and Syntax Errors	78

Chapter 9 Writing your First Real Programs ... 81

9.1	Introduction	81
	Exercise 9.1.1 — Calculating the Area of a Rectangle	81
	Exercise 9.1.2 — Calculating the Area of a Circle	82
	Exercise 9.1.3 — Fahrenheit to Celsius	83
9.2	Review Exercises	83
9.3	Review Questions	84

Chapter 10 Manipulating Numbers ... 85

10.1	Introduction	85
10.2	Useful Functions and Methods	85
10.3	Review Questions: True/False	89
10.4	Review Exercises	89

Chapter 11 Manipulating Strings ... 91

11.1	Introduction	91
11.2	Retrieving Individual Characters from a String	91
11.3	Retrieving a Portion of a String	94
	Exercise 11.3.1 — Displaying a String Backward	95
11.4	Useful Functions and Methods	96
	Exercise 11.4.1 — Creating a Login ID	98
	Exercise 11.4.2 — Switching the Order of Names	98
	Exercise 11.4.3 — Creating a Random Word	99
11.5	Review Questions: True/False	100
11.6	Review Questions: Multiple Choice	101
11.7	Review Exercises	102
11.8	Review Questions	103

Chapter 12 Making Questions ... 105

12.1	Introduction	105
12.2	How to Write Simple Questions	105
	Exercise 12.2.1 — Filling in the Table	106
12.3	Logical Operators and Complex Questions	107
12.4	Python's Membership Operators	109
12.5	What is the Order of Precedence of Logical Operators?	110

12.6	What is the Order of Precedence of Arithmetic, Comparison, and Logical Operators?	110
	Exercise 12.6.1 — Filling in the Truth Table	111
12.7	Converting English Sentences to Boolean Expressions	112
12.8	Review Questions: True/False	114
12.9	Review Questions: Multiple Choice	115
12.10	Review Exercises	116
12.11	Review Questions	117

Chapter 13 Asking Questions - The `if` Structure 119

13.1	The `if` Structure	119
	Exercise 13.1.1 — Find Out What is Displayed	121
	Exercise 13.1.2 — Are you Allowed to Drive a Car?	121
	Exercise 13.1.3 — Finding Minimum and Maximum Values with `if` Structures	122
	Exercise 13.1.4 — Finding the Name of the Heaviest Person	123
13.2	Review Questions: True/False	124
13.3	Review Questions: Multiple Choice	125
13.4	Review Exercises	126
13.5	Review Questions	127

Chapter 14 Asking Questions - The `if-else` Structure 129

14.1	The `if-else` Structure	129
	Exercise 14.1.1 — Finding the Output Message	130
	Exercise 14.1.2 — Who is the Greatest?	130
	Exercise 14.1.3 — Converting Gallons to Liters, and Vice Versa	131
14.2	Review Questions: True/False	132
14.3	Review Questions: Multiple Choice	132
14.4	Review Exercises	134

Chapter 15 Asking Questions - The `if-elif` Structure 135

15.1	The `if-elif` Structure	135
	Exercise 15.1.1 — Find Out What is Displayed	136
	Exercise 15.1.2 — Counting the Digits	137
	Exercise 15.1.3 — The Days of the Week	138
	Exercise 15.1.4 — Where is the Tollkeeper?	139
15.2	Review Questions: True/False	140
15.3	Review Exercises	140

Chapter 16 Asking Questions - Nested Structures 145

16.1	Nested Decision Structures	145
	Exercise 16.1.1 — Find Out What is Displayed	146
	Exercise 16.1.2 — Positive, Negative, or Zero?	146
	Exercise 16.1.3 — The Most Scientific Calculator Ever!	147

16.2	Review Questions: True/False	148
16.3	Review Exercises	148
16.4	Review Questions	149

Chapter 17 Doing Loops 151

17.1	What is a Loop Structure?	151
17.2	From Sequence to Loop Structure	151
17.3	Review Questions: True/False	153

Chapter 18 Doing Loops - The while Structure 155

18.1	The while Structure	155
	Exercise 18.1.1 — Counting the Total Number of Iterations	156
	Exercise 18.1.2 — Finding the Sum of Four Numbers	156
	Exercise 18.1.3 — Finding the Sum of Positive Numbers	157
	Exercise 18.1.4 — Finding the Sum of N Numbers	158
	Exercise 18.1.5 — Finding the Sum of an Unknown Quantity of Numbers	159
	Exercise 18.1.6 — Finding the Product of Five Numbers	160
18.2	Review Questions: True/False	160
18.3	Review Questions: Multiple Choice	161
18.4	Review Exercises	163

Chapter 19 Doing Loops - The for Structure 165

19.1	The for Structure	165
	Exercise 19.1.1 — Find Out What is Displayed	167
	Exercise 19.1.2 — Find Out What is Displayed	167
	Exercise 19.1.3 — Finding the Sum of Four Numbers	167
	Exercise 19.1.4 — Finding the Average Value of N Numbers	168
19.2	Review Questions: True/False	169
19.3	Review Questions: Multiple Choice	169
19.4	Review Exercises	171

Chapter 20 Doing Loops - Nested Structures 173

20.1	Nested Loop Structures	173
	Exercise 20.1.1 — Counting the Total Number of Iterations.	174
	Exercise 20.1.2 — Find Out What is Displayed	175
20.2	Review Questions: True/False	175
20.3	Review Questions: Multiple Choice	176
20.4	Review Exercises	178

Chapter 21 Tips and Tricks with Loop Structures 181

21.1	Introduction	181
21.2	Choosing a Loop Structure	181

21.3 The "Ultimate" Rule 182
21.4 Breaking Out of a Loop 184
21.5 Endless Loops and How to Avoid Them 185
21.6 The "From Inner to Outer" Method 186
21.7 Review Questions: True/False 187
21.8 Review Questions: Multiple Choice 188
21.9 Review Exercises 188

Chapter 22 More Exercises with Loop Structures 191

22.1 Exercises of a General Nature with Loop Structures 191
    Exercise 22.1.1 — Finding the Sum of 1 + 2 + 3 + ... + 100 191
    Exercise 22.1.2 — Finding the Product of 2 × 4 × 6 × 8 × 10 192
    Exercise 22.1.3 — Finding the Average Value of Positive Numbers 193
    Exercise 22.1.4 — Counting the Numbers According to Which is Greater 193
    Exercise 22.1.5 — Counting the Numbers According to Their Digits 194
    Exercise 22.1.6 — How Many Numbers Fit in a Sum 195
    Exercise 22.1.7 — Iterating as Many Times as the User Wants 195
    Exercise 22.1.8 — Finding Minimum Value with Loop Structures 197
    Exercise 22.1.9 — Fahrenheit to Kelvin, from 0 to 100 198
    Exercise 22.1.10 — Rice on a Chessboard 198
    Exercise 22.1.11 — Game - Find the Secret Number 199
22.2 Review Exercises 200

Chapter 23 Turtle Graphics 203

23.1 Introduction 203
23.2 The x-y Plane 203
23.3 Where is the Turtle? 205
23.4 Moving Forward and Backward 206
23.5 Turning Left and Right 208
    Exercise 23.5.1 — Drawing a Rectangle 210
    Exercise 23.5.2 — Drawing a Rectangle of Custom Size 211
23.6 Set the Orientation to a Specified Angle 212
23.7 Setting the Delay 213
23.8 Changing Pen's Color and Size 215
23.9 Pulling Turtle's Pen Up or Down 216
    Exercise 23.9.1 — Drawing a House 217
23.10 Moving a Turtle Directly to a Specified Position 219
23.11 Using Decision and Loop Structures with Turtles 221
    Exercise 23.11.1 — Drawing Squares of Different Sizes 225
    Exercise 23.11.2 — Drawing Houses of Different Sizes 226
    Exercise 23.11.3 — Drawing Polygons 229

       Exercise 23.11.4 — Drawing a Star 230

       Exercise 23.11.5 — Drawing Random Stars at Random Positions 231

       Exercise 23.11.6 — Using Decision Structures to Draw Stars 233

  23.12 Review Exercises 234

Chapter 24 Data Structures in Python 239

  24.1 Introduction to Data Structures 239

  24.2 What is a List? 240

       Exercise 24.2.1 — Designing a Data Structure 240

       Exercise 24.2.2 — Designing Data Structures 241

  24.3 Creating Lists in Python 242

  24.4 What is a Tuple? 244

  24.5 Creating Tuples in Python 244

  24.6 How to Get a Value from a List or Tuple 244

       Exercise 24.6.1 — Find What is Displayed 246

       Exercise 24.6.2 — Using a Non-Existing Index in Lists 246

  24.7 How to Alter the Value of a List Element 247

       Exercise 24.7.1 — Find the Error 247

  24.8 How to Iterate Through a List or Tuple 248

       Exercise 24.8.1 — Finding the Sum 249

  24.9 How to Add User-Entered Values to a List 250

       Exercise 24.9.1 — Displaying Words in Reverse Order 251

       Exercise 24.9.2 — Displaying Positive Numbers in Reverse Order 252

       Exercise 24.9.3 — Finding the Sum 252

       Exercise 24.9.4 — Finding the Average Value 253

       Exercise 24.9.5 — Displaying Reals Only 254

       Exercise 24.9.6 — Displaying Odd Indexes Only 255

  24.10 What is a Dictionary? 256

  24.11 Creating Dictionaries in Python 256

  24.12 How to Get a Value from a Dictionary 257

       Exercise 24.12.1 — Using a Non-Existing Key in Dictionaries 257

  24.13 How to Alter the Value of a Dictionary Element 258

       Exercise 24.13.1 — Assigning a Value to a Non-Existing Key 258

  24.14 How to Iterate Through a Dictionary 258

  24.15 Useful Statements, Functions and Methods 260

  24.16 Review Questions: True/False 263

  24.17 Review Questions: Multiple Choice 267

  24.18 Review Exercises 270

  24.19 Review Questions 273

Chapter 25 More Exercises with Data Structures 275

25.1	Simple Exercises with Data Structures	275
	Exercise 25.1.1 — Creating a List with the Greatest Values	275
	Exercise 25.1.2 — On Which Days Was There a Possibility of Snow?	275
	Exercise 25.1.3 — Was There Any Possibility of Snow?	276
25.2	How to Use More Than One Data Structures in a Program	278
	Exercise 25.2.1 — Finding the Average Value	278
	Exercise 25.2.2 — Using a List Along with a Dictionary	279
25.3	Finding Minimum and Maximum Values in Lists	280
	Exercise 25.3.1 — Which Depth is the Greatest?	280
	Exercise 25.3.2 — Which Lake is the Deepest?	281
	Exercise 25.3.3 — Which Lake, in Which Country, Having Which Average Area, is the Deepest?	282
	Exercise 25.3.4 — Which Students are the Shortest?	284
25.4	Searching Elements in Data Structures	285
	Exercise 25.4.1 — Searching in a List That May Contain the Same Value Multiple Times	285
	Exercise 25.4.2 — Display the Last Names of All Those People Who Have the Same First Name	286
	Exercise 25.4.3 — Searching in a Data Structure that Contains Unique Values	286
	Exercise 25.4.4 — Searching for a Given Social Security Number	287
25.5	Review Questions: True/False	288
25.6	Review Exercises	288

Chapter 26 Introduction to Subprograms 291

26.1	What is a Subprogram?	291
26.2	What is Procedural Programming?	291
26.3	What is Modular Programming?	292
26.4	Review Questions: True/False	293
26.5	Review Questions	294

Chapter 27 User-Defined Subprograms 295

27.1	Subprograms that Return Values	295
27.2	How to Call a Function that Returns Values	296
27.3	Subprograms that Return no Values	299
27.4	How to Call a Function that Returns no Values	299
27.5	Formal and Actual Arguments	300
27.6	How Does a Subprogram Execute?	301
27.7	Can Two Subprograms Use Variables of the Same Name?	302
27.8	Can a Subprogram Call Another Subprogram?	303
27.9	Default Argument Values and Keyword Arguments	304
27.10	The Scope of a Variable	305
27.11	Review Questions: True/False	307
27.12	Review Exercises	309
27.13	Review Questions	310

Chapter 28 More Exercises with Subprograms ... 311
28.1 Some More Exercises for Extra Practice ... 311
Exercise 28.1.1 — Back to Basics – Calculating the Sum of Two Numbers ... 311
Exercise 28.1.2 — Calculating the Sum of Two Numbers Using Fewer Lines of Code! ... 311
Exercise 28.1.3 — A Simple Currency Converter ... 312
Exercise 28.1.4 — A More Complete Currency Converter ... 313
Exercise 28.1.5 — Finding the Average Values of Positive Integers ... 314
Exercise 28.1.6 — Roll, Roll, Roll the… Dice! ... 315
28.2 Review Exercises ... 316

Chapter 29 Object-Oriented Programming ... 319
29.1 What is Object-Oriented Programming? ... 319
29.2 Classes and Objects in Python ... 320
29.3 The Constructor and the Keyword `self` ... 322
29.4 Passing Initial Values to the Constructor ... 324
29.5 Class Variables vs Instance Variables ... 325
29.6 Getter and Setter Methods vs Properties ... 328
Exercise 29.6.1 — The Roman Numerals ... 332
29.7 Can a Method Call Another Method of the Same Class? ... 334
Exercise 29.7.1 — Doing Math ... 335
29.8 Class Inheritance ... 336
29.9 Review Questions: True/False ... 339
29.10 Review Exercises ... 340
29.11 Review Questions ... 343

Some Final Words from the Authors ... 345
Index ... 347

Preface

About the Authors

Aristides S. Bouras

Aristides[1] S. Bouras was born in 1973. During his early childhood, he discovered a love of computer programming. He got his first computer at the age of 12, a Commodore 64, which incorporated a ROM-based version of the BASIC programming language and 64 kilobytes of RAM!!!

He holds a degree in Computer Engineering from the Technological Educational Institute of Piraeus, and a Dipl. Eng. degree in Electrical and Computer Engineering from the Democritus University of Thrace.

He worked as a software developer at a company that specialized in industrial data flow and labelling of products. His main job was to develop software applications for data terminals, as well as PC software applications for collecting and storing data on a database server.

He has developed many applications such as warehouse managing systems and websites for companies and other organizations. Nowadays, he works as a high school teacher. He mainly teaches courses in computer networks, programming tools for the Internet/intranets, and databases.

He has written a number of books, mainly about algorithmic and computational thinking through the use of Python, C#, Visual Basic, Java, C++, and PHP programming languages.

He is married to Loukia V. Ainarozidou and they have two children.

Loukia V. Ainarozidou

Loukia V. Ainarozidou was born in 1975. She got her first computer at the age of 13, an Amstrad CPC6128 with 128 kilobytes of RAM and an internal 3-inch floppy disk drive!!!

She holds a degree in Computer Engineering from the Technological Educational Institute of Piraeus, and a Dipl. Eng. degree in Electrical and Computer Engineering from the Democritus University of Thrace.

She worked as a supervisor in the data logistics department of a company involved in the packaging of fruit and vegetables. Nowadays, she works as a high school teacher. She mainly teaches courses in computer networks, computer programming, and digital design.

She has written a number of books, mainly about algorithmic and computational thinking through the use of Python, C#, Visual Basic, Java, C++, and PHP programming languages.

She is married to Aristides S. Bouras and they have two children.

---

1. Aristides (530 BC–468 BC) was an ancient Athenian statesman and general. The ancient historian Herodotus cited him as "the best and most honorable man in Athens." He was so fair in all that he did that he was often referred to as "Aristides the Just." He flourished in the early quarter of Athens's Classical period and helped the Athenians defeat the Persians at the battles of Salamis and Plataea.

Acknowledgments

We would like to express our thanks, with particular gratefulness, to our friend and senior editor Victoria (Vicki) Austin for generously spending her time answering all of our questions—even the foolish ones—and for her assistance in copy editing. Without her, this book might not have reached its full potential. With her patient guidance and valuable and constructive suggestions, she helped us bring this book up to a higher level!

Who Should Buy This Book?

Algorithmic Thinking involves more than just learning code. It is a problem solving process that involves learning *how to* code! This book teaches computational and algorithmic thinking by taking very seriously one thing for granted—that the reader knows absolutely nothing about computer programming!

Python is unquestionably a very popular programming language and this book can help you enter the programming world with Python. With 350 pages (many of which are illustrated), and more than 100 solved and 200 unsolved exercises, over 250 true/false, 100 multiple choice, and 100 review questions (the solutions and the answers to which can be found on the Internet), this book is ideal for kids 10+ and their parents, students, teachers, or for anyone who wants to start learning or teaching computer programming using the proper conventions and techniques.

Where to Find Answers to Review Questions and Exercises

Answers to all of the review questions, as well as the solutions to all review exercises, are available free of charge on the Internet. You can download them from the following address:

http://www.bouraspage.com

How to Report Errata

Although we have taken great care to ensure the accuracy of our content, mistakes do occur. If you find a mistake in this book, either in the text or the code, we encourage you to report it to us. By doing so, you can save other readers from frustration and, of course, help us to improve the next version of this book. If you find any errata, please feel free to report them by visiting the following address:

http://www.bouraspage.com

Once your errata are verified, your submission will be accepted and the errata will be uploaded to our website, and added to any existing list of errata.

Conventions Used in This Book

Following are some explanations on the conventions used in this book. "Conventions" are the standard ways in which certain parts of the text are displayed.

Python Statements

This book uses plenty of examples written in Python language. Python statements are shown in a typeface that looks like this.

```
This is a Python statement
```

Keywords, Variables, Functions, and Arguments within the Text of a Paragraph

Keywords, variables, functions, and arguments are sometimes shown within the text of a paragraph. When they are, the special text is shown in a typeface different from that of the rest of the paragraph. For instance, `first_name = 5` is an example of a Python statement within the paragraph text.

Special Text in Italics

You may notice that some of the special words (the keywords, variables, functions, and arguments) are also displayed in italics. When you see these special words italicized, this means they are general types that must be replaced with the specific name appropriate for your data. For example, a Python statement may be presented as

```
def name (arg1, arg2):
```

This statement is written in *general form* which means that it is not quite complete. This form just shows you how the real statement might look. In order to complete the statement, the keywords *name*, *arg1*, and *arg2* must be replaced with something meaningful. When you use this statement in your program, you might use it in the following form:

```
def display_rectangle (width, height):
```

Three Dots (…) - an Ellipsis

In the general form of a statement you may also notice three dots (…), known as an *ellipsis*, following a list in an example. The dots are not part of the statement. An ellipsis means that you can have as many items in the list as you want. For example, the ellipsis in the general form of the statement

```
display_messages (arg1, arg2, …)
```

shows that the list may contain more than two arguments. When you use this statement in your program, your statement might be something like this:

```
display_messages (message_A, message_B, message_C, message_D)
```

Square Brackets

The general form of some statements or functions may contain square brackets [ ], which mean that the enclosed section is optional. For example, the general form of the statement

```
subject.sort([reverse = True])
```

shows the section `[reverse = True]` can be omitted.

The following two statements produce different results but they are both syntactically correct (that is, they both use the correct syntax):

```
x.sort()
x.sort(reverse = True)
```

The Dark Header

Most of this book's examples are in a typeface that looks like this.

```
                          file_29_2_3
a = 2
b = 3

c = a + b

print(c)
```

The dark header `file_29_2_3` on top shows the name of the file that you must open to test the program. All the examples that contain this header are free of charge on the Internet. You can download them from the following address:

http://www.bouraspage.com

Notices

Very often this book uses notices to help you better understand the meaning of a concept. Notices look like this.

> *Notice*: This typeface designates a note.

Something Already Known or Something to Remember

Very often this book can help you recall something you have already learned (probably in a previous chapter). Other times, it will point out something you should memorize. Reminders look like this:

> *Remember!* This typeface shows something to recall or something that you should memorize.

Chapter 1
How a Computer Works

1.1 Introduction

These days, almost every task requires the use of a computer. In schools, students use computers to search the Internet and to send email. At work, people use them to make presentations, to analyze data, and to communicate with customers. At home, people use computers to play games, to connect to social networks and to chat with other people all over the world. Of course, don't forget smartphones such as iPhones. They are computers as well!

Computers can perform so many different tasks because of their ability to be programmed. In other words, a computer can perform any job that a program tells it to. A *program* is a set of *statements* (often called *instructions* or *commands*) that a computer follows in order to perform a specific task.

Programs are essential to a computer, because without them a computer is a dummy machine that can do nothing at all. It is the program that actually tells the computer what to do and when to do it. On the other hand, the *programmer* is the person who designs, creates, and tests computer programs.

This book introduces you to the basic concepts of computer programming using the Python language.

1.2 What is Hardware?

The term *hardware* refers to all devices or components that make up a computer. If you have ever opened the case of a computer or a laptop you have probably seen many of its components, such as the microprocessor (CPU), the memory, and the hard disk. A computer is not a device but a system of devices that all work together. The basic components of a typical computer system are:

- **The Central Processing Unit (CPU)**

    This is the part of a computer that actually performs all the tasks defined in a program.

- **Main Memory (RAM – Random Access Memory)**

    This is the area in the computer that holds the program (while it is being *executed*, or run) as well as the data that the program is working with. All programs and data stored in this type of memory are lost when you shut down your computer or you unplug it from the wall outlet.

- **Main Memory (ROM – Read Only Memory)**

    ROM or Read Only Memory is a special type of memory which can only be *read* by the computer (but cannot be changed). All programs and data stored in this type of memory are **not** lost when the computer is switched off. ROM usually contains manufacturer's instructions as well as a program called the *bootstrap loader* whose function is to start the operation of computer system once the power is turned on.

- **Secondary Storage Devices**

    This is usually the hard disk, and sometimes (but more rarely) the CD/DVD drive. In contrast to main memory (RAM), this type of memory can hold data for a longer period of time, even if there is no power to the computer. However, programs stored in this memory cannot be directly executed. They must be transferred to a much faster memory; that is, the main memory (RAM).

- **Input Devices**

    Input devices are all those devices that collect data from the outside world and enter them into the computer for processing. Keyboards, mice, and microphones are all input devices.

- **Output Devices**

    Output devices are all those devices that output data to the outside world. Monitors (screens) and printers are output devices.

1.3 What is Software?

Everything that a computer does is controlled by software. There are two categories of software: system software and application software.

- *System software* is the program that controls and manages the basic operations of a computer. For example, system software controls the computer's internal operations. It manages all devices that are connected to it, and it saves data, loads data, and allows other programs to be executed. The three main types of system software are:
    - the *operating system*. Windows, Linux, Mac OS X, Android, and iOS are all examples of operating systems.
    - the *utility software*. This type of software is usually installed with the operating system. It is used to make the computer run as efficiently as possible. Antivirus utilities and backup utilities are considered utility software.
    - the *device driver software*. A device driver controls a device that is attached to your computer, such as a mouse or a graphic card. A device driver is a program that acts like a translator. It translates the instructions of the operating system to instructions that a device can actually understand.
- *Application software* refers to all the other programs that you use for your everyday tasks, such as browsers, word processors, notepads, games, and many more.

1.4 How a Computer Executes (Runs) a Program

When you turn on your computer, the main memory (RAM) is completely empty. The first thing the computer needs to do is to transfer the operating system from the hard disk to the main memory (RAM).

After the operating system is loaded to the main memory (RAM), you can execute (run) any program (application software) you like. This is usually done by clicking, double clicking, or tapping the program's corresponding icon. For example, let's say you click on the icon of your favorite video game. This action orders your computer to load (or copy) the video game from your hard disk to the main memory (RAM) so the CPU can execute it.

> *Remember!* *Programs are stored on secondary storage devices such as hard disks. When you install a program on your computer, the program is copied to your hard disk. Then, when you execute a program, the program is copied (loaded) from your hard disk to the main memory (RAM), and that copy of the program is executed.*

> *Notice:* *The terms "run" and "execute" mean the same thing.*

1.5 Compilers and Interpreters

Computers can only execute programs that are written in a strictly defined computer language. You cannot write a program using a natural language such as English or Greek, because your computer won't understand you!

But what does a computer actually understand? A computer can understand a special low-level language called *machine language*. In machine language, all statements (or commands) are made up of zeros and ones. The following is an example of a program that calculates the sum of two numbers, written in a machine language.

```
0010 0001 0000 0100
0001 0001 0000 0101
0011 0001 0000 0110
0111 0000 0000 0001
```

Shocked? Don't worry, you are not going to write programs this way. Hopefully, no one writes computer programs this way anymore. These days, all programmers write their programs in a "high-level language" and then they use a special program to translate them into a machine language.

> *Notice:* *A high-level language is one that is not limited to a particular type of computer.*

There are two types of programs that programmers use to perform translation: compilers and interpreters.

A *compiler* is a program that translates statements written in a high-level language into a separate machine language program. You can then execute the machine language program any time you wish. After the translation, you do not need the compiler to translate that program again.

An *interpreter* is a program that simultaneously translates and executes the statements written in a high-level language. As the interpreter reads each individual statement in the program, it translates it into machine language code and then directly executes it. This process is repeated for every statement in the program.

1.6 What is Source Code?

The statements (instructions or commands) that the programmer writes in a high-level language are called *source code* or simply *code*. The programmer first types the source code into a program known as a *code editor*, and then uses either a compiler to translate it into a machine language program, or an interpreter to translate and execute it at the same time.

1.7 Review Questions: True/False

Choose **true** or **false** for each of the following statements.

1. Modern computers can perform so many different tasks because they have many gigabytes of RAM.
2. A computer can operate without a program.
3. A hard disk is an example of hardware.
4. Data can be stored in main memory (RAM) for a long period of time, even if there is no power to the computer.
5. Data is stored in main memory (ROM), but programs are not.
6. Speakers are an example of an output device.
7. Windows and Linux are examples of software.
8. A device driver is an example of hardware.
9. A media player is an example of system software.
10. When you turn on your computer, the main memory (RAM) already contains the operating system.
11. When you open your word processing application, it is actually copied from a secondary storage device to the main memory (RAM).
12. In a machine language, all statements (commands) are a sequence of zeros and ones.
13. Nowadays, a computer cannot understand zeros and ones.
14. Nowadays, software is written in a language composed of ones and zeros.
15. "Software" refers to the physical components of a computer.
16. The compiler and the interpreter are software.
17. The compiler translates source code into an executable file.
18. The interpreter creates a machine language program.
19. After the translation, the interpreter is not required anymore.
20. Source code can be executed by a computer without being compiled or interpreted.
21. A program written in machine language requires compilation (translation).
22. A compiler translates a program written in a high-level language.

Chapter 1
How a Computer Works

1.8 Review Questions: Multiple Choice

Select the correct answer for each of the following statements.

1. Which of the following is **not** computer hardware?
    a. a hard disk
    b. a DVD disc
    c. a sound card
    d. the main memory (RAM)

2. Which of the following is **not** a secondary storage device?
    a. a DVD reader/writer device
    b. a hard disk
    c. a USB flash drive
    d. RAM

3. A touch screen is
    a. an input device.
    b. an output device.
    c. both of the above

4. Which of the following is **not** software?
    a. Windows
    b. Linux
    c. iOS
    d. a video game
    e. a web browser
    f. a device driver
    g. All of the above are software.

5. Which of the following statements is correct?
    a. Programs are stored on the hard disk.
    b. Programs are stored on DVD discs.
    c. Programs are stored in main memory (RAM).
    d. All of the above are correct.

6. Which of the following statements is correct?
    a. Programs can be executed directly from the hard disk.
    b. Programs can be executed directly from a DVD disc.
    c. Programs can be executed directly from the main memory (RAM).
    d. All of the above are correct.
    e. None of the above is correct.

7. Programmers can**not** write computer programs in
    a. machine language.
    b. natural language such as English, Greek, and so on.

c. Python.
8. A compiler translates
    a. a program written in machine language into a high-level language program.
    b. a program written in a natural language (English, Greek, etc.) into a machine language program.
    c. a program written in a high-level language into a machine language program.
    d. none of the above
    e. all of the above
9. Machine language is
    a. a language that machines use to communicate with each other.
    b. a language made up of numerical instructions that is used directly by a computer.
    c. a language that uses English words for operations.
10. If two identical statements are one after the other, the interpreter
    a. translates the first one and executes it, then it translates the second one and executes it.
    b. translates the first one, then translates the second one, and then executes them both.
    c. translates only the first one (since they are identical) and then executes it two times.

1.9 Review Questions

Answer the following questions.
1. What is hardware?
2. List the six basic components of a typical computer system.
3. What does the "bootstrap loader" program?
4. Which part of the computer actually executes the programs?
5. Which part of the computer holds the program and its data while the program is running?
6. Which parts of the computer hold data for a long period of time, even when there is no power to the computer?
7. What do you call the device that collects data from the outside world and enters it into the computer?
8. List some examples of input devices.
9. What do you call the device that outputs data from the computer to the outside world?
10. List some examples of output devices.
11. What is software?
12. How many software categories are there, and what are their names?
13. A word processing program belongs to what category of software?
14. A device driver belongs to what category of software?
15. What is a compiler?
16. What is an interpreter?
17. What is meant by the term "machine language"?
18. What is source code?

Chapter 2
Python and Integrated Development Environments (IDEs)

2.1   What is Python?

Python is a high-level computer programming language that allows programmers to create applications, web pages, and many other types of software. It is the perfect language for teaching algorithmic thinking and programming, especially at the introductory level. It is widely used in scientific and numeric computing. It is a very flexible and powerful language and its coding style is very easy to understand.

There are millions—probably even billions—of lines of code already written in Python and so many possibilities to re-use code! This is why many people prefer using Python to any other programming language. This is also a very good reason why you should actually learn Python!

2.2   How Python Works

Computers do not understand natural languages such as English or Greek, so you need a computer language such as Python to communicate with them. Python is a very powerful high-level computer language. The Python interpreter (or, actually, a combination of a compiler and an interpreter) converts Python language to a machine language that computers can actually understand.

2.3   How to Set Up Python

To install Python, you must download it for free from the following address:

https://www.python.org/downloads/

Python is available for Windows, Linux/UNIX, Mac OS X, and many more. Choose the version that is suitable for your platform and download the latest version. This book shows how to install Python on a Windows platform. When the download completes, run the setup.

In the popup window that appears (see **Figure 2-1**), check the field "Add Python 3.6 to PATH" and click on the "Install Now" option.

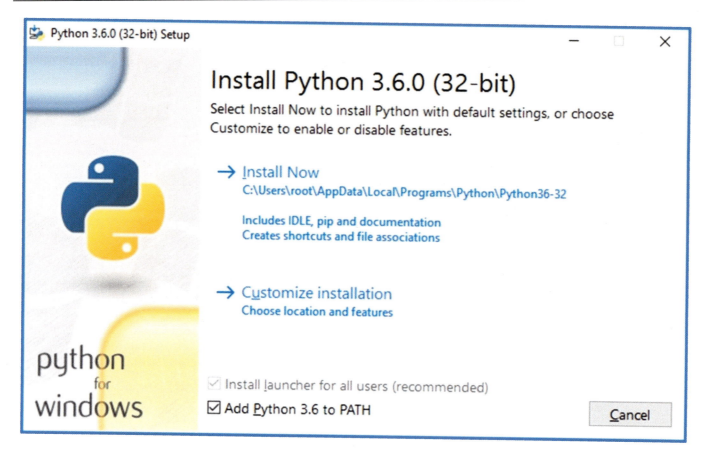

Figure 2-1 The "Python Setup" window

When the installation process is complete, click on the "Close" button.

2.4 Integrated Development Environments

An *Integrated Development Environment*, or *IDE*, is a type of software that includes all the basic tools programmers need to write and test programs. An IDE usually contains a source code editor, a compiler or interpreter, and a *debugger*. IDLE and Eclipse are two example of IDEs that let programmers write and execute their source code.

> *Notice: A "debugger" is a tool that helps programmers to find and correct many of their mistakes.*

2.5 IDLE

IDLE is an IDE that provides a very simple environment suitable for beginners, especially in an educational setting. Using IDLE, novice programmers can easily write and execute their Python programs!

2.6 How to Set Up IDLE

You don't have to install IDLE since it has already been installed in your system. When did that happen? It happened when you installed Python, following the steps described in paragraph 2.3! In Chapter 7, however, you will learn how to use IDLE to write Python programs and execute them. You'll also learn so many tips and tricks that will be useful in your first steps as a budding programmer!

2.7 Eclipse

Eclipse is an IDE that provides a great set of tools for many programming languages such as Java, C, C++, and PHP. Eclipse lets you create applications as well as websites, web applications and web services. Using plugins that are installed separately, Eclipse can support Python or even other languages such as Perl, Lisp, or Ruby.

Eclipse is not a simple code editor. Eclipse can indent lines, match words and brackets, and highlight errors in source code. It also provides automatic code, which means that as you type, it displays a list of possible completions. The IDE also provides hints to help you analyze your code and find any potential problems. It even suggests some simple solutions to fix those problems.

Eclipse is free of charge and open source (which means it's available to the general public). It has a large community of users and developers all around the world.

> ***Notice:*** *You can use Eclipse not only to write but also to execute your programs directly from its environment.*

2.8 How to Set up Eclipse

First of all, if you have decided to use IDLE instead of Eclipse, you can skip reading this paragraph!

If you insist, however, and wish to install Eclipse, you can download it free of charge from the following address:

https://www.eclipse.org/downloads/eclipse-packages/

The Eclipse IDE can be installed on all operating systems that support Java, from Windows to Linux to Mac OS X systems. On the Eclipse web page, there is a dropdown list that lets you choose the required platform (Windows, Linux, or Mac OS X). Choose the platform that matches yours. This book shows the process of installing Eclipse on a Windows platform.

From all the "Package Solutions" available on eclipse.org, select and download the one called "Eclipse IDE for Java Developers." Don't worry, you are not going to learn Java! When the download is complete, unzip the corresponding file to "C:\".

Locate the file "C:\eclipse\eclipse.exe" and execute it.

> ***Notice:*** *It is advisable to create a desktop shortcut that points to "C:\eclipse\eclipse.exe" for easier access.*

Notice*: Eclipse is written mostly in Java. During installation, you may get the following message. This means that the Java Virtual Machine (JVM) was not found on your system.*

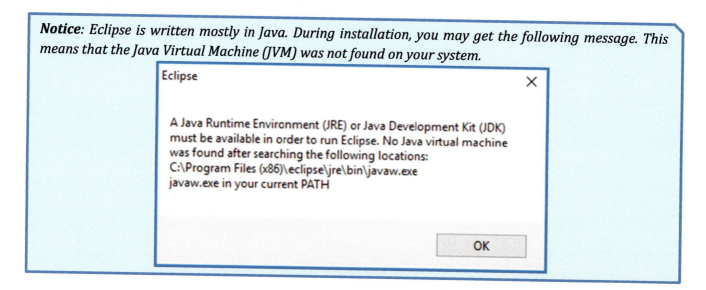

Notice*: You can download Java Virtual Machine (JVM) free of charge from the following address: https://java.com/en/download/*

The first screen in Eclipse prompts you to select the workspace directory (folder). You can keep the proposed folder that appears there and check the field "Use this as the default and do not ask again," as shown in **Figure 2-2**.

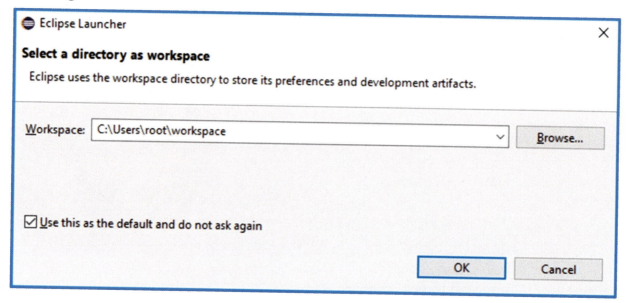

Figure 2-2 Selecting the workspace folder (directory)

Notice*: The folder proposed on your computer may differ from the one in **Figure 2-2** depending on the versions of Eclipse or Windows that you have.*

When the Eclipse environment opens, it should appear as shown in **Figure 2-3**.

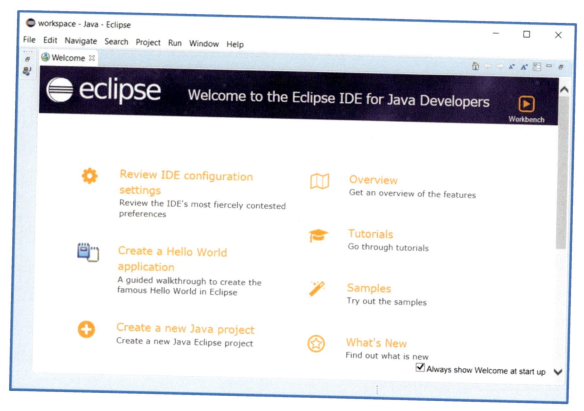

Figure 2-3 The Eclipse IDE

Now it's time to configure Eclipse so it will support Python. From the main menu, select "Help→Eclipse Marketplace". In the popup window that appears, search for the keyword "PyDev" as shown in **Figure 2-4**. Locate the plugin "PyDev – Python IDE for Eclipse" and click on the "Install" button.

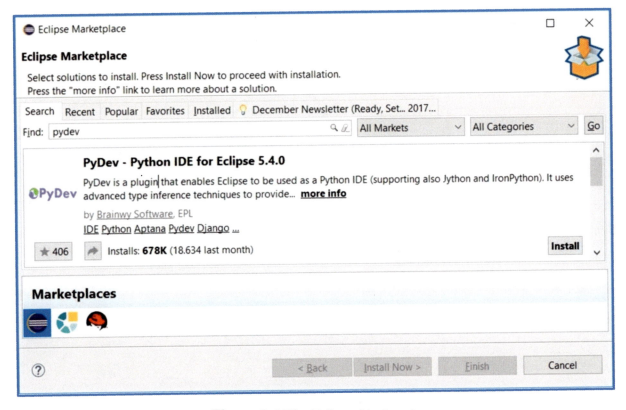

Figure 2-4 The Eclipse Marketplace

In the next window, leave all features checked and click on the "Confirm" button.

When the license agreement pops up (**Figure 2-5**), you must read and accept its terms. Click on the "Finish" button.

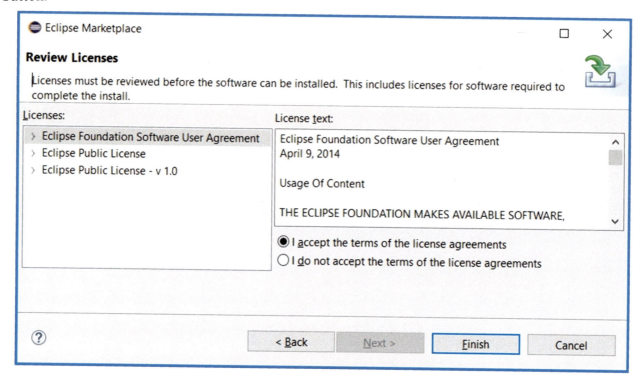

Figure 2-5 The License agreement

During the installation process you may receive a prompt asking you if you trust the "Brainwy Software" certificate as shown in **Figure 2-6**. You must check the corresponding field and click on the "OK" button.

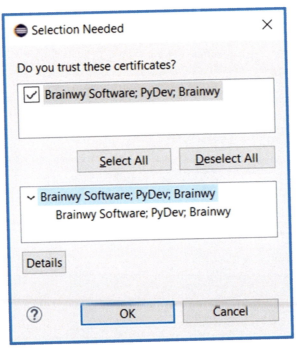

Figure 2-6 The "Brainwy Software" certificate

When the installation is complete, you will be prompted to restart Eclipse in order for the changes to take effect. Click on the "Yes" button.

Eclipse has been configured properly! Now it's time to conquer the world of Python!

2.9 Review Questions

Answer the following questions.
1. What is Python?
2. What are some of the possible uses of Python?
3. What is an Integrated Development Environment (IDE)?
4. What are IDLE and Eclipse?

Chapter 3
Basic Algorithmic Concepts

3.1 What is an Algorithm?

In technical terms, an *algorithm*[1] is a strictly defined finite sequence of well-defined statements (instructions or commands) that provides the solution to a problem. In other words, an algorithm is a step-by-step procedure to solve a given problem. The term "finite" means that the algorithm must reach an end point and cannot run forever.

You can find algorithms everywhere in real life, not just in computer science. For example, the process for preparing toast or a cup of tea can be expressed as an algorithm. You must follow certain steps, in a certain order, in order to achieve your goal.

3.2 The Algorithm for Making a Cup of Tea

The following is an algorithm for making a cup of tea.

1. Put the teabag in a cup.
2. Fill the kettle with water.
3. Boil the water in the kettle.
4. Pour some of the boiled water into the cup.
5. Add milk to the cup.
6. Add sugar to the cup.
7. Stir the tea.
8. Drink the tea.

As you can see, certain steps must be followed. These steps are in a specific order, even though some of the steps could be rearranged. For example, steps 5 and 6 could be reversed. You could add the sugar first, and the milk afterwards.

> ***Notice:*** *Keep in mind that the order of some steps can probably be changed but you can't move them far away from where they should be. For example, you can't move step 3 ("Boil the water in the kettle.") to the end of the algorithm, because you will end up drinking a cup of iced tea which is totally different from your initial goal!*

---

1. The word "algorithm" derives from the word "algorism" and the Greek word "arithmos". The word "algorism" comes from the Latinization of the name of Al-Khwārizmī[2] whereas the Greek word "arithmos" means "number."

2. Muḥammad ibn Al-Khwārizmī (780–850) was a Persian mathematician, astronomer, and geographer. He is considered one of the fathers of algebra.

3.3 Okay about Algorithms. But what is a Computer Program Anyway?

A *computer program* is nothing more than an algorithm that is written in a language that computers can understand, like Python, Java, C++, or C#.

A computer program cannot actually *make* you a cup of tea or cook your dinner, although an algorithm can guide you through the steps to do it yourself. However, programs can (for example) be used to calculate the average value of a set of numbers, or to find the maximum value among them. Artificial intelligence programs can even play chess or solve logic puzzles.

3.4 The Three Parties!

There are always three parties involved in an algorithm—the one that writes the algorithm, the one that executes it, and the one that uses or enjoys it.

Let's take an algorithm for preparing a meal, for example. Someone writes the algorithm (the author of the recipe book), someone executes it (probably your mother, who prepared the meal following the steps from the recipe book), and someone uses it (probably you, who enjoys the meal).

Now consider a real computer program. Let's take a video game, for example. Someone writes the algorithm in a computer language (the programmer), someone or something executes it (usually a laptop or a computer), and someone else uses it or plays with it (the *user*).

Be careful, because sometimes the term "programmer" is confused with the term "user". When you *write* a computer program, for that period of time you are "the programmer." However, when you *use* your own program, you are "the user."

3.5 The Three Main Stages Involved in Creating an Algorithm

Three main stages are involved in creating an algorithm: *data input*, *data processing*, and *results output*. This order is specific and cannot be changed.

Consider a computer program that finds the average value of three numbers. First, the program must prompt (ask) the user to enter the numbers (the data input stage). Next, the program must calculate the average value of the numbers (the data processing stage). Finally, the program must display the result on the computer's screen (the results output stage).

Let's take a look at these stages in more detail.

First stage – Data input
1. Prompt the user to enter a number.
2. Prompt the user to enter a second number.
3. Prompt the user to enter a third number.

Second stage – Data processing
4. Calculate the sum of the three numbers.
5. Divide the sum by 3.

Third stage – Results output
6. Display the result on the screen.

Chapter 3
Basic Algorithmic Concepts

In some rare situations, the input stage may be absent and the computer program may consist of only two stages. For example, consider a computer program that is written to calculate the following sum.

$$1 + 2 + 3 + 4 + 5$$

In this example, the user must enter no values at all because the computer program knows exactly what to do. It must calculate the sum of the numbers 1 to 5 and then display the value of 15 on the user's screen. The two required stages (data processing and results output) are shown here.

First stage – Data input

Nothing to do

Second stage - Data processing

1. Calculate the sum of 1+2+3+4+5.

Third stage – Results output

2. Display the results on the screen.

However, what if you want to let the user decide the upper limit of that sum? What if you want to let the user decide whether to sum the numbers 1 to 10 or the numbers 1 to 20? In that case, the program must include an input stage at the beginning of the program to let the user enter that upper limit. Once the user enters that upper limit, the computer can calculate the result. The three required stages are shown here.

First stage – Data input

1. Prompt the user to enter a number.

Second stage – Data processing

2. Calculate the sum 1 + 2 + … (up to and including the upper limit the user entered).

Third stage – Results output

3. Display the results on the screen.

For example, if the user enters the number 6 as the upper limit, the computer would find the result of 1 + 2 + 3 + 4 + 5 + 6.

3.6 What are "Reserved Words"?

In a computer language, a *reserved word* (or *keyword*) is a word that has a strictly predefined meaning—it is reserved for special use and cannot be used for any other purpose. For example, the words `if`, `while`, `elif`, and `for` in Python all have predefined meanings so they cannot be used for any other purposes.

> **Notice:** Reserved words exist in all high-level computer languages. However, each language has its own reserved words. For example, the reserved word `elif` in Python is written as `else if` in C++, C#, PHP, and Java.

3.7 Your First Python Program

A Python program is nothing more than a text file that includes Python statements. Python programs can even be written in your text editor application! Keep in mind, though, that using IDLE or Eclipse to write Python programs is a much better solution because all of their included features can make your life easier.

Here is a very simple Python program that displays just three messages on the screen.

```python
print("Hello World!")
print("Hello people.")
print("The End")
```

> *Notice:* A Python source code is saved on your hard disk with the default .py file extension.

3.8 What is the Difference between a Syntax Error, a Logic Error, and a Runtime Error?

When programmers write code in a high-level language there are three types of errors that might happen: syntax errors, logic errors, and runtime errors.

A *syntax error* is a mistake such as a misspelled keyword, a missing punctuation character, or a missing closing bracket. Some IDEs, such as Eclipse, detect these errors as you type and underline the erroneous statements with a wavy red line. If you try to execute a Python program that contains a syntax error, you will get an error message on your screen and the program won't execute. You must correct any errors and then try to execute the program again.

A *logic error* is an error that prevents your program from doing what you expected it to do. With logic errors you get no warning at all. Your code compiles and runs but the result is not the expected one. Logic errors are hard to detect. You must review your program thoroughly to find out where your error is. For example, consider a Python program that prompts the user to enter three numbers, and then calculates and displays their average value. In this program, however, the programmer made a typographic error (a "typo"); one of his or her statements divides the sum of the three numbers by 5, and not by 3 as it should. Of course the Python program executes as normal, without any error messages, prompting the user to enter three numbers and displaying a result, but obviously not the correct one! It is the programmer who has to find and correct the erroneously written Python statement, not the computer or the interpreter! Computers are not that smart after all!

A *runtime error* is an error that occurs during the execution of a program. A runtime error can cause a program to end abruptly or even cause system shut-down. Such errors are the most difficult errors to detect. There is no way to be sure, before executing the program, whether this error is going to happen, or not. You can suspect that it may happen though! For example, running out of memory or a division by zero causes a runtime error.

> *Notice:* A logic error can be the cause of a runtime error!

> *Notice:* Logic errors and runtime errors are commonly referred to as "bugs," and are often found during the debugging process, before the software is released. When runtime errors are found after a software has been released to the public, programmers often release patches, or small updates, to fix the errors.

3.9 What Does "Debugging" Mean?

Debugging is the process of finding and reducing the number of defects (*bugs*) in a computer program in order to make it perform as expected. There is a myth about the origin of the term "debugging." In 1940, while Grace Hopper[3] was working on a Mark II Computer at Harvard University, her associates discovered a bug (a moth) stuck in a relay (an electrically operated switch). This bug was blocking the proper operation of the Mark II computer. So, while her associates where trying to remove the bug, Grace Hopper remarked that they were "debugging" the system!

3.10 Commenting Your Code

When you write a small and easy program, anyone can understand how it works just by reading it line-by-line. However, long programs are difficult to understand, sometimes even by the same person who wrote them.

Comments are extra information that can be included in a program to make it easier to read and understand. Using comments, you can add explanations and other pieces of information, including:

- who wrote the program
- when the program was created or last modified
- what the program does
- how the program works

> **Notice:** Comments are for human readers. Compilers and interpreters ignore any comments you may add to your programs.

However, you should not over-comment. There is no need to explain every line of your program. Add comments only when a particular portion of your program is hard to follow.

In Python, you can add comments using the hash character (#), as shown here.

```
#Created By Bouras Aristides
#Date created: 12/25/2003
#Date modified: 04/03/2008
#Description: This program displays some messages on the screen

print("Hello Zeus!")    #display a message on the screen

#display a second message on the screen
print("Hello Hera!")

#This is a comment         print("The End")
```

---

3. Grace Murray Hopper (1906–1992) was an American computer scientist and US Navy admiral. She was one of the first programmers of the Harvard Mark I computer, and developed the first compiler for a computer programming language known as A-0 and later a second one, known as B-0 or FLOW-MATIC.

As you can see in the preceding program, you can add comments above a statement or at the end of it, but not in front of it. Look at the last statement, which is supposed to display the message "The End." This statement is never executed since it is considered part of the comment.

> *Notice*: Comments are not visible to the user of a program while the program runs.

3.11 Review Questions: True/False

Choose **true** or **false** for each of the following statements.

1. The process for preparing a meal is actually an algorithm.
2. Algorithms are used only in computer science.
3. An algorithm can run forever.
4. In an algorithm, you can relocate a step in any position you wish.
5. Computers can play chess.
6. An algorithm can always become a computer program.
7. Programming is the process of creating a computer program.
8. There are always three parties involved in a computer program: the programmer, the computer, and the user.
9. The programmer and the user can sometimes be the same person.
10. It is possible for a computer program to output no results.
11. Reserved words are all those words that have a strictly predefined meaning.
12. A misspelled keyword is considered a logic error.
13. A program can be executed even though it contains logic errors.
14. Logic errors are caught during compilation.
15. Runtime errors are caught during compilation
16. Syntax errors are the most difficult errors to detect.
17. A program that calculates the area of a triangle but outputs the wrong results contains logic errors.
18. When a program includes no output statements, it contains syntax errors.
19. A program must always contain comments.
20. If you add comments to a program, the computer can more easily understand it.
21. You can add comments anywhere in a program.
22. Comments are not visible to the user of a program.

3.12 Review Questions: Multiple Choice

Select the correct answer for each of the following statements.

1. An algorithm is a strictly defined finite sequence of well-defined statements that
    a. provides the solution to a problem.
    b. can cook you a meal.
    c. none of the above

2. A computer program is
    a. an algorithm.
    b. a sequence of instructions.
    c. both of the above
    d. none of the above
3. When someone prepares a meal, he or she is the
    a. "programmer."
    b. "user."
    c. none of the above
4. Which of the following does **not** belong in the three main stages involved in creating an algorithm?
    a. data production
    b. data input
    c. results output
    d. data processing
5. Which of the following Python statements contains a syntax error?
    a. `print(Hello Poseidon)`
    b. `print("It's me! I contain a syntax error!!!")`
    c. `print("Hello Athena")`
    d. none of the above
6. Which of the following `print()` statements is actually executed?
    a. `#print("Hello Apollo")  #This is executed`
    b. `#This is executed  print("Hello Ares")`
    c. `print("Hello Aphrodite") #This is executed`
    d. none of the above

3.13 Review Questions

Answer the following questions.
1. What is an algorithm?
2. Give the algorithm for making a cup of coffee.
3. Can an algorithm execute forever?
4. What is a computer program?
5. What are the three parties involved in an algorithm?
6. What are the three stages that make up a computer program?
7. Can a computer program be made up of two stages?
8. What is meant by the term "reserved words"?
9. What is a syntax error? Give one example.
10. What is a logic error? Give one example.
11. What is a runtime error? Give one example.

12. What type of error is caused by a misspelled keyword, a missing punctuation character, or a missing closing bracket?
13. What does the term "debugging" mean?
14. Why should a programmer add comments in his or her code?

Chapter 4
Variables and Constants

4.1 What is a Variable?

In computer science, a *variable* is a location in the computer's main memory (RAM) where a program can store a value and change it as the program executes.

Picture a variable as a transparent box in which you can insert and hold one thing at a time. Because the box is transparent, you can also see what it contains. Also, if you have two or more boxes you can give each box a unique name. For example, you could have three boxes, each containing a different number, and you could name the boxes numberA, numberB, and numberC.

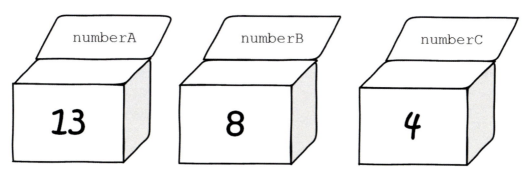

The boxes named numberA, numberB and numberC in this example contain the numbers 13, 8, and 4, respectively. Of course, you can examine or even alter the contained value of each one of these boxes at any time.

Now, let's say that someone asks you to find the sum of the values of the first two boxes and then store the result in the last box. The steps you must follow are:

1. Look at the first two boxes and examine the values they contain.
2. Use your CPU (this is your brain) to calculate the sum (the result).
3. Insert the result (which is the value of 21) in the last box. However, since each box can contain only one single value at a time, the value 4 is actually replaced by the number 21.

The boxes now look like this.

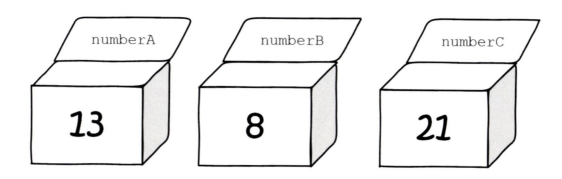

In real computer science, the three boxes are actually three individual regions in main memory (RAM), named numberA, numberB and numberC. You can imagine them as shown here.

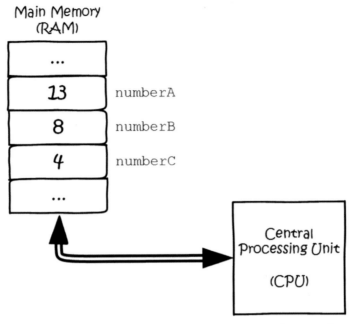

When a program instructs the CPU to add numberA and numberB and store the result to numberC it follows the same three-step process as in the previous example.

1. The numbers 13 and 8 are transferred from the RAM's regions named numberA and numberB to the CPU.

    (This is the first step, in which you examined the values contained in the first two boxes.)

2. The CPU calculates the sum of 13 + 8.

    (This is the second step, in which you used your brain to calculate the sum, or result.)

3. The result, 21, is transferred from the CPU to the RAM's region named numberC, replacing the existing number 4.

    (This is the third step, in which you inserted the result in the last box.)

After execution, the RAM looks like this.

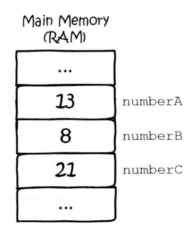

Chapter 4
Variables and Constants

> **Remember!** While a Python program is running, a variable can hold various values, but only one value at a time. When you assign a value to a variable, this value remains stored until you assign a new value, replacing the old one.

A variable is one of the most important elements in computer science because it helps you interact with data stored in the main memory (RAM). Soon, you will learn all about how to use variables in Python.

4.2 How Many Types of Variables Exist?

Many different types of variables exist in most computer languages. The reason for this diversity is the different types of data each variable can hold. Most of the time, variables hold the following types of data.

- **Integers**: An *integer* value is a positive or negative number without any fractional part, such as 5, 135, 0, −25, and −5123.
- **Reals**: A *real* value is a positive or negative number that includes a fractional part, such as 7.56, 5.0, 3.14, and −23.78976. Real values are also known as *floats*.
- **Booleans**[1]: A *Boolean* variable can hold only one of two values: True or False.
- **Characters**: A character is an *alphanumeric* value (a letter, a symbol, or a number), and it is always enclosed in single or double quotes, such as "a", "c", "Hello Zeus", "I am 25 years old", or 'Peter Loves Jane for Ever'. In computer science, a sequence of characters is also known as a *string*.

4.3 Rules for Naming Variables in Python

You must follow certain rules when you choose a name for your variable.

- The name of a variable can contain only English uppercase or lowercase characters, numbers, and the underscore character (_). Examples of variable names are firstName, last_name1, and age.
- Variable names are case sensitive, which means there is a distinct difference between uppercase and lowercase characters. For example, myVAR, myvar, MYVAR, and MyVar are actually four different variables.
- No space characters are allowed. If a variable is described by more than one word, you can use the underscore character (_) between the words. For example, the variable name student age is wrong. Instead, you might use student_age, or even studentAge.

---

1. George Boole (1815–1864) was an English mathematician, philosopher, and logician. He is best known as the architect of what is now called Boolean logic (Boolean algebra), the basis of the modern digital computer.

- A valid variable name can start with a letter, or an underscore. Numbers are allowed, but they cannot be used at the beginning of the variable name. For example, the variable name `1student_name` is not properly written. Instead, you might use something like `student_name1` or `student1_name`.
- A variable name is usually chosen in a way that describes the meaning and the role of the data it contains. For example, a variable that holds a temperature value might be named `temperature`, `temp`, or even `t`.

4.4 What Does the Phrase "Declare a Variable" Mean?

Declaration is the process of reserving a portion in main memory (RAM) for storing the contents of a variable. In many high-level computer languages, the programmer must write a specific statement to reserve that portion in the RAM. In most cases, they even need to specify the variable type so the compiler or the interpreter knows exactly how much space to reserve.

Here are some examples showing how to declare a variable in different high-level computer languages.

Declaration Statement	High-level Computer Language
`Dim sum As Integer`	Visual Basic
`int sum;`	C#, C++, Java, and many more
`sum: Integer;`	Pascal, Delphi
`var sum;`	JavaScript

In Python, there is no need to declare variables. Variables are declared automatically when first used. For example, the statement

`number1 = 0`

declares the variable `number1` and initializes it to 0.

4.5 Review Questions: True/False

Choose **true** or **false** for each of the following statements.

1. A variable is a location in the computer's secondary storage device.
2. A variable can change its content while the program executes.
3. The value 10.5 is an integer.
4. A Boolean variable can hold only one of two values.
5. The value "10.0" enclosed in double quotes is a real value.
6. The name of a variable can contain numbers.
7. A variable can change its name while the program executes.
8. The name of a variable cannot be a number.
9. The name of a variable must always be a descriptive one.
10. The name `student name` is not a valid variable name.
11. In Python, the name of a variable can contain uppercase and lowercase letters.
12. In Python, there is no need to declare a variable.
13. A Python program must use at least one variable.

Chapter 4
Variables and Constants

4.6 Review Questions: Multiple Choice

Select the correct answer for each of the following statements.

1. A variable is a place in
    a. a hard disk.
    b. a DVD disc.
    c. a USB flash drive.
    d. all of the above
    e. none of the above

2. A variable can hold
    a. one value at a time.
    b. many values at a time.
    c. all of the above
    d. none of the above

3. Which one of the following is an integer?
    a. 5.0
    b. −5
    c. "5"
    d. none of the above is an integer.

4. A Boolean variable can hold the value
    a. one.
    b. "True".
    c. True.
    d. none of the above

5. In Python, strings are
    a. enclosed in single quotes.
    b. enclosed in double quotes.
    c. both of the above

6. Which of the following is **not** a valid Python variable?
    a. `city_name`
    b. `cityName`
    c. `cityname`
    d. `city-name`

4.7 Review Exercises

Complete the following exercises.

1. Match each element in the first column with the correct element from the second column.

Value	Data Type
1. "True"	a. Boolean
2. 123	b. Real
3. False	c. String
4. 10.0	d. Integer

2. Match each element in the first column with the correct element from the second column.

Value	Data Type
1. The name of a person	a. Boolean
2. The age of a person	b. Real
3. The result of the division 5/2	c. Integer
4. Is it true or not?	d. String

4.8 Review Questions

Answer the following questions.

1. What is a variable?
2. In which part of a computer are the values of the variables stored?
3. What does the phrase "declare a variable" mean?

Chapter 5
Handling Input and Output

5.1 Which Statement Outputs Messages and Results to a User's Screen?

Python uses the reserved word `print` to display messages or the final results to the user's screen. The following statement:

```python
print("Hello World")
```

displays the message "Hello World" (without the double quotes) to the user's screen.

The `print()` statement can also print two values (also known as "arguments"), as long as you separate them with a comma character. The following code:

```python
name = "Aphrodite"
print(name, "was the Greek goddess of beauty!")
```

displays the message shown in **Figure 5-1**.

Figure 5-1 Two arguments displayed on the screen

If you now suspect that you can have more than two arguments within a `print()` statement, your suspicion is correct! The following example

```python
name1 = "Hera"
name2 = "Zeus"
print(name1, "was the wife of", name2, "and the Queen of Olympus")
```

displays four values, as shown in **Figure 5-2**.

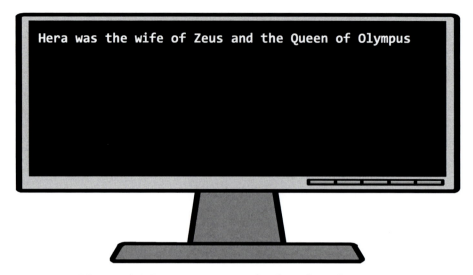

Figure 5-2 Four arguments displayed on the screen

> **Notice:** *If you want to display a string on the screen, the string must be enclosed in single or double quotes. But, if you want to display the **content** of a string variable, this variable must **not** be enclosed in single or double quotes.*

You can also calculate the result of a mathematical expression directly in a `print()` statement. The following statement:

```python
print("The sum of 5 and 6 is", 5 + 6)
```

displays the message shown in **Figure 5-3**.

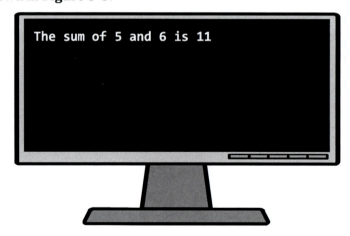

Figure 5-3 The result of an expression displayed on the screen

5.2 How to Alter the Default Behavior of a `print` Statement

As you may have noticed, Python automatically outputs a space between arguments. The following example:

```python
print("Morning", "Evening", "Night")
```

displays what is shown in **Figure 5-4**.

Figure 5-4 The output result displays a space between arguments

Also keep in mind that the following three statements produce the same output result:

```python
print("Morning","Evening","Night")
print("Morning", "Evening", "Night")
print("Morning",    "Evening",    "Night")
```

as shown in **Figure 5-5**.

Figure 5-5 The output result always displays one space between arguments

If you wish to customize the separator character, you need to use a value for argument sep as shown here:

```python
print("Morning", "Evening", "Night", sep = "#")
```

and the output result now becomes as shown in **Figure 5-6**.

Figure 5-6 The output result with a customized separator

Now, look carefully at the following example.

```python
a = "Ares"
print("Hello", a)
print("Halo", a)
```

```python
print("Salut", a)
```

The `print()` statement in Python automatically prints a "line break" after the last argument (variable a); therefore, these three messages are displayed one under the other, as shown in **Figure 5-7**.

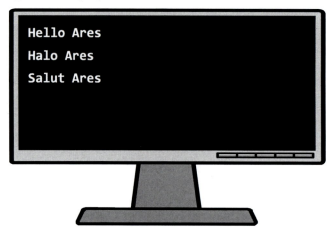

Figure 5-7 The output result displays on three lines

You can alter this behavior by customizing the value of the end argument, as shown here:

```python
a = "Ares"
print("Hello", a, end = " - ")
print("Halo", a, end = " - ")
print("Salut", a)
```

The output result now becomes as shown in **Figure 5-8**.

Figure 5-8 The output result displays on one line

A line break can also be printed by using the special sequence of the character \n as shown here:

```python
print("Hello Ares\nHalo Ares\nSalut Ares")
```

and the output result is shown in **Figure 5-9**.

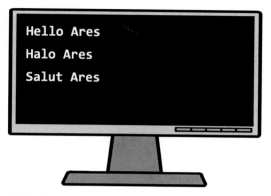

Figure 5-9 The output result displays on three lines

Another interesting sequence of characters is the tab character, \t, which can be used to output a "tab stop." The tab character is useful for aligning output.

```
print("John\tGeorge")
print("Sofia\tMary")
```

The output result now appears in **Figure 5-10**.

Figure 5-10 The output result now displays tabs

Of course, you can accomplish the same result with one single statement.

```
print("John\tGeorge\nSofia\tMary")
```

5.3 Which Statement Lets the User Enter Data? Which Statement Prompts the User to Enter Data?

Do you recall the three main stages (paragraph 3.5) involved in creating an algorithm or a computer program? In the first stage (data input), the computer prompts the user to enter data such as numbers, their name, their address, or their year of birth. In Python, data input is done using the `input()` statement. The following example prompts the user to enter his or her name and then displays a message.

```
name = input("What is your name? ")
print("Hello", name)
```

When the `input()` statement executes, the message "What is your name?" (without the double quotes) is displayed and the flow of execution stops, waiting for the user to enter his or her name. The `print()` statement is not yet executed! As long as the user doesn't enter anything, the computer just waits! When the user finally enters his or her name and hits the "Enter ↵" key, the flow of execution then continues to the next `print()` statement.

To read a float, that is, a number that contains a fractional part, you need to use a slightly different statement. The following example prompts the user to enter the price of a product.

```python
product_price = float(input("Enter product price: "))
```

The following example prompts the user to enter the name and the price of a product.

```python
product_name = input("Enter product name: ")
product_price = float(input("Enter product price: "))
```

If you need to read an integer (that is, a number without a fractional part), you must use another statement. The following example prompts the user to enter his or her age.

```python
age = int(input("What is your age? "))
```

The following code fragment prompts the user to enter his or her name and age and then displays a message.

```python
name = input("What is your name? ")
age = int(input("What is your age? "))
print("Wow, you are already", age, "years old,", name, "!")
```

In this book there is a slight difference between the words "prompts" and "lets." When an exercise says "Write a Python program that **prompts** the user to enter…" this means that you *must* include a prompt message. However, when the exercise says "Write a Python program that **lets** the user enter…" this means that you are not actually required to include a prompt message; that is, it is not wrong to include one but you don't have to! The following example lets the user enter his or her name and age (but does not prompt them to).

```python
name = input()
age = int(input())
print("Wow, you are already", age, "years old,", name, "!")
```

What happens here (when the program is executed) is that the computer displays a text cursor without any prompt message and waits for the user to enter two values – one for name and one for age. The user, though, must be a prophet and guess what to enter! Does he have to enter his name first and then his age, or is it the opposite? So, obviously a prompt message is pretty much required, because it makes your program more user-friendly.

> **Notice**: What is a "user-friendly" program? It's one the user considers a friend instead of an enemy, one that is easy for a novice user. If you want to write user-friendly programs you have to put yourself in the shoes of the user. A user wants the computer to do their job their way, with a minimum of effort. Hidden menus, unclear labels and directions, and misleading error messages can all make a program user-**unfriendly**!

Chapter 5
Handling Input and Output

5.4 Review Questions: True/False

Choose **true** or **false** for each of the following statements.
1. In Python, the word `print` is a reserved word.
2. The `print()` statement can be used to display a message or the content of a variable.
3. When the `input()` statement is executed, the flow of execution is interrupted until the user has entered a value.
4. One single `input()` statement can be used to enter multiple data values.
5. Before data input, a prompt message must always be displayed.

5.5 Review Questions: Multiple Choice

Select the correct answer for each of the following statements.
1. The statement `print("Hello")` displays
   a. the word "Hello" (without the double quotes).
   b. the word "Hello" (including the double quotes).
   c. the content of the variable `Hello`.
   d. none of the above
2. The statement `print("Hello\nHermes")` displays
   a. the message "Hello Hermes" (without the double quotes).
   b. the word "Hello" in one line and the word "Hermes" in the next one (without the double quotes).
   c. the message "HelloHermes" (without the double quotes).
   d. the message "Hello\nHermes" (without the double quotes).
   e. none of the above
3. The statement `data1_data2 = input()`
   a. lets the user enter a value and assigns it to variable `data1`. Variable `data2` remains empty.
   b. lets the user enter a value and assigns it to variable `data1_data2`.
   c. lets the user enter two values and assigns them to variables `data1` and `data2`.
   d. none of the above

5.6 Review Questions

1. What statement is used in Python to display a message?
2. What special sequence of characters is used in Python to output a line break?
3. What special sequence of characters is used in Python to output a tab stop?
4. What statement is used in Python to let the user enter data?
5. A program is called "user-friendly" if it can be used easily by a novice user.
6. Why should a programmer write user-friendly programs?

Chapter 6
Operators

6.1 The Value Assignment Operator

The most commonly used operator in Python is the value assignment operator (=). For example, the Python statement

```
x = 5
```

assigns a value of 5 to variable x.

Be careful though! The (=) sign is not equivalent to the one used in mathematics. In mathematics, the following two lines are equivalent and both are correct!

```
x = 5
5 = x
```

The first one can be read as "*x is equal to 5*" and the second one as "*5 is equal to x.*"

In Python, however, these two statements are **not** equivalent. In Python, the statement x = 5 is correct and can be read as "*assign the value 5 to x*" or "*set x equal to 5.*" The statement 5 = x, though, is considered wrong! Python cannot assign the value of x to 5!

> **Remember!** *In Python, the variable on the left side of the (=) sign represents a region in main memory (RAM) where a value can be stored. Thus, on the left side only one single variable must exist! However, on the right side there can be a number, a variable, a string, or even a complex mathematical expression.*

In **Table 6.1-1** you can find some examples of value assignments.

Table 6.1-1 Examples of Value Assignments

`a = 9`	Assign a value of 9 to variable a.
`b = c`	Assign the content of variable c to variable b.
`d = "Hello Zeus"`	Assign the string "Hello Zeus" without the double quotes to variable d.
`d = a + b`	Calculate the sum of the contents of variables a and b and assign the result to variable d.
`x = a + 1`	Calculate the sum of the content of variable a and 1, and assign the result to variable x. Note that the content of variable a is not altered.
`x = x + 1`	Calculate the sum of the content of variable x and 1, and assign the result back to variable x. In other words, increase variable x by one.

Confused about the last one? Are you thinking about your math teacher right now? What would he/she say if you had written x = x + 1 on the blackboard? Can you personally think of a number that is equal to the number itself plus one? Are you serious? This means that 5 is equal to 6 and 10 is equal to 11!

Obviously, things are different in computer science. The statement x = x + 1 is quite acceptable! It instructs the CPU to retrieve the value of variable x from main memory (RAM), to increase the value by one, and to assign the result to variable x. The old value of variable x is replaced by the new one.

And now that you understand everything, let's see something else. In Python, you can assign a single value to multiple variables with one single statement. The following statement:

```
a = b = c = 4
```

assigns the value 4 to all three variables a, b, and c.

And in Python, you can also assign multiple values to multiple variables with one single statement. This is called *simultaneous assignment*. The following statement:

```
a, b, c = 2, 10, 3
```

assigns the value 2 to variable a, the value of 10 to variable b, and the value of 3 to variable c.

6.2 Arithmetic Operators

Just like every high-level programming language, Python supports almost every type of *arithmetic operator*, as shown in the table that follows. Python can do addition, subtraction, multiplication, and division, among other mathematical operations that we won't go into right now.

Arithmetic Operator	Description
+	Addition
-	Subtraction
*	Multiplication
/	Division
**	Exponentiation

The first two operators are straightforward and need no further explanation.

If you need to multiply two numbers or the content of two variables you have to use the asterisk (*) symbol. For example, if you want to multiply 2 times y, you must write 2 * y. Likewise, to perform a division, you must use the slash (/) symbol. For example, if you want to divide 10 by 2, you must write 10 / 2.

> ***Notice:*** *One other thing that is legal in mathematics (but not in Python) is that you can skip the multiplication operator and write 3y, meaning "3 times y." In Python, however, you must always use an asterisk anywhere a multiplication operation exists. This is one of the most common mistakes novice programmers make when they write mathematical expressions in Python.*

The exponentiation operator (**) raises the number on the left of the operator to the power of the number on the right. For example, the operation

```
f = 2 ** 3
```

calculates 2 to the power of 3 (2^3) and assigns a value of 8 to variable f.

In mathematics, as you may already know, you are allowed to use parentheses (round brackets) as well as braces (curly brackets) and square brackets, as shown in the expression that follows.

$$y = 5\left\{3 + 2\left[4 + 7\left(6 - \frac{4}{3}\right)\right]\right\}$$

However, in Python there is no such thing as braces and brackets. Parentheses are all you have; therefore, the same expression must be written using parentheses instead of braces or brackets.

```
y = 5 * (3 + 2 * (4 + 7 * (6 - 4 / 3)))
```

6.3 What is the Precedence of Arithmetic Operators?

Arithmetic operators follow the same precedence rules as in mathematics, and these are: perform exponentiation operations first, perform multiplication and division operations next, and perform addition and subtraction operations last.

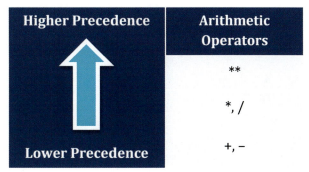

Sometimes multiplication and division operations exist in the same expression. Since both have the same precedence, you must perform them left to right (the same way as you read). This means that the expression

```
y = 6 / 3 * 2
```

is equivalent to $y = \frac{6}{3} \cdot 2$, and assigns a value of 4 to variable y (division is performed before multiplication).

However, if you want to perform the multiplication before the division, you can use parentheses to change the precedence. This means that

```
y = 6 / (3 * 2)
```

is equivalent to $y = \frac{6}{3 \cdot 2}$, and assigns a value of 1 to variable y (multiplication is performed before division).

> **Notice:** All fractions must be written on one single line. For example, $\frac{6}{3}$ must be written as 6 / 3, and $\frac{4x+5}{6}$ must be written as (4 * x + 5) / 6.

The order of operations is summarized as follows:
1. Any operations enclosed in parentheses are performed first.
2. Any exponentiation operations are performed next.
3. Then, any multiplication and division operations are performed from left to right.
4. In the end, any addition and subtraction operations are performed from left to right.

So, let's take the following statement:

```
y = (20 + 3) - 12 + 2 ** 3 / 4 * 3
```

Without looking below, can you calculate the result?

If you found 17, you are correct!

If you didn't, then read below. The sequence of operations is presented in a more graphical way:

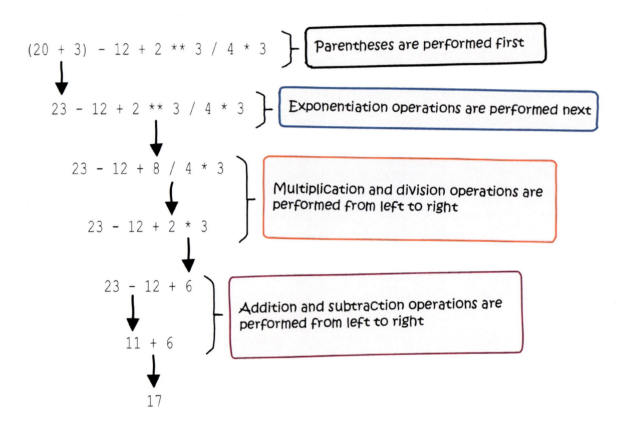

6.4 Compound Assignment Operators

Python offers a special set of operators known as *compound assignment operators*, which can help you write code faster.

Operator	Description
+=	Addition assignment
-=	Subtraction assignment
*=	Multiplication assignment
/=	Division assignment
**=	Exponentiation assignment

Chapter 6
Operators

Let's see some examples:
- the statement `a = a + 1` can be written more concisely as `a += 1`
- the statement `a = a + b` can be written more concisely as `a += b`
- the statement `a = a - 2` can be written more concisely as `a -= 2`

Exercise 6.4.1 – Which Python Statements are Syntactically Correct?

Which of the following Python assignment statements are syntactically correct?

i.	`x = -10`	v.	`x = COWS`	ix.	`x = True`
ii.	`10 = b`	vi.	`a + b = 40`	x.	`y /= 2`
iii.	`a_b = a_b + 1`	vii.	`a = 3 b`	xi.	`y += 1`
iv.	`x = "COWS"`	viii.	`x = "True"`	xii.	`y =* 2`

Solution

i. The statement `x = -10` is **correct**. It assigns the integer value –10 to variable x.

ii. The statement `10 = b` is **wrong**. On the left side of the assignment operator, only variables can exist.

iii. The statement `a_b = a_b + 1` is **correct**. It increases variable `a_b` by one.

iv. The statement `x = "COWS"` is **correct**. It assigns the string (the text) "COWS" without the double quotes to variable x.

v. The statement `x = COWS` is **correct**. It assigns the content of variable COWS to variable x.

vi. The statement `a + b = 40` is **wrong**. On the left side of the assignment operator, only variables can exist.

vii. The statement `a = 3 b` is **wrong**. It should have been written as `a = 3 * b`.

viii. The statement `x = "True"` is **correct**. It assigns the string (the text) "True" without the double quotes to variable x.

ix. The statement `x = True` is **correct**. It assigns the value True to variable x.

x. The statement `y /= 2` is **correct**. This is equivalent to `y = y / 2`.

xi. The statement `y += 1` is **correct**. This is equivalent to `y = y + 1`.

xii. The statement `y =* 2` is **wrong**. It should have been written as `y *= 2`.

Exercise 6.4.2 – Finding Variable Types

What is the type of each of the following variables?

i.	`x = 15`	iii.	`b = "15"`	v.	`b = True`
ii.	`width = "10 meters"`	iv.	`temp = 13.5`	vi.	`b = "True"`

Solution

i. In the statement `x = 15`, the value 15 belongs to the set of integers; therefore, the variable `x` is an integer.

ii. In the statement `width = "10 meters"`, the "10 meters" is a text string; therefore, the `width` variable is a string.

iii. In the statement b = "15", the "15" is a text string (due to the double quotes); therefore, the b variable is a string.
iv. In the statement temp = 13.5, the value 13.5 belongs to the set of real numbers; therefore, the variable temp is real.
v. In the statement b = True, the value True is Boolean; therefore, variable b is a Boolean.
vi. In the statement b = "True", the value "True" is a text string (due to the double quotes); therefore, variable b is a string.

6.5 String Operators

Joining two separate strings into a single one is called *concatenation*. There are two operators that you can use to concatenate (join) strings.

Operator	Description
+	Concatenation
+=	Concatenation assignment

The following example displays "What's up, dude?" without the double quotes on the user's screen.

```
a = "What's up "
b = "dude?"
c = a + b
print(c)
```

The following example displays "Hello my friend!" without the double quotes on the user's screen.

```
a = "Hello"
a += " my friend!"
print(a)
```

Exercise 6.5.1 — Concatenating Names

Write a Python program that prompts the user to enter their first name and last name (assigned to two different variables). It then joins them in a single string (concatenation) and displays them on the user's screen.

Solution

The Python program is shown here.

```
first_name = input("Enter first name: ")
last_name = input("Enter last name: ")

full_name = first_name + " " + last_name
print(full_name)
```

Notice: *Please note the extra space character added between the first and last names.*

Chapter 6
Operators

6.6 Review Questions: True/False

Choose **true** or **false** for each of the following statements.

1. In computer science, the statement x = 5 can be read as *"Variable x is equal to 5."*
2. The value assignment operator assigns the result of an expression to a variable.
3. A string can be assigned to a variable only by using the input() statement.
4. The statement 5 = y assigns the value 5 to variable y.
5. On the right side of a value assignment operator an arithmetic operator must always exist.
6. On the left side of a value assignment operator two variables can exist, but they must be separated with a space character.
7. You cannot use the same variable on both sides of a value assignment operator.
8. The statement x = x + 1 decrements (decreases) variable x by one.
9. Division and multiplication have the higher precedence among the arithmetic operators.
10. When division and multiplication operators co-exist in an expression, multiplication operations are performed before division.
11. The expression 8 / 4 * 2 is equal to 1.0.
12. The expression 4 + 6 / 6 + 4 is equal to 9.0.
13. The statement 2 ** 3 is equal to 9.
14. The expression a + b + c / 3 calculates the average value of three numbers.
15. The statement a += 1 is equivalent to a = a + 1.
16. The statement a = "True" assigns a Boolean value to variable a.
17. The statement a = 2·a doubles the content of variable a.
18. The statements a += 2 and a = a - (-2) are not equivalent.
19. The statement y = "George" + " Malkovich" assigns value "GeorgeMalkovich" (without the double quotes) to variable y.

6.7 Review Questions: Multiple Choice

Select the correct answer for each of the following statements.

1. Which of the following Python statements assigns a value of 10.0 to variable x?
    a. 10.0 = x
    b. x ← 10.0
    c. x = 100 / 10
    d. none of the above

2. In computer science, the statement x = b can be read as
    a. assign the content of variable x to variable b.
    b. variable b is equal to variable x.
    c. assign the content of variable b to variable x.
    d. none of the above

3. The expression `0 / 10 + 2` is equal to
   a. 7.
   b. 2.
   c. 12.
   d. none of the above

4. Which of the following calculates the result of variable x raised to the power of 2?
   a. `y = x * x`
   b. `y = x ** 2`
   c. `y = x * x / x * x`
   d. all of the above

5. Which of the following Python statements is syntactically correct?
   a. `x = 4 * 2 y - 8 / (4 * q)`
   b. `x = 4 * 2 * y - 8 / 4 * q)`
   c. `x = 4 * 2 * y - 8 / (4 */ q)`
   d. none of the above

6. Which of the following Python statements is syntactically correct?
   a. `a ** 5 = b`
   b. `y = a ** 5`
   c. `a =** 5`
   d. none of the above

7. Which of the following Python statements assigns value "George Malkovich" (without the double quotes) to variable x?
   a. `x = "George" + " " + "Malkovich"`
   b. `x = "George" + " Malkovich"`
   c. `x = "George " + "Malkovich"`
   d. all of the above

8. The following code fragment:

   ```
   x = 2
   x += 1
   print(x)
   ```

   displays a value of
   a. 3.
   b. 2.
   c. 1.
   d. none of the above

Chapter 6
Operators

6.8 Review Exercises

Complete the following exercises.

1. Which of the following Python assignment statements are syntactically correct?

   i.   a ← a + 1
   ii. a += b
   iii. a b = a b + 1
   iv. a = a + 1
   v.   a = hello
   vi. a = 40"
   vii. a = b · 5
   viii. a =+ "True"
   ix. fdadstwsdgfgw = 1
   x.   a = a**5

2. What is the type of each of the following variables?

   i.   a = "False"
   ii. w = False
   iii. b = "15 meters"
   iv. weight = "40"
   v.   b = 13.0
   vi. b = 13

3. Match each element from the first column with one element from the second column.

Operation		Result	
i.	1 / 2	a.	100
ii.	4 / 2 * 2	b.	0.5
iii.	0 / 10 * 10	c.	0
iv.	10 / 2 + 3	d.	4
		e.	8
		f.	1
		g.	2

4. What displays on the screen after executing each of the following code fragments?

   i. a = 5
       b = a * a + 1
       print(b + 1)

   ii. a = 9
       b = a / 3 * a
       print(b + 1)

5. What displays on the screen after executing each of the following code fragments?

   i. a = 5
       a += - 5
       print(a)

   ii. a = 5
       a = a - 1
       print(a)

6. What displays on screen after executing each of the following code fragments?

   i. a = 6
       b = 2
       c = a / (b + 1)
       print(c)

   ii. a = 4
       b = 8
       a += 1
       c = a * b
       print(c)

7. What displays on the screen after executing the following code fragment?
   ```
   a = "My name is Alex"
   a += "ander"
   a = a + " the Great"
   print(a)
   ```

8. Fill in the gaps in each of the following code fragments so they display a value of 5.

   i.
   ```
   a = 8
   a = a - ......
   print(a)
   ```

   ii.
   ```
   a = 4
   b = a * 0.5
   b += a
   a = b - ......
   print(a)
   ```

9. What displays on the screen after executing the following code fragment?
   ```
   city = "California"
   California = city
   print(city, California, "California")
   ```

6.9 Review Questions

1. Which symbol is used in Python as a value assignment operator?
2. What are the five most common arithmetic operators supported by Python?
3. Summarize the rules for the precedence of arithmetic operators in Python.
4. Which compound assignment operators does Python support?
5. Which string operators does Python support?

Chapter 7
Using IDLE

7.1 Introduction

So far you have learned some rood basics about Python programs. Now it's time to learn how to enter programs into the computer, execute them, see how they perform, and see how they display the results.

As already stated in paragraph 2.4, an Integrated Development Environment (IDE) is a type of software that enables programmers to both write and execute their source code. IDLE and Eclipse are such examples. This book covers both of them, so it's up to you to choose which one you are going to use. If you decide to use Eclipse, then you don't have to read anything about IDLE. You can skip this chapter and go directly to the next one!

If you don't know which IDE to choose (IDLE or Eclipse), the answer is simple. IDLE is light, simple, and suitable for a novice programmer. It is installed along with Python and needs no further configuration. Eclipse, on the other hand, is more complicated, suitable for programmers who are a bit more advanced.

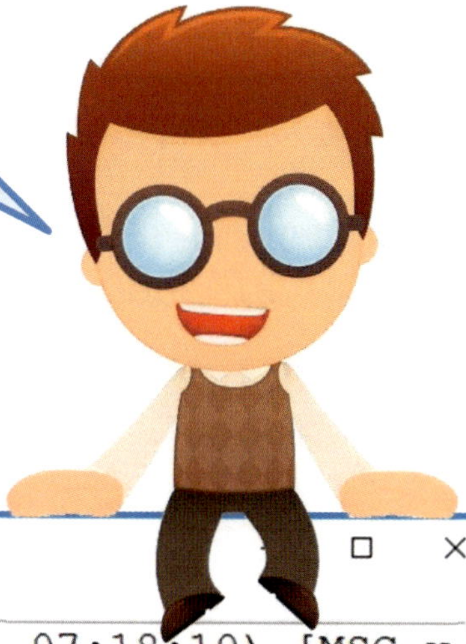

7.2 IDLE - Creating a New Python Module

Once you open IDLE, the first thing you see is the "Python Shell" window, as shown in **Figure 7-1**.

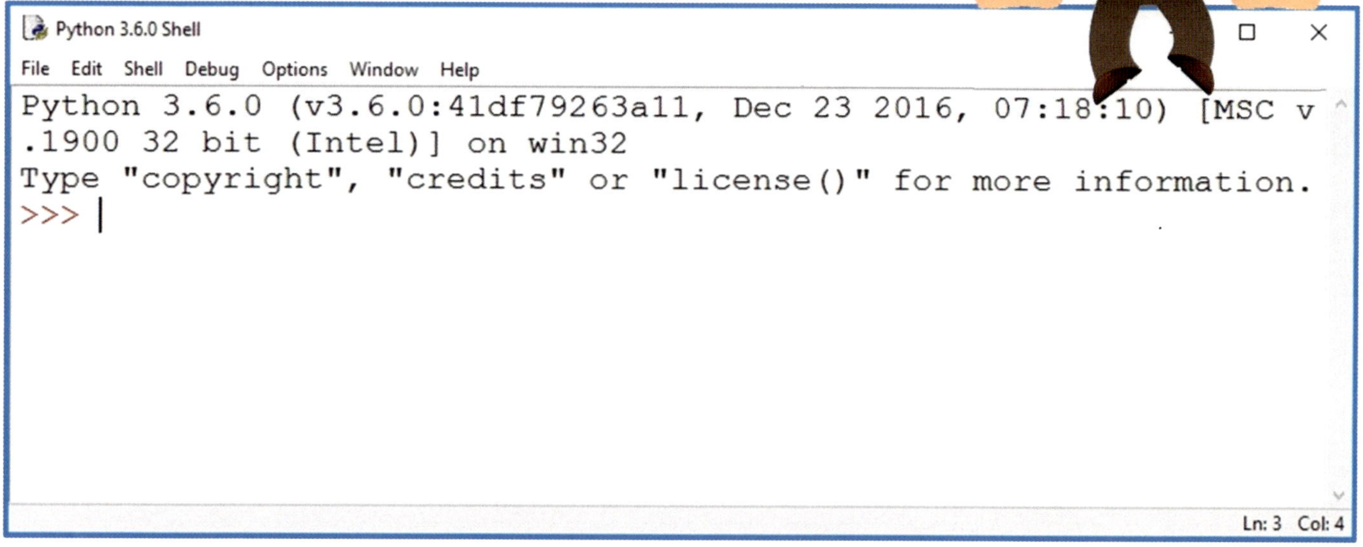

Python 3.6.0 Shell
File Edit Shell Debug Options Window Help
Python 3.6.0 (v3.6.0:41df79263a11, Dec 23 2016, 07:18:10) [MSC v
.1900 32 bit (Intel)] on win32
Type "copyright", "credits" or "license()" for more information.
>>>
Ln: 3 Col: 4

Figure 7-1 The Python Shell

Notice: *To open IDLE on Linux, type into the terminal "idle3" without the double quotes.*

Python Shell is an environment where you can type statements that are immediately executed. For example, if you type 7 + 3 and hit the "Enter ↵" key, the Python Shell will directly display the result of this addition.

However, you should not write a Python program within the Python Shell window. To write a Python program, create a new Python file (known as a Python *module*). From Python Shell's main menu select "File→New File" as shown in **Figure 7-2**.

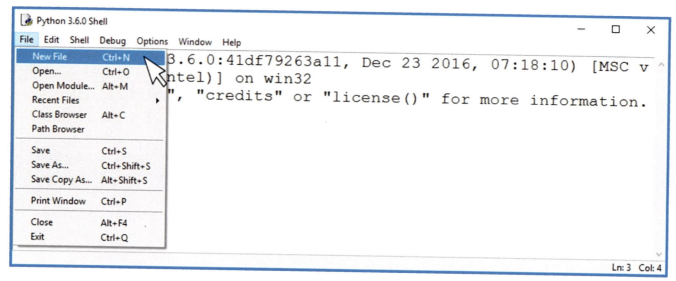

Figure 7-2 Creating a new Python file (module) from within Python Shell

Notice: In simple terms, a "module" is a file containing Python code. Its file name is the module name followed by the .py file extension.

A new window opens, as shown in **Figure 7-3**. This is a new empty module where you will write your Python programs!

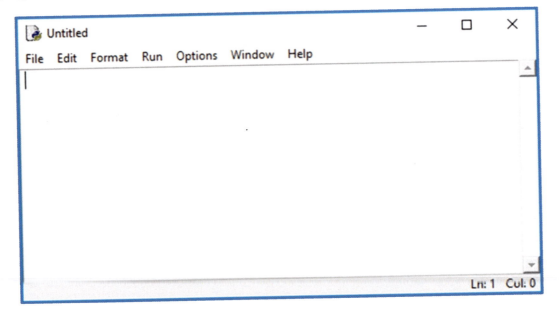

Figure 7-3 A new empty Python module

7.3 IDLE – Writing and Executing a Python Program

You have just seen how to create a new Python module. In the recently created window "Untitled", type the following (terrifying, and quite horrifying!) Python program.

```python
print("Hello World")
```

Now let's try to execute the program! From the main menu, select "Run→Run Module" as shown in **Figure 7-4**, or hit the F5 key.

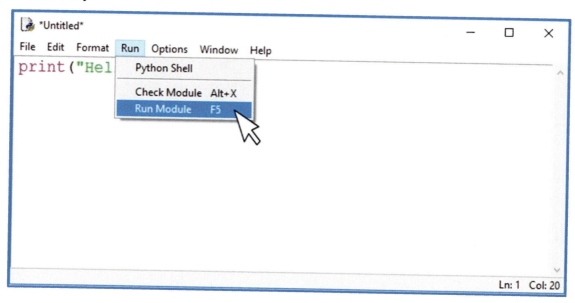

Figure 7-4 Executing your first Python program

IDLE prompts you to save the source code. Click on the "OK" button, select a folder and a filename for your first program, and click on the "Save" button. The Python program is saved, executed, and then the output is displayed in the Python Shell window, as shown in **Figure 7-5**.

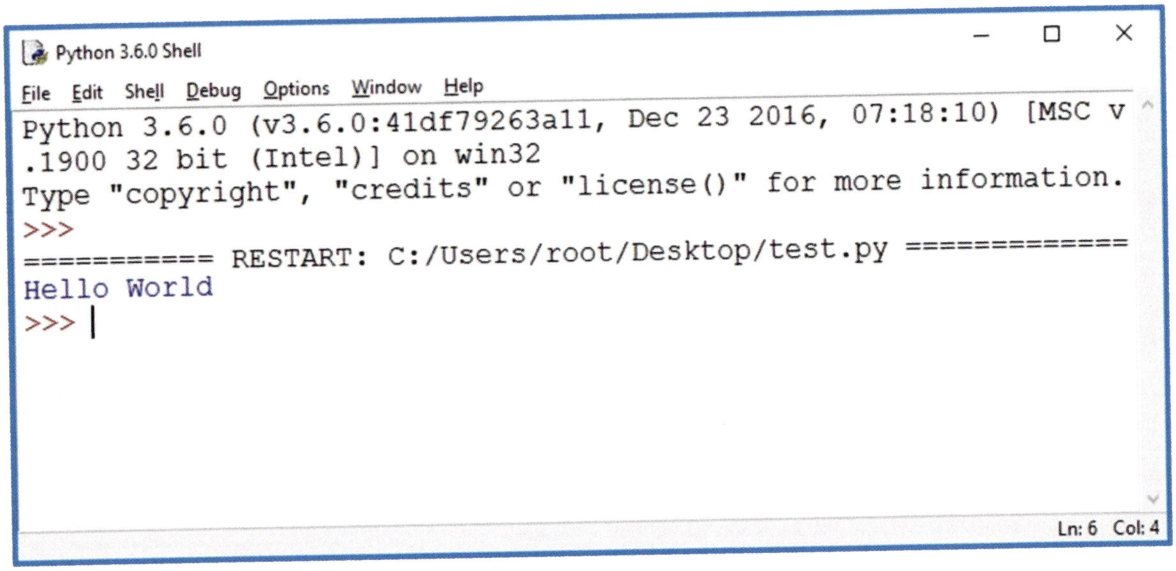

Figure 7-5 Viewing the results of the executed program in the Python Shell window

Congratulations! You have just written and executed your first Python program!

Now let's write another Python program, one that prompts the user to enter his or her name. Type the following Python program and hit F5 to execute the file.

file_7_3
```python
name = input("Enter your name: ")
print("Hello", name)
print("Have a nice day!")
```

> **Remember!** You can execute a program by selecting "Run→Run Module" from the main menu, or by hitting the F5 key.

Once you execute the program, the message "Enter your name: " without the double quotes is displayed in the Python Shell window. The program waits for you to enter your name, as shown in **Figure 7-6**.

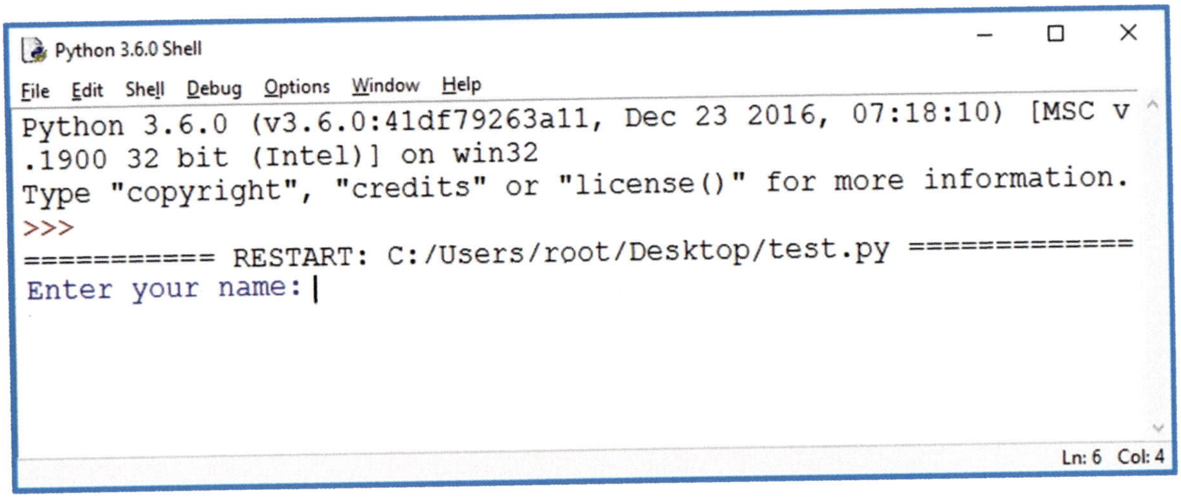

Figure 7-6 Viewing a prompt in the Python Shell window

Type your name and hit the "Enter ↵" key. Once you do that, your computer continues to execute the rest of the statements. When execution finishes, the final output is as shown in **Figure 7-7**.

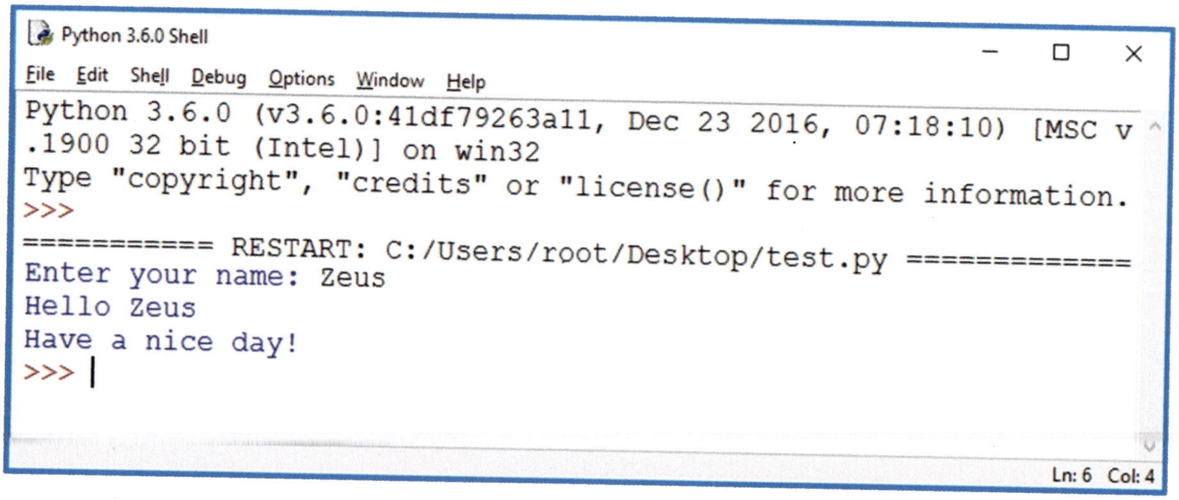

Figure 7-7 Responding to the prompt in the Python Shell window

7.4 IDLE - Finding Runtime and Syntax Errors

When someone writes code in a high-level language they might make some mistakes. Look at the following Python program

```python
num1 = float(input("Enter number A: "))
num2 = float(input("Enter number B: "))
c = num1 / num2
print(c)
```

The program may look perfect, but have you thought about the possibility of num2 being zero? Unfortunately, the way this program is written permits the user to enter a value of zero for variable num2. If you try to execute this program, and enter a value of zero for num2, Python's interpreter complains and displays the error "float division by zero" (see **Figure 7-8**). Also, the interpreter tells you that this runtime error happened when line 3 was executed!

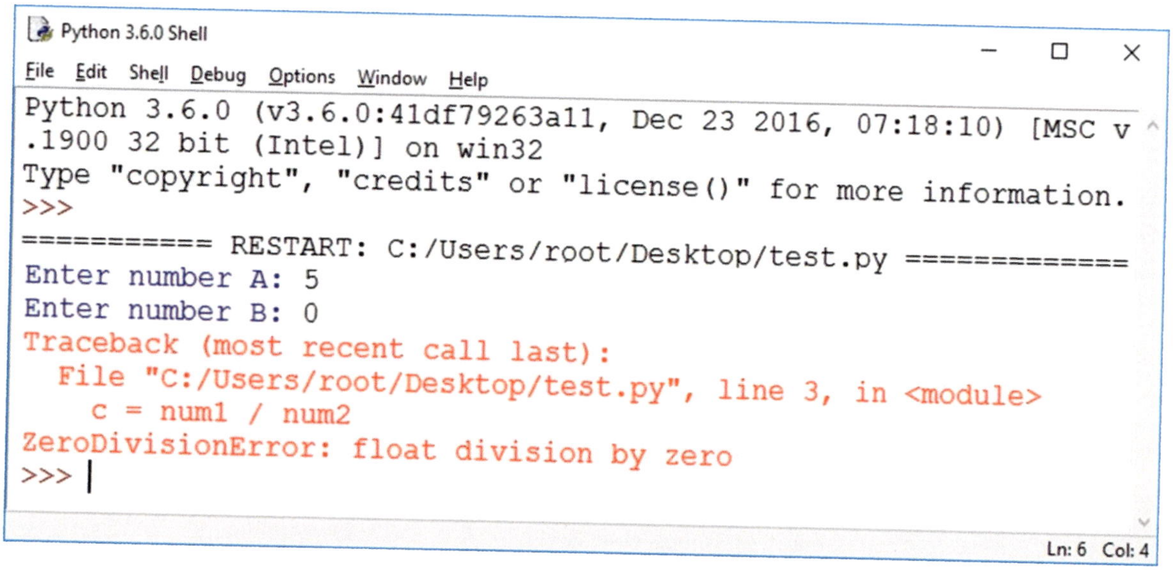

Figure 7-8 Python Shell window displays a runtime error

You cannot deal with this problem right now! You have to wait until **Chapter 12** where you will learn all about decision structures.

> *Notice:* Using a decision structure, the computer can decide whether or not it should perform this division.

Now, look at the following Python program

```python
num1 = 5
num2 = 10
c = num1 + num2 +
print(c)
```

Here, the programmer made a typographic error (a "typo"); the third statement contains an unnecessary addition operator (+). If you try to execute this program, Python's interpreter displays the error "invalid syntax" as shown in **Figure 7-9**.

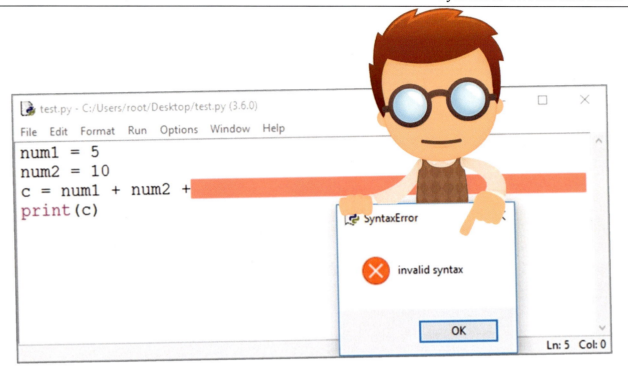

Figure 7-9 Python displays a syntax error

All you have to do is correct the erroneous line and try to execute the program again!

Chapter 8
Using Eclipse

8.1 Introduction

As already stated in paragraph 2.4, an Integrated Development Environment (IDE) is software that enables programmers to both write and execute their source code. IDLE and Eclipse are such examples. This book covers both of them, so, it's up to you to choose which one you are going to use. If you have decided to use IDLE, then you don't have to read anything about Eclipse. You can skip this chapter!

8.2 Eclipse – Creating a New Python Project

Once you open Eclipse, you must first create a new Python project. Eclipse provides a wizard to help you do that. Start Eclipse, and from its main menu select "File→New→ PyDev Project" as shown in **Figure 8-1**.

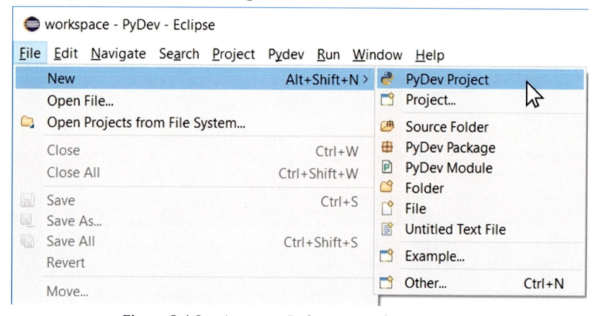

Figure 8-1 Starting a new Python project from Eclipse

If there is no such option in your Eclipse, you can instead select "File→New→ Other" and in the popup window that appears, select the "PyDev Project" wizard, as shown in **Figure 8-2**.

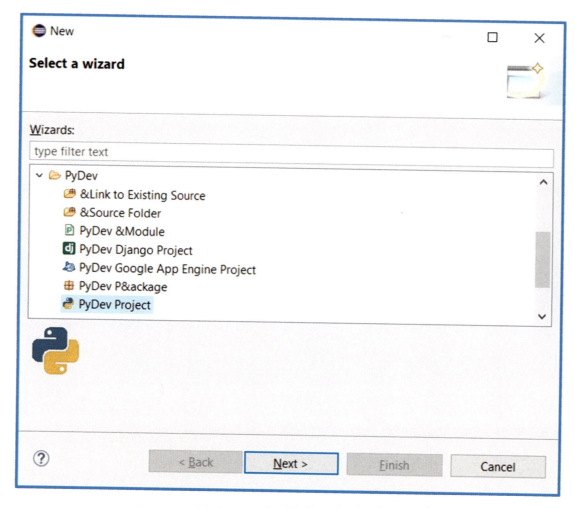

Figure 8-2 Selecting the "PyDev Project" wizard

Then, click on the "Next" button.

The "PyDev Project" dialog box appears, allowing you to create a new PyDev Project. In the "Project name" field, type any name you wish, for example "testingProject" and in the "Grammar Version" field select the option "3.6" (or later), as shown in **Figure 8-3**.

Chapter 8
Using Eclipse

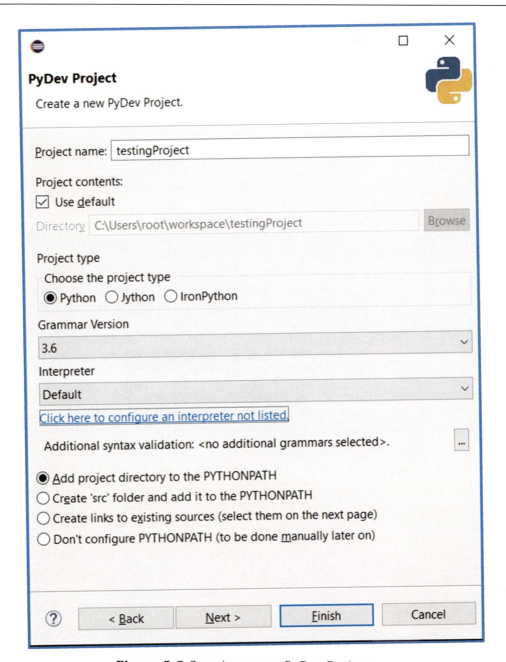

Figure 8-3 Creating a new PyDev Project

Notice: *If the error message "Project interpreter not specified" displays in the "PyDev Project" dialog box, you must click on the link "Please configure an interpreter before proceeding." Then, in the popup window that appears click on the "Quick Auto-Config" button.*

Click on the "Finish" button. If the popup window of **Figure 8-4** appears, check the "Remember my decision" field and click on the "Yes" button.

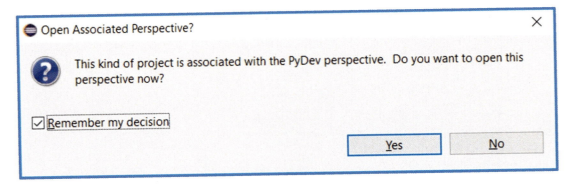

Figure 8-4 The "Open Associated Perspective" popup window

The project is created in your Eclipse environment. If the "PyDev Package Explorer" window is minimized, click on the "Restore" button (shown in **Figure 8-5**) to restore it.

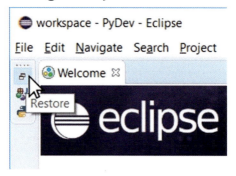

Figure 8-5 Restoring the "PyDev Package Explorer" window

In the "PyDev Package Explorer" window, select the "testingProject" that you have just created. From the main menu select "File→New→ PyDev Module". If there is no such option in your Eclipse, you can instead select "File→New→ Other" and in the popup window that appears, select the "PyDev Module" wizard. Then, click on the "Next" button.

In the popup window that appears (shown in **Figure 8-6**), make sure that the "Source Folder" field contains the value "/testingProject". In the "Name" field, type "test" and click on the "Finish" button.

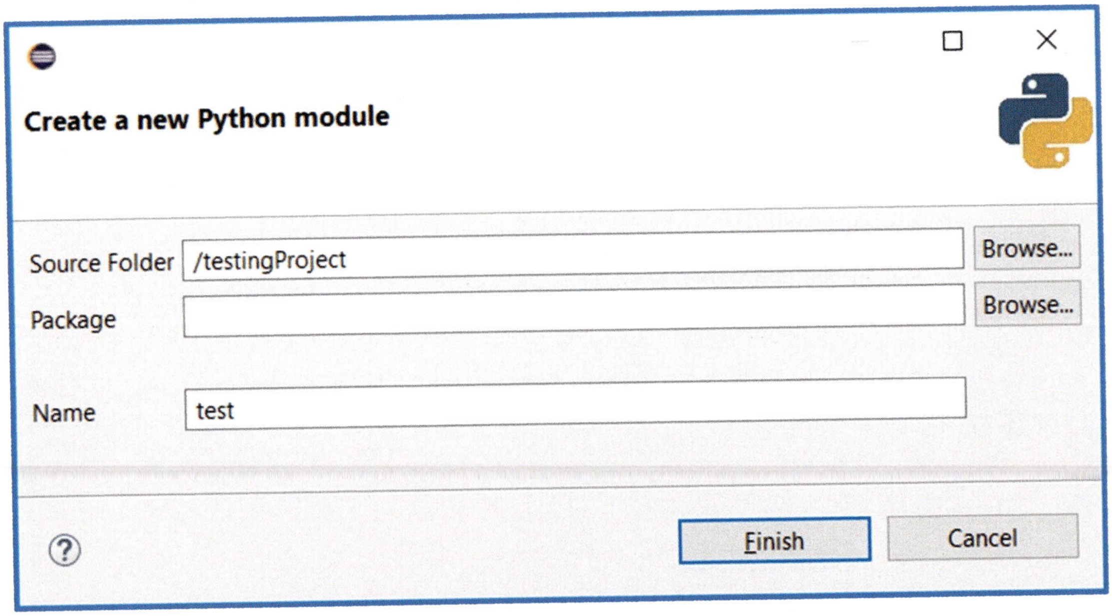

Figure 8-6 Creating a new PyDev module

If the popup window of **Figure 8-7** appears, leave all fields checked and click on the "OK" button.

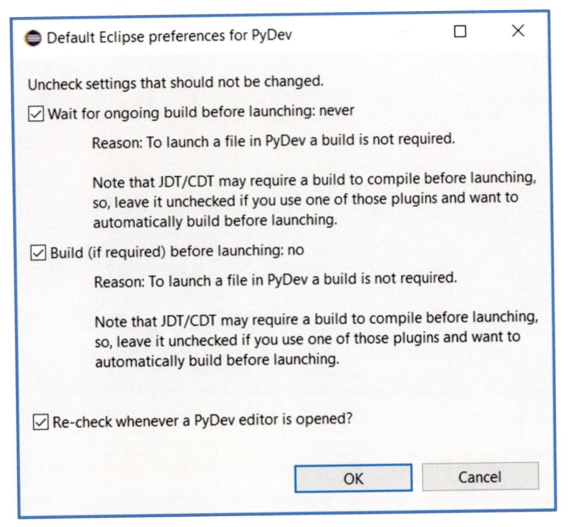

Figure 8-7 Selecting the default Eclipse preferences for PyDev

The next window that appears prompts you to select a template. Since you need no template you can just click on the "Cancel" button.

You should now see the following components (see **Figure 8-8**):

- the "PyDev Package Explorer" window, which contains a tree view of the components of the projects, including source files, libraries that your code may depend on, and so on.
- the "Source Editor" window with the file called "test.py" open. In this file you can write your Python code. Of course, one single project can contain many such files.
- the "Console" window in which Eclipse displays the output results of your Python programs, as well as messages useful for the programmer.

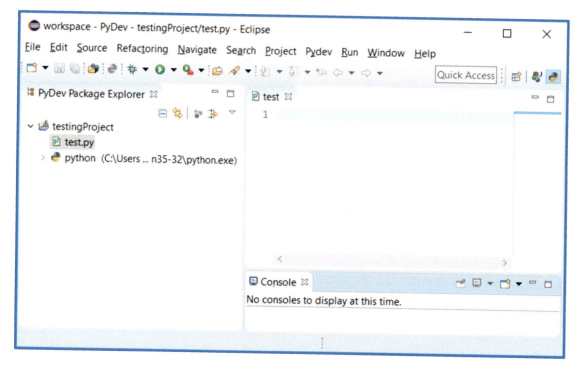

Figure 8-8 Viewing the "Package Explorer", "Source Editor", and "Console" windows in Eclipse

Notice: If the "Console" window is not open, you can open it by selecting "Window→Show View→Console" from the main menu.

8.3   Eclipse – Writing and Executing a Python Program

You have just seen how to create a new Python project. In the window "test", type the following (terrifying, and quite horrifying!) Python program.

```python
print("Hello World")
```

Now let's try to execute the program! From the toolbar, click on the "Run As" icon. Alternatively, from the main menu, you can select "Run→Run" or even hit the CTRL + F11 key combination. The Python program executes and the output is displayed in the "Console" window, as shown in **Figure 8-9**.

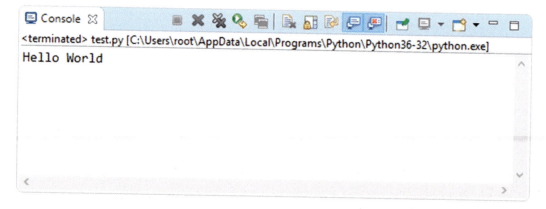

Figure 8-9 Viewing the results of the executed program in the Console window

> **Notice**: *If, while you are trying to execute your first program, the following popup window asks you to select a way to run 'test.py' select the "Python Run" option and click on the "OK" button.*

Congratulations! You have just written and executed your first Python program!

Now let's write another Python program, one that prompts the user to enter his or her name. Type the following Python program into Eclipse and hit CTRL + F11 to execute the file.

file_8_3
```python
name = input("Enter your name: ")
print("Hello", name)
print("Have a nice day!")
```

> **Remember**! *You can execute a program by clicking on the "Run As" ⏵ toolbar icon, or by selecting "Run→Run" from the main menu, or even by hitting the CTRL + F11 key combination.*

Once you execute the program, the message "Enter your name: " is displayed in the "Console" window. The program waits for you to enter your name, as shown in **Figure 8-10**.

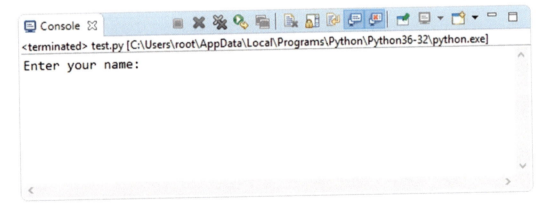

Figure 8-10 Viewing a prompt in the Console window

To enter your name, however, you must place the text cursor inside the "Console" window. Then you can type your name and hit the "Enter ↵" key. Once you do that, your computer continues to execute the rest of the statements. When execution finishes, the final output is as shown in **Figure 8-11**.

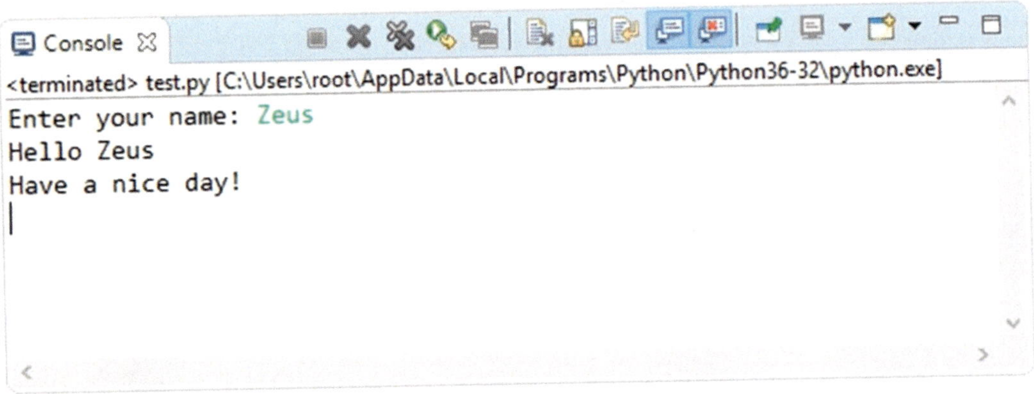

Figure 8-11 Responding to the prompt in the Console window

8.4 Eclipse - Finding Runtime and Syntax Errors

When someone writes code in a high-level language, he or she might make some mistakes. Fortunately, Eclipse provides all the necessary tools to help you debug your programs.

Look at the following Python program

```
num1 = float(input("Enter number A: "))
num2 = float(input("Enter number B: "))
c = num1 / num2
print(c)
```

The program may look perfect, but have you thought about the possibility of num2 being zero? Unfortunately, the way this program is written permits the user to enter a value of zero for variable num2. If you try to execute this program, and enter a value of zero for num2, Python's interpreter complains and displays the error "float division by zero" (see **Figure 7-8**). Also, the interpreter tells you that this runtime error happened when line 3 was executed!

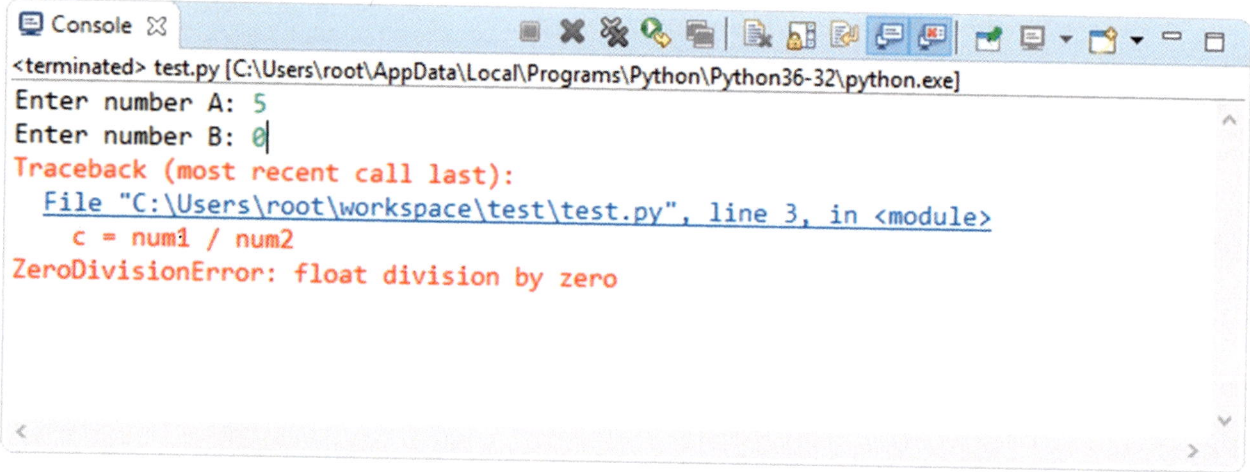

Figure 8-12 Python Shell window displays a runtime error

You cannot deal with this problem right now! You have to wait until **Chapter 12** where you will learn all about decision structures.

> *Notice: Using a decision structure, the computer can decide whether or not it should perform this division.*

Another interesting feature of Eclipse is that it detects syntax errors while you are typing and underlines them with a wavy red line as shown in **Figure 8-13.**

Figure 8-13 In Eclipse, syntax errors are underlined with a wavy red line

All you have to do is correct the error and the red line will disappear at once. However, if you are not certain about what is wrong with your code, you can just place your mouse cursor on the erroneous line. Eclipse will try to help you by showing a popup window with a brief explanation of the error, as shown in **Figure 8-14**.

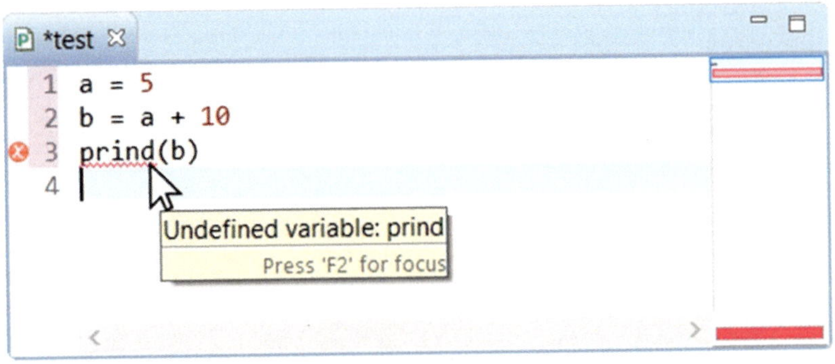

Figure 8-14 Eclipse shows an explanation of a syntax error

Chapter 9
Writing your First Real Programs

9.1 Introduction

In this chapter, you will see some very simple programs in which the statements are executed one after the other (sequentially), in the same order in which they appear in the program. In computer science, a structure that contains statements that are executed sequentially, in the same order in which they appear in the program, without skipping any of them, is called a *sequence structure*. This structure might, for example, carry out a series of input or output operations, arithmetic operations, or assignments to variables.

> ***Notice:*** *The sequence structure is one of the three basic control structures used in computer science. The other two structures are "decision structure" and "loop structure." All problems in computer programming can be solved using only these three structures!*

> ***Notice:*** *The structured programming concept was formalized in 1966 by Corrado Böhm and Giuseppe Jacopini. They demonstrated theoretical computer program design using sequences, decisions, and iterations (loops).*

The following program shows an example of Python statements that are executed sequentially.

file_9_1
```python
#Prompt the user to enter value for num
num = int(input("Enter a number: "))

#Calculate the square of num
result = num ** 2

#Display the result on user's screen
print("The square of", num, "is", result)
```

> ***Remember!*** *In Python, you can add comments using the hash character (#). Comments are for human readers. Compilers and interpreters ignore them.*

Exercise 9.1.1 — Calculating the Area of a Rectangle

Write a Python program that prompts the user to enter the length of the base and the height of a rectangle, and then calculates and displays its area.

Solution

You probably know from school that you can calculate the area of a rectangle using the following formula:

$$Area = Base \times Height$$

In paragraph 3.5, you learned about the three main stages of creating an algorithm: data input, data processing, and results output.

In this exercise, these three main stages are as follows:
- **Data input** - the user must enter values for *Base* and *Height*
- **Data processing** - the program must calculate the area of the rectangle
- **Results output** – the program must display the area of the rectangle calculated in previous stage

The solution to this problem is shown here.

file_9_1_1

```python
#Data input - Prompt the user to enter values for base and height
base = float(input("Enter the Length of Base: "))
height = float(input("Enter the Length of Height: "))

#Data processing - Calculate the area of the rectangle
area = base * height

#Results output - Display the result on user's screen
print("The area of the rectangle is", area)
```

Exercise 9.1.2 — Calculating the Area of a Circle

Write a Python program that prompts the user to enter the length of the radius of a circle, and then calculates and displays its area.

Solution

You can calculate the area of a circle using the following formula:

$$Area = \pi \cdot Radius^2$$

The value of π is a known quantity, which is 3.14159. Therefore, the only value the user must enter is the value for *Radius*.

In this exercise, the three main stages that you learned in paragraph 3.5 are as follows:
- **Data input** - the user must enter a value for *Radius*
- **Data processing** - the program must calculate the area of the circle
- **Results output** – the program must display the area of the circle calculated in previous stage.

The solution to this problem is shown here.

file_9_1_2

```python
#Data input - Prompt the user to enter a value for radius
radius = float(input("Enter the Length of Radius: "))

#Data processing - Calculate the area of the circle
area = 3.14159 * radius ** 2

#Results output - Display the result on user's screen
print("The area of the circle is", area)
```

Chapter 9
Writing your First Real Programs

> **Remember!** The exponentiation operation has a higher precedence and is performed before the multiplication operation.

Exercise 9.1.3 – Fahrenheit to Celsius

Write a Python program that prompts the user to enter a temperature in degrees Fahrenheit[1], and then converts it into its degrees Celsius[2] equivalent. The required formula is

$$C = \frac{5}{9}(F - 32)$$

Solution

In this program the user must enter a temperature value in degrees Fahrenheit, and then calculate its degrees Celsius equivalent using the formula given above. The Python program is shown here.

file_9_1_3
```python
#Data input - Prompt the user to enter a temperature value
#             in degrees Fahrenheit
fahrenheit = float(input("Enter a temperature in Fahrenheit: "))


#Data processing - Calculate the degrees Celsius equivalent
celsius = 5 / 9 * (fahrenheit - 32)


#Results output - Display the result on user's screen
print("The temperature in Celsius is", celsius)
```

9.2 Review Exercises

Complete the following exercises.

1. Write a Python program that prompts the user to enter values for base and height, and then calculates and displays the area of a triangle using the following formula:

$$Area = \frac{Base \times Height}{2}$$

2. Write a Python program that prompts the user to enter a temperature in degrees Fahrenheit, and then converts it into its degrees Kelvin[3] equivalent. The required formula is

---

1. Daniel Gabriel Fahrenheit (1686–1736) was a German physicist, engineer, and glass blower who is best known for inventing both the alcohol and the mercury thermometers, and for developing the temperature scale, which takes his name.

2. Anders Celsius (1701–1744) was a Swedish astronomer, physicist, and mathematician. He founded the Uppsala Astronomical Observatory in Sweden and proposed the Celsius temperature scale, which takes his name.

3. William Thomson, 1st Baron Kelvin (1824–1907), was an Irish-born British mathematical physicist and engineer. He is widely known for developing the basis of absolute zero (the Kelvin temperature scale), and for this reason a unit of

$$Kelvin = \frac{Fahrenheit + 459.67}{1.8}$$

3. Write a Python program that prompts the user to enter two angles of a triangle, and then calculates and displays the third angle.

   Hint: The sum of the interior angles of any triangle is always 180 degrees.

4. Write a Python program that prompts a student to enter their grades from four tests, and then calculates and displays the average grade.

5. Write a Python program that prompts the user to enter a value for the radius of a circle, and then calculates and displays the perimeter of the circle using the following formula:

$$Perimeter = 2 \times \pi \times Radius$$

   It is given that:

$$\pi = 3.14159$$

6. The Body Mass Index (BMI) is often used to determine whether a person is overweight or underweight for his or her height. The formula used to calculate the BMI is

$$BMI = \frac{weight \cdot 703}{height^2}$$

   Write a Python program that prompts the user to enter his or her weight (in pounds) and height (in inches), and then calculates and displays the user's BMI.

7. Write a Python program that prompts the user to enter two numbers, which correspond to current month and current day of the month. The program then calculates the number of days until the end of the year. Assume that each month has 30 days.

9.3 Review Questions

1. What is a sequence structure?
2. Which operations can a sequence structure perform?
3. Name the three basic control structures used in computer science.

---

temperature measure is named after him. He discovered the Thomson effect in thermoelectricity and helped develop the second law of thermodynamics.

Chapter 10
Manipulating Numbers

10.1 Introduction

Just like every high-level programming language, Python has many ready-to-use functions and methods (called *subprograms*) that you can use whenever and wherever you wish.

> **Notice:** A "subprogram" is simply a group of statements packaged as a single unit. Each subprogram has a descriptive name and performs a specific task.

Even though Python supports many mathematical functions (and methods), this chapter covers only those that are necessary for this book's purpose. However, if you need even more information on functions and methods, you can visit

https://docs.python.org/3.6/library/math.html

10.2 Useful Functions and Methods

Integer value

```
int(value)
```

This function returns the integer portion of *value*. You can also use it to convert a string representation of an integer to its numeric equivalent.

Example

file_10_2a

```
a = 5.4
b = int(a)
print(b)                    #It displays: 5

print(int(34))              #It displays: 34
print(int(34.9))            #It displays: 34
print(int(-34.999))         #It displays: -34


c = "15"
d = "3"
print(c + d)                #It displays: 153
print(int(c) + int(d))      #It displays: 18
```

Maximum value

```
max(sequence)
max(value1, value2, value3, …)
```

This function returns the largest value of *sequence,* or the largest of two or more arguments.

Example

file_10_2b

```
a = 5
b = 6
c = 3
d = 4
y = max(a, b, c, d)
print(y)                        #It displays: 6

print(max(5, 3, 2, 6, 7, 1, 5)) #It displays: 7

seq = [2, 8, 4, 6, 2]           #This is a sequence of integers
print(max(seq))                 #It displays: 8
```

Minimum value

```
min(sequence)
min(value1, value2, value3, …)
```

This function returns the smallest value of *sequence,* or the smallest of two or more arguments.

Example

file_10_2c

```
a = 5
b = 6
c = 3
d = 4
y = min(a, b, c, d)
print(y)                        #It displays: 3

print(min(5, 3, 2, 6, 7, 1, 5)) #It displays: 1

seq = [2, 8, 4, 6, 2]           #This is a sequence of integers
print(min(seq))                 #It displays: 2
```

Chapter 10
Manipulating Numbers

Real value

```
float(value)
```

This function converts a string representation of a real to its numeric equivalent.

Example

file_10_2d

```
a = "5.2"
b = "3.4"

print(a + b)                  #It displays: 5.23.4
print(float(a) + float(b))    #It displays: 8.6
```

Range

```
range([initial_value,] final_value [, step])
```

This function returns a sequence of integers between *initial_value* and *final_value* - 1. The argument *initial_value* is optional. If omitted, its default value is 0. The argument *step* is the difference between each number in the sequence. This argument is also optional. If omitted, its default value is 1.

> **Notice:** Please note that initial_value, final_value, and step must be integers. Negative values are also permitted!

Example

file_10_2f

```
#Assign sequence [1, 2, 3, 4, 5] to variable a
a = range(1, 6)

#Assign sequence [0, 1, 2, 3, 4, 5] to variable b
b = range(6)

#Assign sequence [0, 10, 20, 30, 40] to variable c
c = range(0, 50, 10)

#Assign sequence [100, 95, 90, 85] to variable d
d = range(100, 80, -5)
```

Random Integer

```
random.randrange([minimum_value,] maximum_value [, step])
```

This function returns a random integer from a given range. The parameters of randrange() follow the same logic as those of function range().

Example

file_10_2e

```python
import random           #import random module

#Display a random integer between 10 and 100
print(random.randrange(10, 101))

#Assign a random integer between 0 and 10 to variable y
y = random.randrange(11)
#and display it
print(y)

#Display a random integer between -20 and 20
print(random.randrange(-20, 21))

#Display a random odd integer between 1 and 99
print(random.randrange(1, 99, 2))

#Display a random even integer between 0 and 100
print(random.randrange(0, 100, 2))
```

> *Notice: Random numbers are widely used in computer games. For example, an "enemy" may show up at a random time or move in random directions. Also, random numbers are used in simulation programs, in statistical programs, in computer security to encrypt data, and so on.*

> *Notice: The function* `randrange()` *is defined in the module* `random`. *It is not accessible directly in Python, so you need to import the* `random` *module.*

> *Notice: The* `random` *module is nothing more than a file that contains many ready-to-use functions (or methods). Python incorporates many such modules. However, if you want to use a function or a method from one of those modules, you need to import that module into your program.*

Sum

`math.fsum(sequence)`

This function returns the sum of the elements of *sequence*.

Example

file_10_2g

```python
import math

seq = [5.1, 3, 2]           #Assign a sequence of numbers to variable seq
print(math.fsum(seq))       #It displays: 10.1
```

> *Notice: The function* `fsum()` *is defined in the module* `math`. *It is not accessible directly in Python, so you need to import the* `math` *module.*

Square root

`math.sqrt(number)`

This method returns the square root of *number*.

Example

```
file_10_2h
import math                      #import math module

print(math.sqrt(9))              #It displays: 3.0
print(math.sqrt(25))             #It displays: 5.0
```

> **Notice**: *The function* `sqrt()` *is defined in the module* `math`. *It is not accessible directly in Python, so you need to import the* `math` *module.*

10.3 Review Questions: True/False

Choose **true** or **false** for each of the following statements.

1. In general, functions are small subprograms that solve small problems.
2. The statement `int(3.59)` returns a result of 3.6.
3. The statement `y = int("two")` is a valid Python statement.
4. The statement `y = int("2")` is a valid Python statement.
5. The statement `int(3)` returns a result of 3.0.
6. The statement `float(3)` returns a result of 3.0.
7. The statement `y = float("3.14")` is not a valid Python statement.
8. The `randrange()` function can return negative random numbers.
9. The statement `max(-5, -1, -8)` returns a result of −1.
10. The statement `b = range(3)` assigns the sequence [0, 1, 2] to variable b.
11. The statement `c = range(0, 10, 0.5)` is a valid Python statement.
12. The statement `math.fsum([1, 9])` returns a result of 10.0.
13. The statement `math.fsum(a, b, c)` is a valid Python statement.

10.4 Review Exercises

Complete the following exercises.

1. Try to determine the values of the variables in each step of the Python program and find out what is displayed on the user's screen.

    ```
    a = 5.0
    b = 2.0

    y = int(a / b)
    ```

print(y)

2. Try to determine the values of the variables in each step of the Python program for two different executions and find out what is displayed on the user's screen.

    The input values for the two executions are: (i) 2.5, and (ii) 5.5.

    ```
    a = float(input())

    a = a * 2 / int(a)

    print(a)
    ```

3. Try to determine the values of the variables in each step of the Python program for two different executions and find out what is displayed on the user's screen.

    The input values for the two executions are: (i) 2.2, and (ii) 3.5

    ```
    a = float(input())

    b = int(a) ** 2

    print(b)
    ```

4. Try to determine the values of the variables in each step of the Python program for two different executions and find out what is displayed on the user's screen.

    The input values for the two executions are: (i) 2, 5.5, 5; and (ii) 3.5, 3.5, 2

    ```
    a = float(input())
    b = float(input())
    c = float(input())

    y = [a, b, c]

    print(max(y))
    ```

5. Try to determine the values of the variables in each step of the Python program for two different executions and find out what is displayed on the user's screen.

    The input values for the two executions are: (i) 1, 30, 15; and (ii) 20, 12, 17

    ```
    import math
    a = float(input())
    b = float(input())
    c = float(input())

    y = max(a, b, c)
    z = min(a, b, c)
    w = math.fsum([y, z])
    print(w)
    ```

Chapter 11
Manipulating Strings

11.1 Introduction

Generally speaking, a string is anything that you can type using the keyboard, including letters, symbols (such as &, *, and @), and digits. In Python, a string is always enclosed in single or double quotes. Below is a Python program that uses strings.

```python
a = "Everything enclosed in double quotes is a string, "
b = "even the numbers below:"
c = "3, 54, 731"
print(a)
print(b)
print(c)
print("You can even mix letters, symbols and ")
print("digits like this:")
print("The result of 3 + 4 equals to 4")
```

Many times programs deal with data that comes in the form of strings. Strings are everywhere—from word processors, to web browsers, to text messaging programs. Many exercises in this book actually make extensive use of strings. Even though Python supports many useful functions and methods for manipulating strings, this chapter covers only those that are necessary for this book's purpose. However, if you need even more information on strings, you can visit

https://docs.python.org/3.6/library/stdtypes.html#string-methods

> **Remember!** Functions and methods are nothing more than small subprograms that solve small problems.

11.2 Retrieving Individual Characters from a String

Let's use the text «Hello World» in the following example. The string consists of 11 characters (including the space character between the two words). The position of each character is shown here.

0	1	2	3	4	5	6	7	8	9	10
H	e	l	l	o		W	o	r	l	d

Python assumes that the first character is at position 0, the second one is at position 1, and so on. Please note that the space between the two words is also considered a character.

> **Remember!** A space is a character just like any other character. Just because nobody can see it, it doesn't mean it doesn't exist!

Python allows you to retrieve the individual characters of a string using what is known as *substring notation*. Substring notation lets you refer to specific characters within a string. So, you can use index 0 to access the first character, index 1 to access the second character, and so on. The index of the last character is 1 less than the length of the string. The following Python program shows an example.

file_11_2a

```
a = "Hello World"

print(a[0])     #it displays the first letter
print(a[6])     #it displays the letter W
print(a[10])    #it displays the last letter
```

> **Notice:** Please note that the space between the words "Hello" and "World" is considered a character as well. So, the letter W exists in position 6—and not in position 5 (as you may have thought).

If you want to start counting from the end of the string (instead of the beginning) you can use negative indexes. For example, an index of –1 refers to the rightmost character.

In the text «Hello World», the position (using negative indexes) of each character is shown here.

-11	-10	-9	-8	-7	-6	-5	-4	-3	-2	-1
H	e	l	l	o		W	o	r	l	d

An example is shown here.

file_11_2b

```
a = "Hello World"

print(a[-1])    #it displays the last letter
print(a[-3])    #it displays the letter r
```

However, if you try to use an invalid index such as an index greater than the length of the string, Python displays an error message as shown in **Figure 11-1** and in **Figure 11-2**.

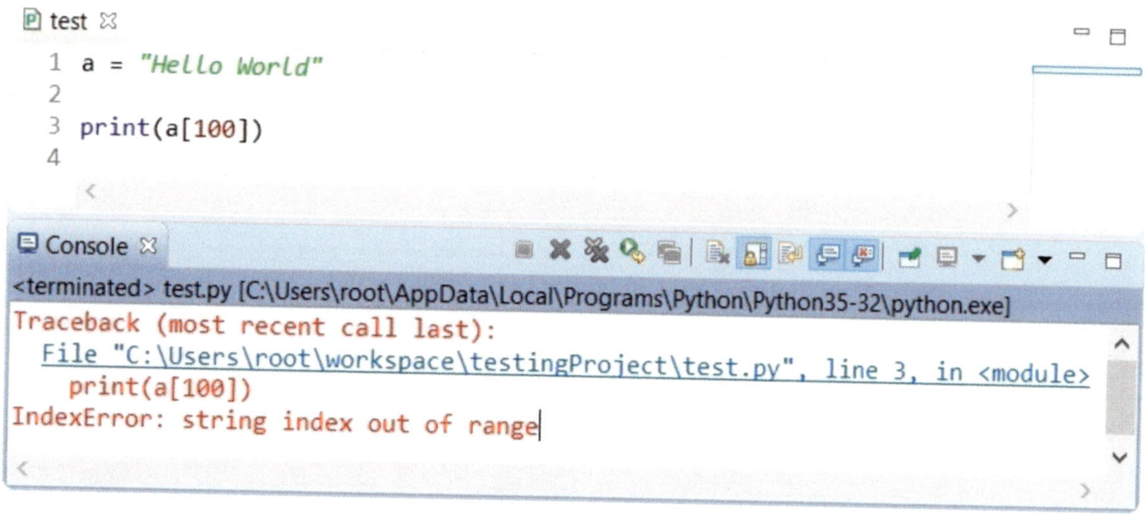

Chapter 11
Manipulating Strings

Figure 11-1 An error message (in Eclipse) indicating an invalid index

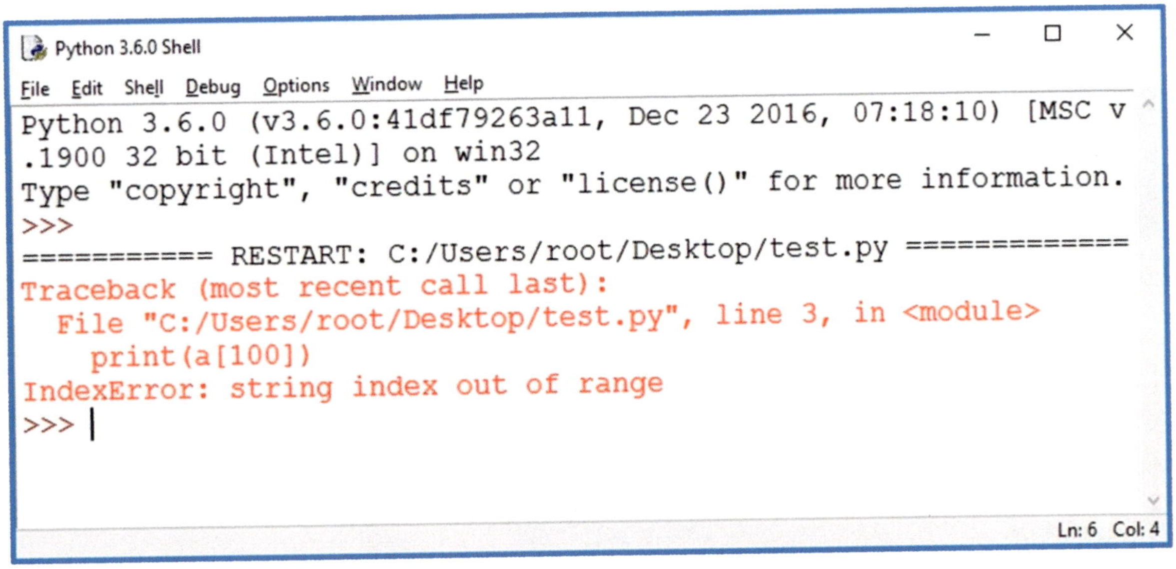

Figure 11-2 An error message (in IDLE) indicating an invalid index

Another way of extracting single characters from strings in Python is to unpack them into individual variables, as shown here.

file_11_2c

```
name = "Zeus"

letter1, letter2, letter3, letter4 = name

print(letter1)      #It displays the letter Z
print(letter2)      #It displays the letter e
print(letter3)      #It displays the letter u
print(letter4)      #It displays the letter s
```

> **Notice:** *This last approach requires you to know in advance how many characters are in the string. If the number of variables you provide does not match the number of characters in the string, Python displays an error.*

11.3 Retrieving a Portion of a String

If you wish to extract a portion of a string (a substring) you can use the following formula:

subject[[*beginIndex*] : [*endIndex*]]

This returns a portion of *subject*. Specifically, it returns the substring starting from position *beginIndex* and running up to, but not including, position *endIndex* as shown in the example that follows.

file_11_3a
```
a = "Hello World"
b = a[6:9]
print(b)         #It displays: Wor
```

Argument *beginIndex* is optional. If omitted, the substring starting from position 0 and running up to, but not including, position *endIndex* is returned as shown in the example that follows.

file_11_3b
```
a = "Hello World"
print(a[:2])     #It displays: He
```

Argument *endIndex* is also optional. If you omit it, the substring starting from position *beginIndex* until the end of *subject* is returned as shown in the example that follows.

file_11_3c
```
a = "Hello World"
print(a[7:])     #It displays: orld
```

> **Notice:** *The practice of selecting a range of elements (in this case, characters) from a sequence (in this case, a string) is called "slicing" in Python.*

The slicing mechanism of Python can have an extra third argument, called *step* as shown in the formula that follows:

subject[[*beginIndex*] : [*endIndex*] [: *step*]]

The argument *step* is optional as well. If omitted, its default value is 1. If supplied, it defines the number of characters you want to move forward after each character is retrieved from the original string. An example is shown here.

file_11_3d
```
a = "Hello World"
print(a[4:10:2])    #step is set to 2. It displays: oWr
```

If you want to start counting from the end of the string (instead of the beginning), use negative indexes as shown in the example that follows.

Chapter 11
Manipulating Strings

file_11_3e

```
a = "Hello World"

print(a[3:-2])      #It displays: lo Wor
print(a[-4:-2])     #It displays: or
print(a[-3:])       #It displays: rld
print(a[:-3])       #It displays: Hello Wo
```

Exercise 11.3.1 – Displaying a String Backward

Write a Python program that prompts the user to enter any word with four letters and then displays its contents backward. For example, if the word entered is "Zeus", the program must display "sueZ".

Solution

Three approaches are presented below.

First Approach

Let's say that the user's input is assigned to variable s. You can access the fourth letter using s[3], the third letter using s[2], and so on. The Python program is shown here.

file_11_3_1a

```
s = input("Enter a word with four letters: ")

s_reversed = s[3] + s[2] + s[1] + s[0]

print(s_reversed)
```

Second Approach

This approach unpacks the four letters into four individual variables, as shown here.

file_11_3_1b

```
s = input("Enter a word with four letters: ")

a, b, c, d = s
s_reversed = d + c + b + a

print(s_reversed)
```

Third Approach

This approach uses the negative value of −1 for argument *step*.

file_11_3_1c

```
s = input("Enter a word with four letters: ")

s_reversed = s[::-1]
```

```
print(s_reversed)
```

11.4 Useful Functions and Methods

String replacement

```
subject.replace(search, replace)
```

This method searches in *subject* and replaces all occurrences of the *search* string with the *replace* string.

Example

file_11_4a
```
a = "I am newbie in Java. Java rocks!"
b = a.replace("Java", "Python")

print(b)        #It displays: I am newbie in Python. Python rocks!
print(a)        #It displays: I am newbie in Java. Java rocks!
```

Counting the number of characters

```
len(subject)
```

This function returns the length of *subject* or, in other words, the number of characters that *subject* consists of (including space characters, symbols, numbers, and so on).

Example

file_11_4b
```
a = "Hello Olympians!"
print(len(a))       #It displays: 16

b = "I am newbie in Python"
k = len(b)
print(k)            #It displays: 21
```

Finding string position

```
subject.find(search)
```

This method finds the numeric position of the first occurrence of *search* in *subject*.

Example

file_11_4c
```
a = "I am newbie in Python. Python rocks!"

i = a.find("newbie")

print(i)                    #It displays: 5
print(a.find("Python"))     #It displays: 15
print(a.find("Java"))       #It displays: -1
```

Remember! The first character is at position 0.

Chapter 11
Manipulating Strings

Converting to lowercase

```
subject.lower()
```

This method returns the *subject*, converted to lowercase.

Example

file_11_4d

```
a = "My NaMe is JohN"
b = a.lower()

print(b)           #It displays: my name is john
print(a)           #It displays: My NaMe is JohN
```

Converting to uppercase

```
subject.upper()
```

This method returns the *subject*, converted to uppercase.

Example

file_11_4e

```
a = "My NaMe is JohN"
b = a.upper()

print(b)           #It displays: MY NAME IS JOHN
print(a)           #It displays: My NaMe is JohN
```

Example

file_11_4f

```
a = "I am newbie in Java. Java rocks!"
b = a.replace("Java", "Python").upper()

print(b)           #It displays: I AM NEWBIE IN PYTHON. PYTHON ROCKS!
print(a)           #It displays: I am newbie in Java. Java rocks!
```

> **Notice:** Please note how the method `replace()` is "chained" to the method `upper()`. The result of the first method is used as a subject for the second method. Chaining is a writing style that most programmers prefer to follow because it helps to save a lot of code lines. Of course you can chain as many methods as you want, but if you chain too many of them, no one will be able to understand your code.

Converting a number to string

```
str(number)
```

This function returns a string version of *number* or, in other words, it converts a number (real or integer) into a string.

Example

file_11_4g

```
age = int(input("Enter your age: "))

new_age = age + 10
message = "You will be " + str(new_age) + " years old in 10 years from now!"

print(message)
```

Exercise 11.4.1 — Creating a Login ID

Write a Python program that prompts the user to enter his or her last name and then creates a login ID from the first four letters of the name (in lowercase) and a random three-digit integer.

Solution

To create a random integer, you can use the `randrange()` function. Since you need a random integer of three digits, the range must be between 100 and 999.

The Python program is shown here.

file_11_4_1

```
import random

last_name = input("Enter last name: ")

#Get a random integer between 100 and 999
random_int = random.randrange(100, 1000)

#Create login ID
login_id = last_name[:4].lower() + str(random_int)

print(login_id)
```

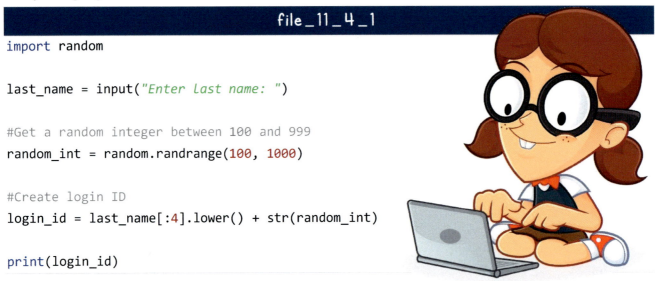

Exercise 11.4.2 — Switching the Order of Names

Write a Python program that prompts the user to enter both a first and a last name into one single string. In the end, the program must change the order of the two names.

Solution

In this exercise, you must split the string and assign each name to a different variable. If you manage to do so, then you can just rejoin them in a different order.

Let's try to understand this exercise using an example. The following shows the string that you must split, and the position of its individual characters.

0	1	2	3	4	5	6	7	8
T	o	m		S	m	i	t	h

The character that visually separates the first name from the last name is the space character between them. The problem is that this character is not always at position 3. Someone can have a short first name like "Tom" and someone else can have a longer one like "Robert". Therefore, you need something that actually finds the position of the space character regardless of the content of the string.

Method `find()` is what you are looking for! If you use it to find the position of the space character in the string "Tom Smith", it returns the value 3. But if you use it to find the space character in another string, such as "Angelina Brown", it returns the value 8 instead.

> **Notice**: *The value 3 is not just the position where the space character exists. The value 3 is also the number of characters that the word "Tom" contains! The same applies to the value 8 that is returned for the string "Angelina Brown". The value 8 is both the position where the space character exists and the number of characters that the word "Angelina" contains!*

The Python program for this algorithm is shown here.

file_11_4_2
```python
full_name = input("Enter your full name: ")

#Find the position of space character. This is also the number
#of characters first name contains
space_pos = full_name.find(" ")

#Get space_pos number of characters starting from position 0
name1 = full_name[:space_pos]

#Get the rest of the characters starting from position space_pos + 1
name2 = full_name[space_pos + 1:]

full_name = name2 + " " + name1
print(full_name)
```

> **Notice**: *Please note that you cannot apply this program to a Spanish name such as "Maria Teresa García Ramírez de Arroyo." The reason is obvious!*

Exercise 11.4.3 — Creating a Random Word

Write a Python program that displays a random word consisting of three letters.

Solution

To create a random word you need a string that contains all 26 letters of the English alphabet. Then you can use the `randrange()` function to choose a random letter between position 0 and 25.

The Python program for this algorithm is shown here.

file_11_4_3a
```python
import random
```

```
ab = "abcdefghijklmnopqrstuvwxyz"

random_letter1 = ab[random.randrange(26)]
random_letter2 = ab[random.randrange(26)]
random_letter3 = ab[random.randrange(26)]

random_word = random_letter1 + random_letter2 + random_letter3
print(random_word)
```

You can also use the `len()` function to get the length of string ab as shown here.

file_11_4_3b
```
import random

ab = "abcdefghijklmnopqrstuvwxyz"

random_letter1 = ab[random.randrange(len(ab))]
random_letter2 = ab[random.randrange(len(ab))]
random_letter3 = ab[random.randrange(len(ab))]

random_word = random_letter1 + random_letter2 + random_letter3
print(random_word)
```

> *Notice:* Please note how the function `len()` is "nested" within the function `randrange()`. The result of the inner (nested) function is used as an argument for the outer function. Nesting is a writing style that most programmers prefer to follow because it helps to save a lot of code lines. Of course, if you nest too many functions (or methods), no one will be able to understand your code. Nesting of up to four levels is acceptable.

11.5 Review Questions: True/False

Choose **true** or **false** for each of the following statements.

1. A string is anything that you can type using the keyboard.
2. Strings must be enclosed in parentheses.
3. The phrase "Hi there!" without the double quotes contains 8 characters.
4. In the phrase "Hi there!" (without the double quotes) the letter "t" is at position 3.
5. The statement `y = x[1]` assigns the second character of the string contained in variable x to variable y.
6. The statement `print("Hi there!".replace("Hi", "Hello"))` displays the message "Hello there!"

7. The following code fragment

   ```
   a = "Hi there"
   index = a.find("the")
   ```

   assigns the value 4 to the variable `index`.

8. The statement `print("hello there".upper())` displays the message "Hello There".

9. The statement `print(a[:len(a)])` displays some letters of the variable a.

10. The following code fragment

    ```
    y = "hello there!"
    print(y[:5].upper())
    ```

    displays the word "HELLO" without the double quotes.

11.6 Review Questions: Multiple Choice

Select the correct answer for each of the following statements.

1. Which of the following is **not** a string?
    a. "Hello there!"
    b. "13"
    c. "13.5"
    d. All of the above are strings.

2. In which position does the space character in the string "Hello Zeus!" exist?
    a. 6
    b. 5
    c. Space is not a character.
    d. none of the above

3. The statement `print(a[len(a) - 1])` displays
    a. the last character of variable a.
    b. the second to last character of variable a.
    c. The statement is not valid.

4. The statement `a.replace(" ", "")`
    a. adds a space between each letter in the variable a.
    b. removes all space characters from the variable a.
    c. empties the variable a.

5. The following code fragment

    ```
    a = ""
    print(len(a))
    ```

    displays
    a. nothing.
    b. 1.
    c. 0.

d. The statement is invalid.

e. none of the above

6. Which value assigns the following code fragment

    ```
    to_be_or_not_to_be = "2b Or Not 2b"
    Shakespeare = to_be_or_not_to_be.find("b")
    ```

    to the variable Shakespeare?

    a. 1

    b. 2

    c. 6

    d. none of the above

7. What does the following code fragment do?

    ```
    a = "Hi there"
    b = a[a.find(" ") + 1:]
    ```

    a. It assigns the word "Hi" to the variable b.

    b. It assigns a space character to the variable b.

    c. It assigns the word "there" to the variable b.

    d. none of the above

11.7 Review Exercises

Complete the following exercises.

1. Write a Python program that prompts the user to enter his or her first name, middle name, last name, and their preferred title (Mr., Mrs., Ms., Dr., and so on) and displays them formatted in all the following ways.

    Title FirstName MiddleName LastName

    FirstName MiddleName LastName

    LastName, FirstName

    LastName, FirstName MiddleName

    LastName, FirstName MiddleName, Title

    FirstName LastName

    For example, assume that the user enters the following:

    First name: Aphrodite

    Middle name: Maria

    Last name: Boura

    Title: Ms.

    The program must display the user's name formatted in all of the following ways:

    Ms. Aphrodite Maria Boura

    Aphrodite Maria Boura

    Boura, Aphrodite

> Boura, Aphrodite Maria
>
> Boura, Aphrodite Maria, Ms.
>
> Aphrodite Boura

2. Write a Python program that creates and displays a random word consisting of four letters. The first letter must be a capital letter.

3. Write a Python program that prompts the user to enter his or her name and then creates a secret password consisting of three letters (in lowercase) randomly picked up from his or her name, and a random four-digit number. For example, if the user enters "Vassilis Bouras" a secret password can probably be one of "sar1359" or "vbs7281" or "bor1459". Space characters are not allowed in the secret password.

11.8 Review Questions

Answer the following questions.

1. What is a function or a method in computer science?
2. What is "slicing" in Python?
3. What does the term "chain a method" mean?
4. What does the term "nest a function" mean?

Chapter 12
Making Questions

12.1 Introduction

All you have learned so far is just the sequence structure, where statements are executed sequentially, in the same order in which they appear in the program. However, in serious Python programming, rarely do you want the statements to be executed sequentially. Many times you want a block of statements to be executed in one situation and an entirely different block of statements to be executed in another situation.

> *Notice:* In a "decision structure" (also known as a "selection structure"), a question is asked, and depending on the answer, the computer decides on whether or not to execute a specific statement or a block of statements.

12.2 How to Write Simple Questions

Let's say that variable x contains a value of 5. This means that if you ask the question "*is x greater than 2?*" the answer is obviously "*Yes.*" For a computer, these questions are called *Boolean expressions*. For example, if you write x > 2, this is a Boolean expression, and the computer must check whether or not the expression x > 2 is True or False.

A *simple Boolean expression* is written as

where

- *Operand1* and *Operand2* can be values, variables, or mathematical expressions
- *Comparison_Operator* can be one of those shown in **Table 12.2-1**

Table 12.2-1 Comparison Operators in Python

Comparison Operator	Description
==	Equal (not assignment)
!=	Not equal
>	Greater than
<	Less than
>=	Greater than or equal to
<=	Less than or equal to

Here are some examples of Boolean expressions:

- x > y. This Boolean expression is a question to the computer and can be read as *"is x greater than y?"*
- x != 3 * y + 4. This Boolean expression is also a question to the computer and can be read as *"is x not equal to the result of the expression 3 * y + 4?"*
- s == "Hello". This can be read as *"is s equal to the word Hello?"* In other words, this question can be read as *"does s contain the word Hello?"*
- x == 5. This can be read as *"is x equal to 5?"*

> **Notice**: *A very common mistake that novice programmers make when writing Python programs is to confuse the assignment operator with the equals operator. They often make the mistake of writing x = 5 when they really want to ask if x == 5.*

> **Remember!** *Boolean expressions are questions and they should be read as "Is something equal to/greater than/less than something else?" and the answer is just a "Yes" or a "No" (True or False).*

Given that a Boolean expression actually returns a value (True or False), this value can be directly assigned to a variable. For example, the expression

```
a = x > y
```

assigns a value of True or False to Boolean variable a. It can be read as *"If the content of variable x is greater than the content of variable y, assign the value True to variable a; otherwise, assign the value False."* This next example displays the value True on the screen.

```
x = 8
y = 5

a = x > y
print(a)
```

Exercise 12.2.1 — Filling in the Table

Fill in the following table with the words "True" or "False" according to the values of the variables a and b.

a	b	a == 10	b <= a
3	-5		
10	2		
4	2		
-4	-2		
10	10		
2	10		

Chapter 12
Making Questions

Solution

Some notes about the table:
- The Boolean expression (the question) `a == 10` is True only when the content of the variable a is 10.
- The Boolean expression (the question) `b <= a` is True only when b is less than or equal to a.

So, the table becomes

a	b	a == 10	b <= a
3	-5	False	True
10	2	True	True
4	2	False	True
-4	-2	False	False
10	10	True	True
2	10	False	False

12.3 Logical Operators and Complex Questions

A more complex question (a complex Boolean expression) can be built of simpler Boolean expressions and can be written as

Boolean_Expression1   Logical_Operator   Boolean_Expression2

where
- *Boolean_Expression1* and *Boolean_Expression2* can be any simple Boolean expression
- *Logical_Operator* can be one of those shown in **Table 12.3-1**

Table 12.3-1 Logical Operators in Python

Logical_Operator
and
or
not

> **Notice:** When you combine simple Boolean expressions with logical operators, the whole Boolean expression is called a "complex Boolean expression". For example, the expression `x == 3 and y > 5` is a complex Boolean expression.

The and operator

When you use the `and` operator between two simple Boolean expressions, it means that the whole complex Boolean expression is `True` only when both simple Boolean expressions are `True`.

You can organize this information in something known as a *truth table*. A truth table shows the result of a logical operation between two or more simple Boolean expressions for all their possible combinations of values. The truth table for the and operator is shown here.

Boolean_Expression1 (BE1)	Boolean_Expression2 (BE2)	BE1 and BE2
False	False	*False*
False	True	*False*
True	False	*False*
True	True	*True*

Are you still confused? You shouldn't be! It is quite simple! Let's see an example. The complex Boolean expression

```
name == "John" and age > 5
```

is True only when the variable name contains the word "John" (without the double quotes) **and** variable age contains a value greater than 5. Both Boolean expressions must be True. If at least one of them is False, for example, the variable age contains a value of 3, then the whole complex Boolean expression is False.

The or operator

When you use the or operator between two simple Boolean expressions, it means the whole complex Boolean expression is True when either the first or the second simple Boolean expression is True (at least one.)

The truth table for the or operator is shown here.

Boolean_Expression1 (BE1)	Boolean_Expression2 (BE2)	BE1 or BE2
False	False	*False*
False	True	*True*
True	False	*True*
True	True	*True*

Let's see an example. The complex Boolean expression

```
name == "John" or name == "George"
```

is True when the variable name contains the word "John" **or** the word "George" (without the double quotes). At least one Boolean expression must be True. If both Boolean Expressions are False, for example, the variable name contains the word "Maria", then the whole complex Boolean expression is False.

The not operator

When you use the `not` operator in front of a simple Boolean expression, it means that the whole complex Boolean expression is `True` when the simple Boolean expression is `False` and vice versa.

The truth table for the `not` operator is shown here.

Boolean_Expression (BE)	not BE
False	*True*
True	*False*

Let's see an example. The complex Boolean expression

$$\text{not age} > 5$$

is `True` when the variable `age` contains a value less than or equal to 5. If, for example, the variable `age` contains a value of 6, then the whole complex Boolean expression is `False`.

> **Remember!** *The logical operator* **not** *reverses the result of a Boolean expression.*

12.4 Python's Membership Operators

In Python, a *membership operator* evaluates whether or not a variable exists in a specified sequence. There are two membership operators, as shown in **Table 12.4-1**.

Table 12.4-1 Membership Operators in Python

Membership Operator	Description
in	It evaluates to `True` if it finds a value in the specified sequence; it evaluates to `False` otherwise.
not in	It evaluates to `True` if it does **not** find a value in the specified sequence; it evaluates to `False` otherwise.

Next are some examples of Boolean expressions that use membership operators.

- `x in [3, 5, 9]`. This can be read as *"is x equal to 3, or equal to 5, or equal to 9?"*. It can also be written as

$$x == 3 \text{ or } x == 5 \text{ or } x == 9.$$

- `x in "ab"`. This can be read as *"is x equal to letter "a", or equal to letter "b", or equal to word "ab"?"* It can also be written as

$$x == \text{"a"} \text{ or } x == \text{"b"} \text{ or } x == \text{"ab"}$$

- `x in ["a", "b"]`. This can be read as *"is x equal to letter "a", or equal to letter "b"?"* It can also be written as

$$x == \text{"a"} \text{ or } x == \text{"b"}$$

- `x not in ["a", "b"]`. This can be read as *"is x **not** equal to letter "a", nor equal to letter "b"?"* It can also be written as

    `not(x == "a" or x == "b")`

12.5 What is the Order of Precedence of Logical Operators?

A more complex Boolean expression may use several logical operators like the expression shown here.

`name == "Peter" or age > 10 and not name == "Maria"`

So, a reasonable question is *"which logical operation is performed first?"*

Python's logical operators follow the same precedence rules that apply to most programming languages. The order of precedence is: perform the not logical operators first, perform the and logical operators next, and perform the or logical operators last.

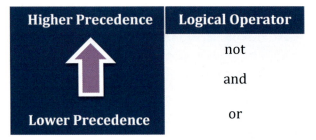

Notice: You can always use parentheses to change the default precedence.

12.6 What is the Order of Precedence of Arithmetic, Comparison, and Logical Operators?

In many cases, an expression may contain different types of operators, such as the expression shown here.

`a * b + 2 > 21 or not(c == b / 2) and c > 13`

In such cases, perform arithmetic operations first, perform comparison operations next, and perform logical operations last, as shown in the following table.

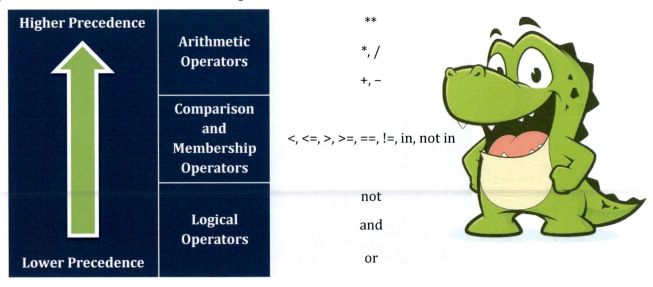

Chapter 12
Making Questions

Exercise 12.6.1 — Filling in the Truth Table

Fill in the following table with the words "True" or "False" according to the values of the variables a, b and c.

a	b	c	a > 2 or c > b and c > 2	not(a > 2 or c > b and c > 2)
1	-5	7		
-4	-2	-9		

Solution

To calculate the result of a complex Boolean expression, you can use the following graphical method.

For a = 1, b = -5, c = 7,

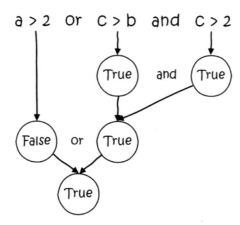

the final result is True.

> **Remember!** The *and* operation has a higher precedence and is performed before the *or* operation.

For a = -4, b = -2, c = -9,

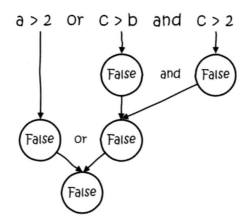

the final result is False.

The values in the table's fifth column can be calculated easily because the Boolean expression in its column heading is almost identical to the one in the fourth column. The only difference is the *not* operator in front of the expression. So, the values in the fifth column can be calculated by simply reversing the results in the fourth column!

The final truth table is shown here.

a	b	c	a > 2 or c > b and c > 2	not(a > 2 or c > b and c > 2)
1	−5	7	True	False
−4	−2	−9	False	True

12.7 Converting English Sentences to Boolean Expressions

A teacher asks her students to raise their hands according to their age. She wants to find the students who are

  i. between the ages of 9 and 12.
 ii. under the age of 8 and over the age of 11.
iii. 8, 10, and 12 years old.
 iv. between the ages of 6 and 8, and between the ages of 10 and 12.
  v. neither 10 nor 12 years old.

Solution

To compose the required Boolean expressions, a variable age is used.

i. The sentence "*Between the ages of 9 and 12*" can be graphically represented as shown here.

Be careful though! It is valid to write 9 ≤ age ≤ 12 in mathematics, as well as in Python where you can write it as

$$9 \;\texttt{<=}\; age \;\texttt{<=}\; 12$$

In most computer languages, however, this is not a valid Boolean expression. What you can do is to split the expression into two parts, as shown here

$$age \;\texttt{>=}\; 9 \;\text{and}\; age \;\texttt{<=}\; 12$$

This last expression is valid in most computer languages, including Python.

For your confirmation, you can test this Boolean expression for several values inside and outside of the *region of interest* (the range of data that you have specified). For example, the result of the expression is False for the age values 7, 8, 13, and 17. On the contrary, for the age values 9, 10, 11, and 12, the result is True.

ii. The sentence "*under the age of 8 and over the age of 11*" can be graphically represented as shown here.

> **Notice:** Please note the absence of the two circles that you saw in solution (i). This means the values 8 and 11 are **not** included within the two regions of interest.

Be careful with the sentence "Under the age of 8 **and** over the age of 11". It's a trap! Don't make the mistake of writing

$$\text{age < 8 and age > 11}$$

There is no person on the planet Earth that can be under the age of 8 **and** over the age of 11 concurrently!

The trap is in the word "**and**". Try to rephrase the sentence and make it *"Children! Please raise your hand if you are under the age of 8 **or** over the age of 11."* Now it's better and the correct Boolean expression becomes

$$\text{age < 8 or age > 11}$$

For your confirmation, you can test this expression for several values inside and outside of the regions of interest. For example, the result of the expression is False for the age values 8, 9, 10 and 11. On the contrary, for the age values 6, 7, 12, and 15, the result is True.

In Python, however, don't make the mistake of writing

$$\text{8 > age > 11}$$

because, if you split the expression into two parts, it is equivalent to

$$\text{age < 8 and age > 11}$$

which, as already mentioned, is incorrect!

iii. Oops! Another trap in the sentence *"8, 10, and 12 years old"* with the "**and**" word again! Obviously, the next Boolean expression is wrong.

$$\text{age == 8 and age == 10 and age == 12}$$

As before, there isn't any student who is 8 **and** 10 **and** 12 years old concurrently! Once again, the correct Boolean expression must use the or operator.

$$\text{age == 8 or age == 10 or age == 12}$$

For your confirmation, you can test this expression for several values inside and outside of the regions of interest. For example, the result of the expression is False for the age values 7, 9, 11, and 13. For the age values 8, 10, and 12, the result is True.

In Python, this complex Boolean expression can also be written as

$$\text{age in [8, 10, 12]}$$

iv. The sentence *"between the ages of 6 and 8, and between the ages of 10 and 12"* can be graphically represented as shown here.

and the Boolean expression is

$$\text{age >= 6 and age <= 8 or age >= 10 and age <= 12}$$

For your confirmation, the result of the expression is False for the age values 5, 9, 13, and 16. For the age values 6, 7, 8, 10, 11, and 12, the result is True.

In Python, this complex Boolean expression can also be written as

$$\text{6 <= age <= 8 or 10 <= age <= 12}$$

v. The Boolean expression for the sentence "*neither 10 nor 12 years old*" can be written as

$$\text{age != 10 and age != 12}$$

In Python, this complex Boolean expression can also be written as

$$\text{age not in [10, 12]}$$

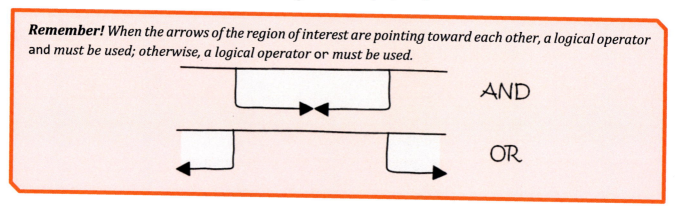

Remember! When the arrows of the region of interest are pointing toward each other, a logical operator *and* must be used; otherwise, a logical operator *or* must be used.

12.8 Review Questions: True/False

Choose **true** or **false** for each of the following statements.

1. A Boolean expression is an expression that always results in one of two values.
2. A Boolean expression includes at least one logical operator.
3. In Python, the expression x = 5 tests if the variable x is equal to 5.
4. The statement a = b == c is not a valid Python statement.
5. The Boolean expression b < 5 tests if the variable b is 5 or less.
6. When two simple Boolean expressions are combined with an or operator the result is definitely True, given that the simple Boolean expressions have different values.
7. The expression c == 3 and d > 7 is considered a complex Boolean expression.
8. The result of the logical operator or is True when both operands (Boolean expressions) are True.
9. The result of the Boolean expression not(x == 5) is True when the variable x contains any value except 5.
10. The not operator has the highest precedence among logical operators.
11. The or operator has the lowest precedence among logical operators.
12. In the Boolean expression x > y or x == 5 and x <= z, the and operation is performed before the or operation.
13. In the Boolean expression a * b + c > 21 or c == b / 2, the program first tests if c is greater than 21.
14. When a teacher wants to find the students who are under the age of 8 and over the age of 11, the corresponding Boolean expression is 8 > a > 11.
15. The Boolean expression x < 0 and x > 100 is, for any value of x, always False.
16. The Boolean expression x > 0 or x < 100 is, for any value of x, always True.
17. The Boolean expression x > 5 is equivalent to not(x < 5).

18. In William Shakespeare's[1] *Hamlet* (Act 3, Scene 1), the main character says "To be, or not to be: that is the question:.... " If you write this down as a Boolean expression

    to_be or not to_be

    the result of the "Shakespearean" expression is always True for the following code fragment.

    ```
    to_be = 1 > 0
    result = to_be or not to_be
    ```

19. The Boolean expression not(not(x > 5)) is equivalent to x > 5.

12.9 Review Questions: Multiple Choice

Select the correct answer for each of the following statements.

1. Which of the following is not a comparison operator?
    a. >=
    b. =
    c. <
    d. All of the above are comparison operators.

2. Which of the following is not a Python logical operator?
    a. nor
    b. not
    c. All of the above are logical operators.
    d. None of the above is a logical operator.

3. If variable x contains a value of 5, what value does the statement y = x > 1 assign to variable y?
    a. True
    b. False
    c. none of the above

4. If variable x contains a value of 5, what value does the statement y = x < 2 or x == 5 assign to variable y?
    a. True
    b. False
    c. none of the above

5. The temperature in a laboratory room should be between 50 and 80 degrees Fahrenheit. Which of the following Boolean expressions tests for this condition?
    a. t >= 50 or t <= 80
    b. 50 < t < 80

---

[1] William Shakespeare (1564–1616) was an English poet, playwright, and actor. He is often referred to as England's national poet. He wrote about 40 plays and several long narrative poems. His works are counted among the best representations of world literature. His plays have been translated into every major living language and are still performed today.

c. `t >= 50 and t <= 80`
d. `t > 50 or t < 80`

12.10 Review Exercises

Complete the following exercises.

1. Match each element in the first column with one or more elements from the second column.

Operator		Sign	
i.	Logical operator	a.	+=
ii.	Arithmetic operator	b.	and
iii.	Comparison operator	c.	==
iv.	Assignment operator (in general)	d.	or
		e.	>=
		f.	not
		g.	=
		h.	*=
		i.	/

2. Fill in the following table with the words "True" or "False" according to the values of variables a, b, and c.

a	b	c	a != 1	b > a	c / 2 > 2 * a
3	−5	8			
1	10	20			
−4	−2	−9			

3. Fill in the following table with the words "True" or "False" according to the values of the Boolean expressions BE1 and BE2.

Boolean Expression1 (BE1)	Boolean Expression2 (BE2)	BE1 or BE2	BE1 and BE2	not(BE2)
False	False			
False	True			
True	False			
True	True			

4. Fill in the following table with the words "True" or "False" according to the values of variables a, b, and c.

a	b	c	a > 3 or c > b and c > 1	a > 3 and c > b or c > 1
4	−6	2		
−3	2	−4		

5. For x = 4, y = -2 and flag = True, fill in the following table with the corresponding values.

Expression	Value
(x + y) ** 3	
(x + y) / (x ** 2 - 14)	
(x - 1) == y + 5	
x > 2 and y == 1	
x == 1 or not(flag == False)	

6. A teacher asks her students to raise their hands according to their age. She wants to find the students who are:
   a. under the age of 12, but not those who are 8 years old.
   b. between the ages of 6 and 9, and also those who are 11 years old.
   c. over the age of 7, but not those who are 10 or 12 years old.
   d. 6, 9, and 11 years old.
   e. between the ages of 6 and 12, but not those who are 8 years old.
   f. neither 7 nor 10 years old.

   To compose the required Boolean expressions, use the variable age.

12.11 Review Questions

Answer the following questions.
1. What is a Boolean expression?
2. Which comparison operators does Python support?
3. When does the logical operator and return a result of True?
4. When does the logical operator or return a result of True?
5. State the order of precedence of logical operators.
6. State the order of precedence of arithmetic, comparison, membership, and logical operators.

Chapter 13
Asking Questions – The if Structure

13.1 The if Structure

This is the simplest decision structure. It includes a statement or block of statements on the "True" path only.

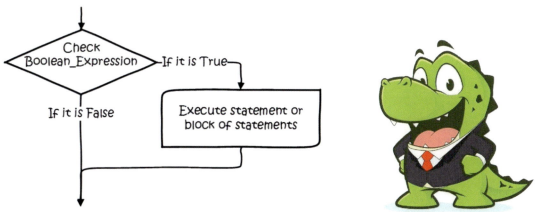

If the Boolean expression evaluates to True, the statement, or block of statements, of the structure is executed; otherwise, the statements are skipped.

The general form of the Python statement is

```
if Boolean_Expression:
    #Here goes
    #a statement or block of statements
```

In the next example, the message "You are underage!" displays only when the user enters a value less than 18. Nothing is displayed when the user enters a value that is greater than or equal to 18.

file_13_1a
```
age = int(input("Enter your age: "))

if age < 18:
    print("You are underage!")
```

Notice: Please note that the `print()` *statement is indented by 4 spaces.*

In the next example, the message "You are underage!" and the message "You have to wait for a few more years" are displayed only when the user enters a value less than 18. Same as previously, no messages are displayed when the user enters a value that is greater than or equal to 18.

file_13_1b
```
age = int(input("Enter your age: "))
```

```python
if age < 18:
    print("You are underage!")
    print("You have to wait for a few more years.")
```

In the next example, the message "You are the King of the Gods!" is displayed only when the user enters the word "Zeus". The message "You live on Mount Olympus", however, is always displayed, no matter what name the user enters.

file_13_1c

```python
name = input("Enter the name of an Olympian: ")

if name == "Zeus":
    print("You are the King of the Gods!")

print("You Live on Mount Olympus.")
```

> **Notice**: A very common mistake that novice programmers make when writing Python programs is to confuse the assignment operator with the "equal" operator. They frequently make the mistake of writing `if name = "Zeus"` when they actually want to say `if name == "Zeus"`.

> **Notice**: Please note that the last `print()` statement is **not** indented, and so it does **not** belong to the block of statements of the `if` structure.

> **Notice**: Python was one of the first programming languages to enforce indentation. Python indicates that several statements are part of a group by indenting them. The indented group is called a "block of statements" or "code block." Indentation is considered good practice in other languages, but in Python indentation is **mandatory**. Code that is part of a block must be indented. For example, all statements that appear inside an `if` statement must be indented to the right by the same number of spaces; otherwise they are not considered part of the `if` statement and you will likely get an error message. There are two simple rules to remember about code block syntax:
> - The statement on the first line of a code block always ends with a colon (:) character.
> - The code underneath the first line must be indented.

> **Notice**: Python's official website recommends the use of 4 spaces per indentation level. If you need more information you can visit
> *https://www.python.org/dev/peps/pep-0008*

> **Notice**: In computer languages other than Python, such as C, C++, C#, Java, or Visual Basic, indentation is not mandatory but it is necessary. Indentation makes your code easier to read and helps programmers to more easily study and understand code written by others.

Chapter 13
Asking Questions – The if Structure

Exercise 13.1.1 — Find Out What is Displayed

Try to determine the values of the variables in each step of the next Python program for two different executions and find out what is displayed on the user's screen.

The input values for the two executions are (i) 6, and (ii) 4.

file_13_1_1
```
x = int(input())

y = 5
if x * 2 > 10:
    y = x * 3
    x = x * 2

print(y, x)
```

Solution

i. For the input value of 6:
   1. The value 6 is assigned to variable x.
   2. The value 5 is assigned to variable y.
   3. The Boolean expression x * 2 > 10 evaluates to True.
   4. The two statements of the if structure are executed.
   5. The values 18 and 12 are displayed on the user's screen.

ii. For the input value of 4:
   1. The value 4 is assigned to variable x.
   2. The value 5 is assigned to variable y.
   3. The Boolean expression x * 2 > 10 evaluates to False. Thus, the two statements of the if structure are **not** executed.
   4. The values 5 and 4 are displayed on user's screen.

Exercise 13.1.2 — Are you Allowed to Drive a Car?

Write a Python program that prompts the user to enter his or her age, and then displays the message "You can drive a car in Kansas (USA)" when the given age is greater than or equal to 15.

Solution

In this exercise, the program must prompt the user to enter his or her age (as an integer, without decimal digits) and then it must check whether to display the given message. The solution to this problem is shown here.

file_13_1_2
```
age = int(input("Enter your age: "))

if age >= 15:
    print("You can drive a car in Kansas (USA)")
```

Exercise 13.1.3 — Finding Minimum and Maximum Values with `if` Structures

Write a Python program that prompts the user to enter the weight of four people and then finds and displays the lightest weight.

Solution

Suppose there are some men and you want to find the lightest one. Let's say that each one of them comes by and tells you his weight. What you must do is, memorize the weight of the first person that has come by and for each new person, you have to compare his weight with the one that you keep memorized. If he is heavier, you ignore his weight. However, if he is lighter, you need to forget the previous weight and memorize the new one. The same procedure continues until all the people have come by.

Let's ask four men to come by in a random order. Assume that their weights, in order of appearance, are 165, 170, 160, and 180 pounds.

Procedure	Value of Variable `minimum` in Your Mind!
The first person comes by. He weighs 165 pounds. Keep his weight in your mind (imagine a variable in your mind named minimum.)	minimum = 165
The second person comes by. He weighs 170 pounds. He does not weigh less than the weight you are keeping in variable minimum, so you must ignore his weight. Variable minimum in your mind still contains the value 165.	minimum = 165
The third person comes by. He weighs 160 pounds, which is less than the weight you are keeping in variable minimum, so you must forget the previous value and keep the value 160 in variable minimum.	minimum = 160
The fourth person comes by. He weighs 180 pounds. He does not weigh less than the weight you are keeping in variable minimum, so you must ignore his weight. Variable minimum still contains the value 160.	minimum = 160

When the procedure finishes, the variable `minimum` in your mind contains the weight of the lightest man!

Following is the corresponding Python program that prompts the user to enter the weight of four people and then finds and displays the lightest weight.

file_13_1_3a
```
w1 = int(input("Enter the weight of the 1st person: "))
w2 = int(input("Enter the weight of the 2nd person: "))
w3 = int(input("Enter the weight of the 3rd person: "))
w4 = int(input("Enter the weight of the 4th person: "))

#memorize the weight of the first person
minimum = w1
```

Chapter 13
Asking Questions – The if Structure

```
#If second one is lighter, forget
#everything and memorize this weight
if w2 < minimum:
    minimum = w2

#If third one is lighter, forget
#everything and memorize this weight
if w3 < minimum:
    minimum = w3

#If fourth one is lighter, forget
#everything and memorize this weight
if w4 < minimum:
    minimum = w4

print(minimum)
```

Notice: *You can find the maximum instead of the minimum value by simply replacing the "less than" with a "greater than" operator in all Boolean expressions.*

Notice: *Please note that this program is trying to find out the lowest value and **not** which variable this value was actually assigned to.*

A more Pythonic way, however, is to use the min() function as shown here.

file_13_1_3b
```
w1 = int(input("Enter the weight of the 1st person: "))
w2 = int(input("Enter the weight of the 2nd person: "))
w3 = int(input("Enter the weight of the 3rd person: "))
w4 = int(input("Enter the weight of the 4th person: "))

print(min(w1, w2, w3, w4))
```

Exercise 13.1.4 — Finding the Name of the Heaviest Person

Write a Python program that prompts the user to enter the weights and the names of three people and then displays the name and the weight of the heaviest person.

Solution

In this exercise, along with the maximum weight, you need to store in another variable the name of the person who actually has that weight. The Python program is shown here.

file_13_1_4
```
w1 = int(input("Enter the weight of the 1st person: "))
n1 = input("Enter the name of the 1st person: ")
```

```python
w2 = int(input("Enter the weight of the 2nd person: "))
n2 = input("Enter the name of the 2nd person: ")

w3 = int(input("Enter the weight of the 3rd person: "))
n3 = input("Enter the name of the 3rd person: ")

maximum = w1
m_name = n1          #This variable holds the name of the heaviest person

if w2 > maximum:
    maximum = w2
    m_name = n2      #Someone else is heavier. Keep his or her name.

if w3 > maximum:
    maximum = w3
    m_name = n3      #Someone else is heavier. Keep his or her name.

print("The heaviest person is", m_name)
print("His or her weight is", maximum)
```

Notice: *If the two heaviest people happen to have the same weight, the first one that the user entered is found and displayed.*

13.2 Review Questions: True/False

Choose **true** or **false** for each of the following statements.

1. The `if` structure is used when a sequence of statements must be executed.
2. You use an `if` structure to allow other programmers to more easily understand your program.
3. It is possible that none of the statements enclosed in an `if` structure will be executed.
4. The following code

    ```
    if = 5
    x = if + 5
    print(x)
    ```

    is syntactically correct.

Chapter 13
Asking Questions – The if Structure

13.3 Review Questions: Multiple Choice

Select the correct answer for each of the following statements.

1. The `if` structure is used when
    a. statements are executed one after another.
    b. a decision must be made before executing some statements.
    c. neither *a* nor *b*
    d. both *a* and *b*

2. The following two programs

    ```
    a = int(input())              a = int(input())
    if a > 40:                    if a > 40:
        print(a * 2)                  print(a * 2)
    if a > 40:                        print(a * 3)
        print(a * 3)
    ```

    a. produce the same results
    b. do not produce the same results.

3. In the following code fragment,

    ```
    if x == 3:
        x = 5
    y += 1
    ```

    the statement `y += 1` is
    a. executed only when variable x contains a value of 3.
    b. executed only when variable x contains a value of 5.
    c. executed only when variable x contains a value other than 3.
    d. always executed.

4. In the following code fragment,

    ```
    x = y
    if x != y:
        y += 1
    ```

    the statement `y += 1` is
    a. always executed.
    b. sometimes executed.
    c. never executed.

13.4 Review Exercises

Complete the following exercises.

1. Identify all five syntax errors in the following Python program:

    ```
    x = float(input())


    5 = y
    if x * y / 2 > 20
        y =* 2
        x = 4 * x²


    print(x  y)
    ```

2. Try to find out the values of the variables in each step of the following Python program for two different executions, and find what is displayed on the user's screen.

    The input values for the two executions are (i) 3, and (ii) 2.

    ```
    x = int(input())


    y = 2
    if x * y > 7:
        y -= 1
        x -= 4


    if x > 2:
        y += 10
        x = x ** 2


    print(x, y)
    ```

3. Write a Python program that prompts the user to enter a number, and then displays the message "Positive" when the given number is positive.

4. Write a Python program that prompts the user to enter two numbers, and then displays the message "Positives" when both given numbers are positives.

5. Write a Python program that prompts the user to enter a string, and then displays the message "Uppercase" when the given string contains only uppercase characters.

    Hint: Use the upper() method.

6. Write a Python program that prompts the user to enter a string, and then displays the message "Many characters" when the given string contains more than 20 characters.

    Hint: Use the len() function.

7. Write a Python program that prompts the user to enter three numbers and, if one of them is negative, it displays the message "Among the given numbers, there is a negative one!"

8. Write a Python program that prompts the user to enter three temperature values measured at three different points in New York, and then displays the message "Heat Wave" if the average value is greater than 60 degrees Fahrenheit.

9. Write a Python program that prompts the user to enter the weight of four people and then finds and displays the heaviest weight.

10. Write a Python program that prompts the user to enter the ages and the names of four people and then displays the name of the youngest person.

11. Write a Python program that prompts the user to enter the ages of three people and then finds and displays the age in the middle.

13.5 Review Questions

Answer the following questions.
1. When must a block of code be indented?
2. Write the Python statement (in general form) of an `if` structure. Describe how this decision structure operates.

Chapter 14
Asking Questions - The `if-else` Structure

14.1 The `if-else` Structure

This is another type of decision structure. In contrast to the `if` structure, this type of decision structure includes a statement or block of statements on both paths, "True" and "False".

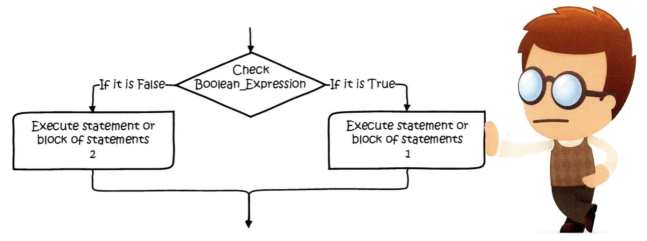

If the Boolean expression evaluates to True, the statement or block of statements 1 is executed; otherwise, the statement or block of statements 2 is executed.

The general form of the Python statement is

```python
if Boolean_Expression:
    #Here goes
    #a statement or block of statements 1
else:
    #Here goes
    #a statement or block of statements 2
```

In the next example, the message "You are an adult" is displayed when the user enters a value greater than or equal to 18. The message "You are underage!" is displayed otherwise.

file_14_1
```python
age = int(input("Enter your age: "))

if age >= 18:
    print("You are an adult!")
else:
    print("You are underage!")
```

Exercise 14.1.1 — Finding the Output Message

For the following Python program, determine the output message for three different executions.

The input values for the three executions are (i) 3, (ii) –3, and (iii) 0.

```python
a = int(input())
if a > 0:
    print("Positive")
else:
    print("Negative")
```

Solution

i. When the user enters the value 3, the Boolean expression evaluates to True and the message "Positive" is displayed.
ii. When the user enters the value –3, the Boolean expression evaluates to False and the message "Negative" is displayed.
iii. When the user enters the value 0, the Boolean expression evaluates to False. Inevitably, the message "Negative" is displayed again!

> **Notice:** Hey, don't jump the gun! Obviously, something is not quite right with this program! Zero is not a negative value! Actually, it is not a positive value either. Later in this book, you will learn how to display a third message that will say "The number entered is zero."

Exercise 14.1.2 — Who is the Greatest?

Write a Python program that prompts the user to enter two numbers, A and B, and then finds and displays the greater of the two numbers. Assume the user enters two different values.

Solution

You can solve this exercise using either the `if` or the `if-else` structure. Also, a third approach shows you how to do this in a more Pythonic way!

First approach - Using an `if-else` structure

This approach tests if the value of number B is greater than that of number A. If so, number B is the greatest; otherwise, number A is the greatest. The Python program is as follows.

file_14_1_2a

```python
a = float(input("Enter number A: "))
b = float(input("Enter number B: "))

if b > a:
    maximum = b
else:
    maximum = a
```

```
print("Greatest value:", maximum)
```

Second approach - Using an `if` structure

This approach first assumes that number A is the greatest value (this is why it assigns the value of variable a to the variable `maximum`). However, if it turns out that number B is a greater than number A, then the greatest value is updated, that is, the variable `maximum` is assigned a new value, the value of variable b. Thus whatever happens, in the end the variable `maximum` always contains the greatest value! The Python program is shown here.

file_14_1_2b
```python
a = float(input())
b = float(input())

maximum = a
if b > a:
    maximum = b

print("Greatest value:", maximum)
```

Third approach - The Pythonic way

This approach is the simplest, without any decision structure. It just uses the `max()` function of Python as shown here.

file_14_1_2c
```python
a = float(input())
b = float(input())

maximum = max(a, b)
print("Greatest value:", maximum)
```

Exercise 14.1.3 — Converting Gallons to Liters, and Vice Versa

Write a Python program that displays the following menu:

1. Convert gallons to liters
2. Convert liters to gallons

Then, the program prompts the user to enter a choice (1 or 2) and a quantity. Finally, it must calculate and display the required value. It is given that

$$1 \text{ gallon} = 3.785 \text{ liters}$$

Solution

The Python program is shown here.

file_14_1_3
```python
COEFFICIENT = 3.785
```

```
print("1: Gallons to liters")
print("2: Liters to gallons")
choice = int(input("Enter choice: "))

quantity = float(input("Enter quantity: "))

if choice == 1:
    result = quantity * COEFFICIENT
    print(quantity, "gallons =", result, "liters")
else:
    result = quantity / COEFFICIENT
    print(quantity, "liters =", result, "gallons")
```

14.2 Review Questions: True/False

Choose **true** or **false** for each of the following statements.

1. It is possible that none of the statements enclosed in an `if-else` structure will be executed.
2. The `if-else` structure must include at least two statements.
3. The statement
   ```
   else = 2
   ```
   is syntactically correct.
4. In an `if-else` structure, the evaluated Boolean expression can return more than two values.

14.3 Review Questions: Multiple Choice

Select the correct answer for each of the following statements.

1. The following two programs

   ```
   a = int(input())
   if a > 40:
       a += 1
       print(a * 2)
   else:
       a += 1
       print(a * 3)
   ```

   ```
   a = int(input())
   a += 1
   if a > 40:
       print(a * 2)
   else:
       print(a * 3)
   ```

   a. produce the same result.
   b. do not produce the same result.

Chapter 14
Asking Questions - The if-else Structure

2. The following two programs

    ```
    a = int(input())

    if a > 40:
        print(a * 2)
    else:
        print(a * 3)
    ```

    ```
    a = int(input())

    if a > 40:
        print(a * 2)
    if a <= 40:
        print(a * 3)
    ```

    a. produce the same result(s).
    b. do not produce the same result(s).
    c. neither of the above

3. In the following code fragment,

    ```
    if x > 5:
        x = 0
    else:
        x += 1
    ```

    the statement x = 0 is executed when

    a. variable x is greater than 5.
    b. variable x is greater than or equal to 5.
    c. variable x is less than 5.
    d. none of the above

4. In the following code fragment,

    ```
    if x > 0:
        x = 0
    else:
        x += 1
    ```

    the statement x += 1 is executed when

    a. variable x is negative.
    b. variable x is equal to zero.
    c. variable x is less than zero.
    d. all of the above

5. In the following code fragment,

    ```
    if x == 3:
        x = 5
    else:
        x = 7
    y += 1
    ```

    the statement y += 1 is executed

    a. when variable x contains a value of 3.
    b. when variable x contains a value other than 3.

c. both of the above

14.4 Review Exercises

Complete the following exercises.

1. Try to determine the values of the variables in each step of the next Python program for two different executions, and find out what is displayed on the user's screen.

    The input values for the two executions are (i) 0, and (ii) 1.5.

    ```
    a = float(input())
    if a >= 1:
        a = 5
    else:
        a = 1
    print(a)
    ```

2. Try to determine the values of the variables in each step of the next Python program for two different executions and find out what is displayed on the user's screen.

    The input values for the two executions are (i) 3, and (ii) 0.5.

    ```
    a = float(input())
    z = a * 3 - 2
    if z >= 1:
        y = 6 * a
    else:
        z += 1
        y = 6 * a + z
    print(z, y)
    ```

3. Using an if-else structure, write a Python program that prompts the user to enter a number, and then displays a message indicating whether the given number is greater than 100.

4. Using an if-else structure, write a Python program that prompts the user to enter a number, and then displays a message indicating whether the given number is between 0 and 100.

5. Using an if-else structure, write a Python program that prompts the user to enter an integer, and then displays a message indicating whether the given integer is a four-digit integer.

    Hint: Four-digit integers are between 1000 and 9999.

6. Using an if-else structure, write a Python program that prompts the user to enter two values, and then determines and displays the smaller of the two values. Assume the user enters two different values.

7. Athletes in the long jump at the Olympic Games in Athens in 2004 took part in three different qualifying jumps. Assume that to qualify, an athlete had to achieve an average jump distance of at least 8 meters. Write a Python program that prompts the user to enter the three performances, and then displays the message "Qualified" when the average value is greater than or equal to 8 meters; it displays "Disqualified" otherwise.

Chapter 15
Asking Questions - The if-elif Structure

15.1 The if-elif Structure

The if-elif structure is used to expand the number of alternatives, as shown here.

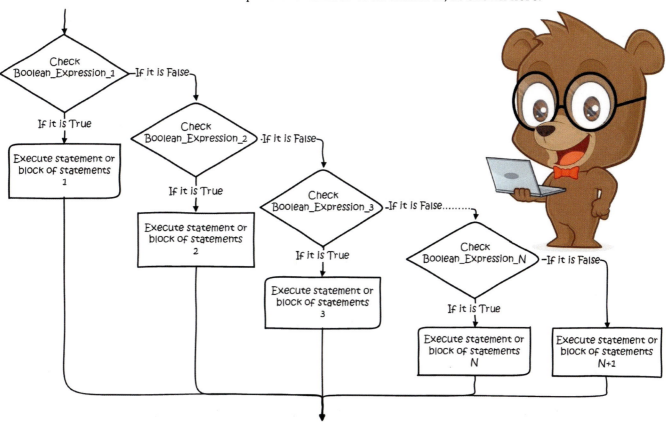

When an if-elif structure is executed, *Boolean_Expression_1* is evaluated. If *Boolean_Expression_1* evaluates to True, the corresponding statement or block of statements that immediately follows it is executed and the rest of the structure is skipped, that is, the flow of execution continues to any statements that may exist **after** the if-elif structure. However, if *Boolean_Expression_1* evaluates to False, the flow of execution evaluates *Boolean_Expression_2*. If *Boolean_Expression_2* evaluates to True, the corresponding statement or block of statements that immediately follows it is executed and the rest of the structure is skipped. This continues until one Boolean expression evaluates to True or until no more Boolean expressions are left.

The last statement or block of statements N+1 executes when none of the previous Boolean expressions has evaluated to True. Also, this last statement or block of statements N+1 is optional and can be omitted. It depends on the algorithm you are trying to solve.

The general form of the Python statement is

```
if Boolean_Expression_1:
    #Here goes a statement or block of statements 1
elif Boolean_Expression_2:
    #Here goes a statement or block of statements 2
elif Boolean_Expression_3:
    #Here goes a statement or block of statements 3
.
.
elif Boolean_Expression_N:
    #Here goes a statement or block of statements N
else:
    #Here goes a statement or block of statements N + 1
```

Notice: The keyword `elif` is an abbreviation for "else if."

A simple example is shown here.

file_15_1

```python
name = input("What is your name? ")

if name == "John":
    print("You are my cousin!")
elif name == "Aphrodite":
    print("You are my sister!")
elif name == "Loukia":
    print("You are my mom!")
else:
    print("Sorry, I don't know you.")
```

Exercise 15.1.1 — Find Out What is Displayed

Try to find out the values of the variables in each step for three different executions of the next Python program, and find out what is displayed on the user's screen.

The input values for the three executions are (i) 5, 8; (ii) 2, 0; and (iii) 1, −1.

file_15_1_1

```python
a = int(input())
b = int(input())

if a > 3:
    print("Message #1")
```

```
    elif a > 1 and b <= 10:
        print("Message #2")
        print("Message #3")
    elif b == 0:
        print("Message #4")
    else:
        print("Message #5")

print("The End!")
```

Solution

i. For the input values of 5 and 8:
   1. The value 5 is assigned to variable a and the value 8 is assigned to variable b.
   2. The first Boolean expression (a > 3) evaluates to True
   3. The message "Message #1" is displayed on the user's screen. Since the first Boolean expression has evaluated to True, the second Boolean expression (a > 1 and b <= 10) is not checked.
   4. The message "The End" is displayed.

ii. For the input values of 2 and 0:
   1. The value 2 is assigned to variable a and the value 0 is assigned to variable b.
   2. The first Boolean expression (a > 3) evaluates to False
   3. The flow of execution continues and evaluates the second Boolean expression (a > 1 and b <= 10). This one evaluates to True
   4. The messages "Message #2" and "Message #3" are displayed.
   5. The message "The End" is displayed.

> **Notice:** *Please note that the third Boolean expression (b == 0) could also have evaluated to True, but it was never checked.*

iii. For the input values of 1 and –1:
   1. The value 1 is assigned to variable a and the value –1 is assigned to variable b.
   2. None of the Boolean expressions evaluates to True, so the message "Message #5" is displayed.
   3. The message "The End" is displayed.

Exercise 15.1.2 — Counting the Digits

Write a Python program that prompts the user to enter an integer between 0 and 999 and then counts its total number of digits. In the end, a message "You entered a N-digit number" is displayed, where N is the total number of digits. For example, if the user enters a value of 87, the message "You entered a 2-digit number" must be displayed, whereas if the user enters a value of 756, the message "You entered a 3-digit number" must be displayed. Assume the user enters a valid number between 0 and 999.

Solution

The following Python program assumes the user enters a valid number between 0 and 999, and therefore it does not check the validity of the data input. The solution to this problem is shown here.

file_15_1_2a
```python
x = int(input("Enter an integer (0 - 999): "))

if x <= 9:
    count = 1
elif x <= 99:
    count = 2
else:
    count = 3

print("You entered a ", count, "-digit number", sep = "")
```

However, if you wish to make your program even better and display an error message to the user when he or she enters a value that is not between 0 and 999, you can do something like this:

file_15_1_2b
```python
x = int(input("Enter an integer (0 - 999): "))

if x < 0 or x > 999:
    print("Wrong number!")
elif x <= 9:
    print("You entered a 1-digit number")
elif x <= 99:
    print("You entered a 2-digit number")
else:
    print("You entered a 3-digit number")
```

Exercise 15.1.3 — The Days of the Week

Write a Python program that prompts the user to enter a number between 1 and 7, and then displays the corresponding day (Sunday, Monday, and so on). If the value entered is invalid, an error message must be displayed.

Solution

The Python program is shown here.

file_15_1_3
```python
day = int(input("Enter a number between 1 and 7: "))

if day == 1:
    print("Sunday")
elif day == 2:
```

```
        print("Monday")
    elif day == 3:
        print("Tuesday")
    elif day == 4:
        print("Wednesday")
    elif day == 5:
        print("Thursday")
    elif day == 6:
        print("Friday")
    elif day == 7:
        print("Saturday")
    else:
        print("Invalid Number")
```

Exercise 15.1.4 — Where is the Tollkeeper?

A toll gate system automatically recognizes each passing vehicle as a motorcycle, a car, or a truck. Write a Python program that prompts the user to enter the type of vehicle (M for motorcycle, C for car, and T for truck). It then displays the corresponding amount of money the driver must pay according to the following table.

Vehicle Type	Amount to Pay
Motorcycle	$1
Car	$2
Track	$4

If the user enters a character other than M, C, or T, a corresponding error message must be displayed.

Solution

The solution to this problem is simple. The Python program is shown here.

file_15_1_4
```
v = input("Enter the type of vehicle (M, C, or T): ")

if v == "M":
    print("You need to pay $1")
elif v == "C":
    print("You need to pay $2")
elif v == "T":
    print("You need to pay $4")
else:
    print("Invalid vehicle")
```

15.2 Review Questions: True/False

Choose **true** or **false** for each of the following statements.

1. The `if-elif` structure is used to expand the number of alternatives.
2. The `if-elif` structure can have at most three alternatives.
3. In an `if-elif` structure, once a Boolean expression evaluates to True, the next Boolean expression is also evaluated.
4. In an `if-elif` structure, the last statement or block of statements N+1 (appearing below the `else` Python keyword) is always executed.
5. In an `if-elif` structure, the last statement or block of statements N+1 (appearing below the `else` Python keyword) is executed when at least one of the previous Boolean expressions has evaluated to True.
6. In an `if-elif` decision structure, the last statement or block of statements N+1, and by extension the `else` Python keyword, can be omitted.
7. In the following code fragment,

    ```
    if w == 1:
        x = x + 5
    elif w == 2:
        x = x - 2
    elif w == 3:
        x = x - 9
    else:
        x = x + 3
        y += 1
    ```

    the statement `y += 1` is executed only when variable w contains a value other than 1, 2, or 3.

15.3 Review Exercises

Complete the following exercises.

1. Try to determine the values of the variables in each step for four different executions of the next Python program and find what is displayed on the user's screen.

    The input values for the four executions are (i) 5, (ii) 100, (iii) 250, and (iv) −1.

    ```
    q = int(input())
    if 0 < q <= 50:
        b = 1
    elif 50 < q <= 100:
        b = 2
    elif 100 < q <= 200:
        b = 3
    else:
        b = 4
    print(b)
    ```

2. Try to find out the values of the variables in each step for three different executions of the next Python program and find what is displayed on the user's screen.

   The input values for the three executions are (i) 5, (ii) 100, and (iii) 200.

   ```python
   amount = float(input())

   if amount < 20:
       discount = 0
   elif 20 <= amount < 100:
       discount = 5
   elif 100 <= amount < 150:
       discount = 10
   else:
       discount = 20
   payment = amount - amount * discount / 100
   print(discount, payment)
   ```

3. Write a Python program that prompts the user to enter an integer between −9999 and 9999, and then counts its total number of digits. In the end, a message "You entered a N-digit number" is displayed, where N is the total number of digits.

4. Write a Python program that prompts the user to enter the number of a month between 1 and 12, and then displays the corresponding season. It is given that
   - Winter includes months 12, 1, and 2
   - Spring includes months 3, 4, and 5
   - Summer includes months 6, 7, and 8
   - Fall (Autumn) includes months 9, 10, and 11

5. The most commonly used grading system in the United States uses discrete evaluation in the form of letter grades. Write a Python program that prompts the user to enter a letter between A and F, and then displays the corresponding percentage according to the following table.

Grade	Percentage
A	90 – 100
B	80 – 89
C	70 – 79
D	60 – 69
E / F	0 – 59

6. Write a Python program that prompts the user to enter the name of a month, and then displays the corresponding number (1 for January, 2 for February, and so on). If the value entered is invalid, an error message must be displayed.

7. Roman numerals are shown in the following table.

Number	Roman Numeral
1	I
2	II
3	III
4	IV
5	V
6	VI
7	VII
8	VIII
9	IX
10	X

Write a Python program that prompts the user to enter a Roman numeral between I and X, and then displays the corresponding number. However, if the choice entered is invalid, an error message must be displayed.

8. An online CD shop awards points to its customers based on the total number of audio CDs purchased each month. The points are awarded as follows:
    - If the customer purchases 1 CD, they are awarded 3 points.
    - If the customer purchases 2 CDs, they are awarded 10 points.
    - If the customer purchases 3 CDs, they are awarded 20 points.
    - If the customer purchases 4 CDs or more, they are awarded 45 points.

    Write a Python program that prompts the user to enter the total number of CDs that he or she has purchased in a month, and then displays the number of points awarded. Assume the user enters values greater than 0.

9. Write a Python program that prompts the user enter a word such as "zero", "one", "two", or "three", and then converts it into the corresponding digit, such as 0, 1, 2, or 3. This must be done for the numbers 0 to 3. Display "I don't know this number!" when the user enters an unknown.

10. The Beaufort scale[1] is an empirical measure that relates wind speed to observed conditions on land or at sea. Write a Python program that prompts the user to enter the Beaufort number, and then displays the corresponding description from the following table. Also, if the number entered is invalid, an error message must be displayed.

---

1. Francis Beaufort (1774 –1857) was an Irish hydrographer and officer in Britain's Royal Navy. He is the inventor of the Beaufort wind force scale.

Beaufort Number	Description
0	Calm
1	Light air
2	Light breeze
3	Gentle breeze
4	Moderate breeze
5	Fresh breeze
6	Strong breeze
7	Moderate gale
8	Gale
9	Strong gale
10	Storm
11	Violent storm
12	Hurricane force

11. Write a Python program that prompts the user to enter the wind speed and then displays the corresponding Beaufort number and description according to the following table. Also, if the number entered is invalid, an error message must be displayed.

Wind Speed (miles per hour)	Beaufort Number	Description
wind speed < 1	0	Calm
1 ≤ wind speed < 4	1	Light air
4 ≤ wind speed < 8	2	Light breeze
8 ≤ wind speed < 13	3	Gentle breeze
13 ≤ wind speed < 18	4	Moderate breeze
18 ≤ wind speed < 25	5	Fresh breeze
25 ≤ wind speed < 31	6	Strong breeze
31 ≤ wind speed < 39	7	Moderate gale
39 ≤ wind speed < 47	8	Gale
47 ≤ wind speed < 55	9	Strong gale
55 ≤ wind speed < 64	10	Storm
64 ≤ wind speed < 74	11	Violent storm
74 ≤ wind speed	12	Hurricane force

12. Write a Python program that displays the following menu:
    1. Convert Kelvin to Fahrenheit
    2. Convert Fahrenheit to Kelvin
    3. Convert Fahrenheit to Celsius
    4. Convert Celsius to Fahrenheit

    It then prompts the user to enter a choice (of 1 to 4) and a temperature value. The program must calculate and display the required value. Also, an error message must be displayed when the user enters a choice other than 1, 2, 3, or 4.

    It is given that
    - $Fahrenheit = 1.8 \times Kelvin - 459.67$
    - $Kelvin = \frac{Fahrenheit + 459.67}{1.8}$
    - $Fahrenheit = \frac{9}{5} \times Celsius + 32$
    - $Celsius = \frac{5}{9}(Fahrenheit - 32)$

Chapter 16
Asking Questions - Nested Structures

16.1 Nested Decision Structures

A nested decision structure is a decision structure that is "nested" (enclosed) within another decision structure. This means that one decision structure can enclose another decision structure (which then becomes the "nested" decision structure). In turn, that nested decision structure can enclose another decision structure, and so on.

An example of a nested decision structure is shown here.

```
if x < 30:
    if x < 15:      ##
        y = y + 2   # This is the
    else:           # nested if-else structure
        y -= 1      ##
else:
    y += 1
```

There are no practical limitations to how deep this nesting can go. As long as the syntax rules are not violated, you can nest as many structures as you wish. For practical reasons however, as you move to three or four levels of nesting, the entire structure becomes very complex and difficult to understand. So, try to keep your code as simple as possible by breaking large nested structures into multiple smaller ones, or by using other types of structures.

Obviously, you can nest **any** structure inside **any other** structure as long as you keep them syntactically and logically correct. In the next example, an `if-elif` structure is nested within an `if-else` structure.

file_16_1

```
x = int(input("Enter a number: "))

if x < 1 or x > 3:
    print("Invalid Number")
else:
    print("Valid Number")
    
    if x == 1:        #This is the nested if-elif structure
        print("1st choice selected")
    elif x == 2:
        print("2nd choice selected")
    else:
        print("3rd choice selected")
```

Exercise 16.1.1 — Find Out What is Displayed

Try to find out the values of the variables in each step of the next Python program for three different executions and find out what is displayed on the user's screen.

The input values for the three executions are (i) 13, (ii) 18, and (iii) 30.

file_16_1_1
```
x = int(input())
y = 10

if x < 30:
    if x < 15:
        y = y + 2
    else:
        y -= 1
else:
    y += 1

print(y)
```

Solution

i. For the input value of 13:
   1. The value 13 is assigned to variable x
   2. The value 10 is assigned to variable y.
   3. The first Boolean expression (x < 30) evaluates to True
   4. The second Boolean expression (x < 15) evaluates to True
   5. The statement y = y + 2 is executed. The value of variable y thus becomes 12.
   6. Finally, the print(y) statement displays the value 12 on the user's screen.

ii. For the input value of 18:
   1. The value 18 is assigned to variable x
   2. The value 10 is assigned to variable y.
   3. The first Boolean expression (x < 30) evaluates to True.
   4. The second Boolean expression (x < 15) evaluates to False.
   5. The statement y -= 1 is executed. The value of variable y now becomes 9.
   6. Finally, the print(y) statement displays the value 9 on the user's screen.

iii. For the input value of 30:
   1. The value 30 is assigned to variable x
   2. The value 10 is assigned to variable y.
   3. The first Boolean expression (x < 30) evaluates to False.
   4. The statement y += 1 is executed. The value of variable y now becomes 11.
   5. Finally the print(y) statement displays the value 11 on the user's screen.

Exercise 16.1.2 — Positive, Negative, or Zero?

Write a Python program that prompts the user to enter a number and then displays the messages "Positive", "Negative", or "Zero" depending on whether the given value is greater than, less than, or equal to zero.

Chapter 16
Asking Questions - Nested Structures

Solution

This program can be written using either an `if-else` structure nested inside another `if-else` structure, or an `if-elif` structure. Let's try them both!

First approach - Using a nested `if-else` structure

file_16_1_2a
```python
a = float(input("Enter a number: "))

if a > 0:
    print("Positive")
else:
    if a < 0:
        print("Negative")
    else:
        print("Zero")
```

Second approach - Using an `if-elif` structure

file_16_1_2b
```python
a = float(input("Enter a number: "))

if a > 0:
    print("Positive")
elif a < 0:
    print("Negative")
else:
    print("Zero")
```

Exercise 16.1.3 — The Most Scientific Calculator Ever!

Write a Python program that prompts the user to enter a number, the type of operation (+, -, *, /), and a second number. Then, the program must execute the required operation and display the result.

Solution

The only thing that you need to take care of in this exercise is the possibility the user could enter zero for the divisor (the second number). As you know from mathematics, division by zero is not possible.

The following Python program uses the `if-elif` structure to check the type of operation.

file_16_1_3
```python
a = float(input("Enter 1st number: "))
op = input("Enter type of operation: ")    #Variable op is of type string
b = float(input("Enter 2nd number: "))

if op == "+":
    print(a + b)
```

```
    elif op == "-":
        print(a - b)
    elif op == "*":
        print(a * b)
    elif op == "/":
        if b == 0:
            print("Error: Division by zero")
        else:
            print(a / b)
```

16.2 Review Questions: True/False

Choose **true** or **false** for each of the following statements.

1. Nesting of decision structures describes a situation in which a decision structure encloses other decision structures.
2. The nesting level can go as deep as the programmer wishes.
3. It is possible to nest an `if-elif` structure within an `if` structure, but not the opposite.

16.3 Review Exercises

Complete the following exercises.

1. Try to determine the values of the variables in each step of the next Python program for three different executions and find what is displayed on the user's screen.

    The input values for the four executions are (i) 20, 3; (ii) 12, 8; and (iv) 50, 1.

    ```
    x = int(input())
    y = int(input())

    if x < 30:
        if y == 1:
            x = x * 3
            y = 5
        elif y == 2:
            x = x * 2
            y = 2
        elif y == 3:
            x = x + 5
            y += 3
        else:
            x -= 2
            y += 1
    else:
        y += 1
    ```

```
    print(x, y)
```

2. Write a Python program that prompts the user to enter two values, one for temperature and one for wind speed. If the temperature is above 75 degrees Fahrenheit, the day is considered hot, otherwise it is cold. If the wind speed is above 12 miles per hour, the day is considered windy, otherwise it is not windy. The program must display one single message, depending on the values given. For example, if a user enters 60 for temperature and 10 for wind speed, the program must display "The day is cold and not windy".

3. The Body Mass Index (BMI) is used to determine whether an adult is overweight or underweight for his or her height. The formula used to calculate the BMI of an adult is

$$BMI = \frac{weight \cdot 703}{height^2}$$

Write a Python program that prompts the user to enter their age, weight (in pounds) and height (in inches) and then displays a description according to the following table.

Body Mass Index	Description
BMI < 15	Very severely underweight
$15.0 \leq BMI < 16.0$	Severely underweight
$16.0 \leq BMI < 18.5$	Underweight
$18.5 \leq BMI < 25$	Normal
$25.0 \leq BMI < 30.0$	Overweight
$30.0 \leq BMI < 35.0$	Severely overweight
$35.0 \leq BMI$	Very severely overweight

The message "Invalid age" must be displayed when the user enters an age less than 18.

16.4 Review Questions

Answer the following questions.

1. What does the term "nesting a decision structure" mean?
2. How deep can the nesting of decision structures go? Is there any practical limit?

Chapter 17
Doing Loops

17.1 What is a Loop Structure?

A *loop structure* is a structure that allows the execution of a statement or block of statements multiple times until a specified condition is met. There are two types of loops:

- In an *indefinite loop structure*, the number of iterations is not known before the loop starts iterating, and it depends on certain conditions. For example, a loop can print a message and ask the user whether or not they want to repeat it. As long as the user does not decide that it is time to stop, the loop can iterate again and again.

- In a *definite loop structure*, the number of iterations is known before the loop starts iterating. For example, a loop can repeat 100 times, printing the message "Loops are superb!"

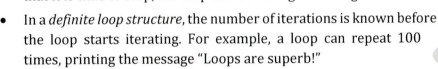

17.2 From Sequence to Loop Structure

The next example lets the user enter four numbers and it then calculates and displays their sum. As you can see, there is no loop structure yet, just your familiar sequence structure.

```
x = float(input())
y = float(input())
z = float(input())
w = float(input())

total = x + y + z + w

print(total)
```

This program is quite short. However, think of an analogous program that lets the user enter 1000 numbers instead of four! Can you imagine writing the statement `float(input())` 1000 times? Wouldn't it be much easier if you could write this statement only once but "tell" the computer to execute it 1000 times? Of course it would be! But for this you need a loop structure!

Let's try to solve a riddle first! Without using a loop structure yet, try to rewrite the previous program, but using only two variables, `x` and `total`. Yes, you heard that right! This program must calculate and display the sum of four given numbers, but it must do it with only two variables! Can you find a way?

Hmmm... it's obvious what you are thinking right now: "*The only thing that I can do with two variables is to read one single value in variable* `x` *and then assign that value to variable* `total`." Your thinking is quite correct, and it is presented in the code fragment that follows.

```
x = float(input())
total = x
```

which can equivalently be written as

```
total = 0

x = float(input())
total = total + x
```

And now what? Now, there are three things that you can do, and these are: think, think, and of course, think!

The first given number has been stored in variable `total`, so variable `x` is now free for further use! Thus, you can re-use variable `x` to read a second value which can also *accumulate* in variable `total`, as follows.

```
total = 0

x = float(input())
total = total + x

x = float(input())
total = total + x
```

> **Notice:** Statement `total = total + x` *accumulates the value of* `x` *to* `total`. *For example, if variable* `total` *contains the value 5 and variable* `x` *contains the value 3, the statement* `total = total + x` *assigns the value 8 to the variable* `total`.

Since the second number has been accumulated in variable `total`, variable `x` can be re-used! Of course, this process can repeat until all four numbers are read and have accumulated in the variable `total`. The final Python program is as follows. Please note that this program does not use any loop structures yet!

```
total = 0

x = float(input())
total = total + x

x = float(input())
total = total + x

x = float(input())
total = total + x

x = float(input())
total = total + x

print(total)
```

> **Notice:** The main difference between this program and the initial one is that this one has four identical pairs of statements.

Of course, we can use this example to read and find the sum of more than four numbers. However, you can't write that pair of statements over and over again because soon you will realize how painful this is. Also, if you forget to write at least one pair of statements, it will eventually lead to incorrect results.

What you need here is to keep only *one* pair of those statements but use a loop structure that executes it four times (or even 1000 times, if you wish). You can use something like the following code fragment.

```
total = 0

execute_these_statements_4_times:
    x = float(input())
    total = total + x

print(total)
```

Obviously there isn't any `execute_these_statements_4_times` statement in Python. This is for demonstration purposes only, but soon enough you will learn everything about all the loop structures that Python supports!

17.3 Review Questions: True/False

Choose **true** or **false** for each of the following statements.

1. A loop structure is a structure that allows the execution of a statement or block of statements multiple times until a specified condition is met.
2. It is possible to use a sequence structure that prompts the user to enter 1000 numbers and then calculates their sum.
3. The following code fragment
   ```
   total = 10
   a = 0
   total = total + a
   ```
   accumulates the value 10 in the variable `total`.
4. The following two code fragments are considered equivalent.

`a = 5`	`total = 0`
`total = a`	`a = 5`
	`total = total + a`

Chapter 18
Doing Loops - The while Structure

18.1 The while Structure

A `while` structure is a structure that allows the execution of a statement or block of statements multiple times. It can be used to create either definite or indefinite loop structures.

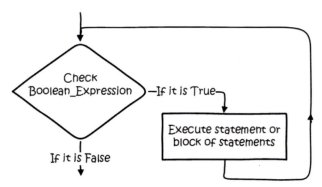

Let's see what happens when the flow of execution reaches a `while` structure. If the Boolean expression evaluates to True, the statement or block of statements of the structure is executed and the flow of execution goes back to check the Boolean expression once more. If the Boolean expression evaluates to True again, the process repeats. The iterations stop when the Boolean expression, at some point, evaluates to False and the flow of execution exits the loop.

The general form of the Python statement is

```
while Boolean_Expression:
    #Here goes
    #a statement or block of statements
```

Notice: In a `while` structure, first the Boolean expression is evaluated, and afterwards the statement or block of statements of the structure is executed.

Notice: Because the Boolean expression is evaluated before entering the loop, a `while` structure may perform from zero to many iterations.

Notice: Each time the statement or block of statements of the structure is executed, the term used in computer science is "the loop is iterating" or "the loop performs an iteration."

The following example displays the numbers 1 to 10.

file_18_1
```
i = 1
while i <= 10:
    print(i)
    i += 1
```

> *Notice: Just as in decision structures, the statements inside the loop structure must be indented.*

Exercise 18.1.1 — Counting the Total Number of Iterations

Try to determine how many iterations this Python program performs, and find out what is displayed on the user's screen.

```
i = 1
while i < 4:
    print("Hello")
    i += 1

print("The End")
```

Solution

The following steps are performed:

1. A value of 1 is assigned to variable `i`.
2. The Boolean expression (`i < 4`) is checked. It evaluates to `True` so the two statements of the `while` structure are executed. The message "Hello" is displayed and variable `i` becomes 2.
3. The Boolean expression (`i < 4`) is checked. It evaluates to `True` again, so the two statements of the `while` structure are executed once more. The message "Hello" is displayed (for the second time), and variable `i` becomes 3.
4. The Boolean expression (`i < 4`) is checked. It evaluates to `True` again, so the two statements of the `while` structure are executed one more time. The message "Hello" is displayed (for the third time), and variable `i` becomes 4.
5. The Boolean expression (`i < 4`) is checked. This time it evaluates to `False`, so the flow of execution exits the loop and the message "The End" is displayed.

Exercise 18.1.2 — Finding the Sum of Four Numbers

Using a `while` structure, write a Python program that prompts the user to enter four numbers and then calculates and displays their sum.

Solution

Do you remember the example in paragraph 17.2 for calculating the sum of four numbers? At the end, after a little work, the proposed Python program became

Chapter 18
Doing Loops - The while Structure

```
total = 0

execute_these_statements_4_times:
    x = float(input())
    total = total + x

print(total)
```

Now, you need a way to "present" the statement *execute_these_statements_4_times* with real Python statements. The while statement is actually able to do this, but you need one extra variable to count the total number of iterations. Then, when the desired number of iterations has been performed, the flow of execution must exit the loop.

Following is a general purpose code fragment that iterates for the number of times specified by *total_number_of_iterations*,

```
i = 1
while i <= total_number_of_iterations:
    #Here goes
    #a statement or block of statements
    i += 1
```

where *total_number_of_iterations* can be a constant value or even a variable or an expression.

> **Notice**: The name of the variable i is not binding. You can use any variable name you wish such as counter, count, k, and more.

After combining this code fragment with the previous one, the final program becomes

file_18_1_2

```
total = 0

i = 1
while i <= 4:
    x = float(input("Enter a number: "))
    total = total + x
    
    i += 1

print(total)
```

Exercise 18.1.3 — Finding the Sum of Positive Numbers

Write a Python program that prompts the user to enter 20 numbers, and then calculates and displays the sum of the positive ones.

Solution

This is quite easy. What the program must do inside the loop is check whether a given number is positive and, if it is, that number must accumulate to the variable `total`; negative numbers and zero must be ignored.

The Python program is as follows.

file_18_1_3

```python
total = 0

i = 1
while i <= 20:
    x = float(input("Enter a number: "))
    if x > 0:
        total = total + x
    i += 1

print(total)
```

Exercise 18.1.4 — Finding the Sum of N Numbers

Write a Python program that lets the user enter N numbers and then calculates and displays their sum. The value of N must be given by the user at the beginning of the program.

Solution

In this exercise, the total number of iterations depends on a value that the user must enter. Following is a general purpose code fragment that iterates for N times, where N is given by the user.

```python
n = int(input())

i = 1
while i <= n:
    #Here goes
    #a statement or block of statements
    i += 1
```

According to what you have learned so far, the final program becomes

file_18_1_4

```python
n = int(input("How many numbers are you going to enter? "))

total = 0

i = 1
while i <= n:
    x = float(input("Enter a number: "))
    total += x
    i += 1

print(total)
```

Chapter 18
Doing Loops - The while Structure

Exercise 18.1.5 — Finding the Sum of an Unknown Quantity of Numbers

Write a Python program that lets the user enter numeric values repeatedly until the value −1 is entered. When data input is completed, the sum of the numbers entered must be displayed. (The value of −1 must not be included in the final sum.).

Solution

In this exercise, the total number of iterations is unknown. If you were to use decision structures, your program would look something like the one that follows.

```python
total = 0

x = float(input())
if x != -1:             #Check x
    total = total + x   #and execute
    x = float(input())
    if x != -1:             #Check x
        total = total + x   #and execute
        x = float(input())
        if x != -1:             #Check x
            total = total + x   #and execute
            x = float(input())
            ...
            ...

print(total)
```

As you can see in the previous example, the part

```python
if x != -1:             #Check x
    total = total + x   #and execute
    x = float(input())
```

is the part that actually repeats. So, let's rewrite it using a `while` structure instead of an `if` structure. The final program is shown next. If you try to follow the flow of execution, you will find that it operates similar to the previous one.

file_18_1_5

```python
total = 0

x = float(input())
while x != -1:          #Check x
    total = total + x   #and execute
    x = float(input())

print(total)
```

Exercise 18.1.6 — Finding the Product of Five Numbers

Write a Python program that lets the user enter five numbers and then calculates and displays their product.

Solution

If you were to use a sequence structure, it would be something like the next code fragment.

```
p = 1

x = float(input())
p = p * x

x = float(input())
p = p * x

x = float(input())
p = p * x

x = float(input())
p = p * x

x = float(input())
p = p * x
```

*Notice: Please note that the variable p is initialized to 1 instead of 0. This is necessary for the statement p = p * x to operate properly; the final product would be zero otherwise.*

Using knowledge from the previous exercises of this chapter, the final program becomes

```
p = 1

i = 1
while i <= 5:
    x = float(input())
    p = p * x

    i += 1

print(p)
```

18.2 Review Questions: True/False

Choose **true** or **false** for each of the following statements.

1. A `while` structure may perform zero iterations.
2. The statement or block of statements of a `while` structure is executed at least one time.
3. A `while` structure stops iterating when its Boolean expression evaluates to `True`
4. In a `while` structure, when the statement or block of statements of the structure is executed N times, the Boolean expression is evaluated N – 1 times.

5. You cannot nest an `if` structure inside a `while` structure.
6. In the following code fragment
    ```
    i = 1
    while i <= 10:
        print("Hello")
    i += 1
    ```
    the word "Hello" is displayed 10 times.
7. In the following Python program
    ```
    i = 1
    while i != 10:
        print("Hello")
        i += 2
    ```
    the word "Hello" is displayed 5 times.

18.3 Review Questions: Multiple Choice

Select the correct answer for each of the following statements.

1. In a `while` structure, the statement or block of statements of the structure
    a. is executed before the loop's Boolean expression is evaluated.
    b. is executed after the loop's Boolean expression is evaluated.
    c. neither of the above
2. In the following code fragment
    ```
    i = 1
    while i < 10:
        print("Hello Hermes")
        i += 1
    ```
    the message "Hello Hermes" is displayed
    a. 10 times.
    b. 9 times.
    c. 1 time.
    d. 0 times.
    e. none of the above
3. In the following code fragment
    ```
    i = 1
    while i < 10:
        print("Hi!")
    print("Hello Ares")
    i += 1
    ```
    the message "Hello Ares" is displayed
    a. 10 times.

b. 1 time.

c. 0 times.

d. none of the above

4. In the following code fragment

```
i = 1
while i < 10:
    i += 1
print("Hi!")
print("Hello Aphrodite")
```

the message "Hello Aphrodite" is displayed

a. 10 times.

b. 1 time.

c. 0 times.

d. none of the above

5. In the following code fragment

```
i = 1
while i >= 10:
    print("Hi!")
    print("Hello Apollo")
    i += 1
```

the message "Hello Apollo" is displayed

a. 10 times.

b. 1 time.

c. 0 times.

d. none of the above

6. The following Python program calculates and displays the sum of

```
n = int(input())
s = 0
i = 1
while i < n:
    a = float(input())
    s = s + a
    i += 1
print(s)
```

a. as many numbers as the value of variable n denotes.

b. as many numbers as the result of the expression n - 1 denotes.

c. as many numbers as the value of variable i denotes.

d. none of the above

18.4 Review Exercises

Complete the following exercises.

1. Identify the syntax error(s) in the following Python program.
    ```
    i = 30.0
    while i > 5
        print(i)
        i =/ 2
    print(The end)
    ```

2. Try to determine how many iterations this Python program performs.
    ```
    i = 3
    x = 0
    while i >= 0:
        i -= 1
        x += i
    print(x)
    ```

3. Try to determine how many iterations this Python program performs.
    ```
    i = -5
    while i > 10:
        i -= 1
    print(i)
    ```

4. Try to determine the values of the variables in each step of the next Python program and find what is displayed on the user's screen. How many iterations does this Python program perform?
    ```
    a = 2
    while a <= 10:
        b = a + 1
        if b == 7:
            print(2 * b)
        elif b == 3:
            print(b - 1)
        elif b == 8:
            print(a, b)
        else:
            print(a - 4)
        a += 4
    ```

5. Fill in the gaps in the following code fragments so that all loops perform exactly four iterations.

   i. ```
       a = 3
       while a > ...... :
           a -= 1
       ```

   ii. ```
       a = 5
       while a < ...... :
           a += 1
       ```

   iii. ```
        a = 9
        while a != 11:
            a = a + ...
        ```

   iv. ```
       a = 1
       while a != ...... :
           a -= 2
       ```

   v. ```
       a = 2
       while a < ...... :
           a = 2 * a
       ```

   vi. ```
       a = 1
       while a < ...... :
           a = a + 0.1
       ```

6. Write a Python program that prompts the user to enter 20 numbers. The program then calculates and displays the sum of all the positive numbers that the user entered.

7. Write a Python program that prompts the user to enter N numbers. It then calculates and displays the product of all the positive numbers that the user entered. The value of N must be given by the user at the beginning of the program.

8. Write a Python program that prompts the user to enter 10 integers. It then calculates and displays the sum of all the numbers that the user entered that are between 100 and 200.

9. Write a Python program that prompts the user to enter 20 integers. The program then calculates and displays the sum of all the numbers that the user entered that consist of three digits.

   Hint: All three-digit integers are between 100 and 999.

10. Write a Python program that prompts the user to enter numeric values repeatedly until the value 0 is entered. When data input is completed, the product of the numbers entered must be displayed. (The last 0 entered must not be included in the final product.)

Chapter 19
Doing Loops - The for Structure

19.1 The for Structure

In Chapter 18, as you noticed, we used the `while` structure to create both definite and indefinite loop structures. In other words, it was used to iterate for a known number of times, but also for an unknown number of times. Since definite loop structures are so often used in computer programming, almost every computer language, including Python, includes a special statement that is much more readable and convenient than the `while` structure—and this is the `for` structure.

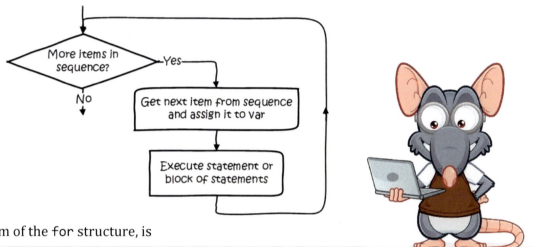

The general form of the `for` structure, is

```
for var in sequence:
    #Here goes
    #a statement or block of statements
```

where *var* is a variable that is assigned each successive value of *sequence*, and the statement or block of statements of the structure is executed once for each value.

The following example

file_19_1a
```
for i in [1, 2, 3, 4, 5]:
    print(i)
```

displays the numbers 1, 2, 3, 4, and 5.

The following example

file_19_1b
```
for letter in "Hello":
    print(letter)
```

displays the letters "H", "e", "l", "l", and "o" (all without the double quotes).

As you learned in paragraph 10.2, the Python's range() function can be used to create a sequence of integers. You can use the range() function along with the for statement, to expand the possibilities of the for statement as shown here.

```
for var in range([initial_value,] final_value [, step ]):
    #Here goes
    #a statement or block of statements
```

where

- initial_value is the starting value of the sequence. This argument is optional. If omitted, its default value is 0.
- the sequence is up to, but not including, final_value.
- step is the difference between each number in the sequence. This argument is optional. If omitted, its default value is 1.

> **Remember!** The arguments initial_value, final_value, and step must be integers.

The following example displays the numbers 0 to 10.

file_19_1c
```
for i in range(0, 11, 1):
    print(i)
```

Of course, when step is 1, you can omit the third argument. The previous example can also be written as

file_19_1d
```
for i in range(0, 11):
    print(i)
```

Moreover, when initial_value is 0, you can omit the first argument as well. The previous example can also be written as

file_19_1e
```
for i in range(11):
    print(i)
```

The next example displays the numbers 2, 4, 6, 8, and 10.

file_19_1f
```
for i in range(2, 12, 2):
    print(i)
```

Last, but not least, if you want a sequence of numbers in reverse order, you can use a negative value for step. The following example displays odd numbers from 11 to 1.

file_19_1g
```
a = 11
b = 0
for i in range(a, b, -2):
```

Chapter 19
Doing Loops - The for Structure

```
    print(i)
```

Exercise 19.1.1 — Find Out What is Displayed

Try to determine the values of the variables in each step of the next Python program when the input value 1 is entered, and find out what is displayed on the user's screen.

```python
x = int(input())

for i in range(-3, 3, 2):
    x = x * 3

print(x)
```

Solution

The steps that are performed are:
1. The value 1 is assigned to variable x.
2. The range() function creates a sequence that includes the numbers −3, −1, and 1. This means that the loop will perform three iterations.
3. The statement x = x * 3 is executed three times.
4. When the loop performs all three iterations, the flow of execution exits the loop and the value 27 is displayed on the user's screen.

Exercise 19.1.2 — Find Out What is Displayed

Try to determine the values of the variables in each step of the next Python program when the input value 3 is entered, and find what is displayed on the user's screen.

```python
x = int(input())

for i in range(6, x - 1, -1):
    print(i)
```

Solution

For the input value of 3:
1. The value 3 is assigned to variable x.
2. The range() function creates a sequence that includes the numbers 6, 5, 4, and 3. This means that the loop will perform four iterations.
3. The statement print(i) is executed four times and the values 6, 5, 4, and 3 are displayed on the user's screen.

Exercise 19.1.3 — Finding the Sum of Four Numbers

Write a Python program that prompts the user to enter four numbers and then calculates and displays their sum.

Solution

In exercise 18.1.2, the solution proposed with a while structure was the following:

```python
total = 0
```

```python
i = 1
while i <= 4:
    x = float(input("Enter a number: "))
    total = total + x

    i += 1

print(total)
```

It's now very easy to rewrite it using a for structure.

file_19_1_3
```python
total = 0

for i in range(4):
    x = float(input("Enter a number: "))
    total = total + x

print(total)
```

Exercise 19.1.4 — Finding the Average Value of N Numbers

Write a Python program that prompts the user to enter N numbers and then calculates and displays their average value. The user must provide the value of N at the beginning of the program.

Solution

The solution is presented here.

file_19_1_4
```python
n = int(input("How many numbers are you going to enter? "))

total = 0
for i in range(n):
    x = float(input("Enter number No" + str(i + 1) + ": "))
    total = total + x

if n > 0:
    average = total / n
    print("The average value is:", average)
else:
    print("You didn't enter any number!")
```

> *Notice: The* `if n > 0` *statement is necessary because if the user enters the value 0 for variable n, the program avoids any division-by-zero errors. Also, if the user enters a negative value for variable n, this check avoids any undesirable results.*

19.2 Review Questions: True/False

Choose **true** or **false** for each of the following statements.

1. In a `for` structure, the variable *var* is automatically assigned each successive value of *sequence* at the beginning of each loop.
2. A definite loop structure can be used when the number of iterations is known.
3. In a definite loop structure, the statement or block of statements of the loop is executed at least one time.
4. In a `range()` function, the value of *initial_value* cannot be greater than the value of *final_value*.
5. In a `range()` function, the value of *initial_value*, *final_value* and *step* cannot be a float.
6. In a `for` structure, the *var* variable can appear in a statement inside the loop.
7. In the following code fragment

    ```
    for i in range(1, 10):
        print("Hello")
    ```

    the word "Hello" is displayed 10 times.
8. In the following code fragment

    ```
    b = int(input())
    for i in range(b):
        print("Hello")
    ```

    the message "Hello" is always displayed at least once.

19.3 Review Questions: Multiple Choice

Select the correct answer for each of the following statements.

1. A `for` structure can be used in a problem in which
    a. the user enters numbers repeatedly until the value –1 is entered.
    b. the user enters numbers repeatedly until the value entered is greater than *final_value*.
    c. both *a* and *b*
    d. none of the above
2. In a `for` structure *initial_value*, *final_value*, and *step* can be
    a. a constant value.
    b. a variable.
    c. an expression.
    d. all of the above

3. In a for structure, when *initial_value*, *final_value*, and *step* are variables, their values
    a. can be reals.
    b. must be reals.
    c. must be integers.
    d. none of the above

4. In a for structure, the initial value of *var*
    a. must be 0.
    b. can be 0.
    c. cannot be a negative value.
    d. none of the above

5. In a for structure, variable *var* is automatically assigned each successive value of *sequence*
    a. at the beginning of each iteration.
    b. at the end of each iteration.
    c. It is not assigned automatically.
    d. none of the above

6. In the following code fragment

    ```
    i = 1
    for i in range(5, 6):
        print("Hello Hera")
    ```

    the message "Hello Hera" is displayed
    a. 5 times.
    b. 1 time.
    c. 0 times.
    d. none of the above

7. In the following code fragment

    ```
    for i in range(40, 51):
        print("Hello Dionysus")
    ```

    the message "Hello Dionysus" is displayed
    a. 1 time.
    b. 2 times.
    c. 10 times.
    d. 11 times.

8. In the following code fragment

    ```
    k = 0
    for i in range(1, 7, 2):
        k = k + i
    print(i)
    ```

    the value displayed is

a. 3.
   b. 6.
   c. 9.
   d. none of the above

9. In the following code fragment
   ```
   k = 0
   for i in range(100, -105, -5):
       k = k + i
   print(i)
   ```
   the value displayed is
   a. −95.
   b. −105.
   c. −100.
   d. none of the above

19.4 Review Exercises

Complete the following exercises.

1. Try to determine the values of the variables in each step of the next Python program and find out what is displayed on the user's screen. How many iterations does this Python program perform?
   ```
   a = 0
   b = 0
   for j in range(0, 10, 2):
       if j < 5:
           b += 1
       else:
           a += j - 1
   print(a, b)
   ```

2. Try to find out the values of the variables in each step of the next Python program for the input value 9, and find what is displayed on the user's screen.
   ```
   a = int(input())
   for j in range(2, a, 3):
       x = j * 3
       y = j * 2
       if x > 10:
           y *= 2
       x += 4
       print(x, y)
   ```

3. Fill in the gaps in the following code fragments so all loops perform exactly five iterations.

   i.   ```
        for a in range(5, ... + 1):
            b += 1
        ```

   ii.  ```
        for a in range(0, ......, 4):
            b += 1
        ```

   iii. ```
        for a in range(......, -17, -2):
            b += 1
        ```

   iv.  ```
        for a in range(-11, -16, ......):
            b += 1
        ```

4. Write a Python program that prompts the user to enter 20 numbers and then calculates and displays their product and their average value.

5. Write a Python program that prompts the user to enter N integers and then displays the total number of those that are positive. The user must provide the value of N at the beginning of the program. Also, if all integers given are negative, the message "You entered no positive integers" must be displayed.

6. Write a Python program that prompts the user to enter 50 integers and then calculates and displays the average value of those that are positive and the average value of those that are negative.

7. Write a Python program that prompts the user to enter two integers into variables, one into `start` and the other into `finish`. The program then displays all the integers from `start` to `finish`.

8. Write a Python program that prompts the user to enter a real and an integer and then displays the result of the first number raised to the power of the second number, without using the exponentiation operator (**). Assume that the user enters values greater than 0.

9. Write a Python program that prompts the user to enter a message and then displays the number of words it contains. For example, if the string entered is "My name is Bill Bouras", the program must display "The message entered contains 5 words". Assume the words are separated by a single space character.

   Hint: Use the `len()` function to get the number of characters that the given message contains.

Chapter 20
Doing Loops - Nested Structures

20.1 Nested Loop Structures

A *nested loop* is a loop within another loop or, in other words, an inner loop within an outer one.

The outer loop controls the number of **complete** iterations of the inner loop. This means that the first iteration of the outer loop triggers the inner loop to start iterating until completion. Then the second iteration of the outer loop triggers the inner loop to start iterating until completion again. This process repeats until the outer loop has performed all of its iterations.

Take the following Python program, for example.

file_20_1
```
for i in range(1, 3):
    for j in range(1, 4):    #This is the nested for structure
        print(i, j)
```

The outer loop, the one that is controlled by variable i, controls the number of complete iterations that the inner loop performs. That is, when variable i contains the value 1, the inner loop performs three iterations (for j = 1, j = 2, and j = 3). The inner loop finishes but the outer loop needs to perform one more iteration (for i = 2). Therefore, the inner loop starts over and performs three new iterations (for j = 1, j = 2 and j = 3).

The previous example is similar to the following one.

```
i = 1    #outer loop assigns value 1 to variable i
for j in range(1, 4):  #and inner loop performs three iterations
    print(i, j)


i = 2    #outer loop assigns value 2 to variable i
for j in range(1, 4):  #and inner loop starts over and
    print(i, j)        #performs three new iterations
```

The output result is as follows.

Remember! As long as the syntax rules are not violated, you can nest as many loop structures as you wish. For practical reasons however, as you move to four or five levels of nesting, the entire loop structure becomes very complex and difficult to understand. However, experience shows that the maximum levels of nesting that you will do in your entire life as a programmer is probably three or four.

Notice: The inner and outer loops do not need to be the same type. For example, a `for` structure may nest (enclose) a `while` structure, or vice versa.

Exercise 20.1.1 — Counting the Total Number of Iterations.

Find the number of times the message "Hello Zeus" is displayed.

```python
for i in range(3):
    for j in range(4):
        print("Hello Zeus")
```

Solution

The values of variables `i` and `j` (in order of appearance) are as follows:
- For `i = 0`, the inner loop performs 4 iterations (for `j = 0`, `j = 1`, `j = 2`, and `j = 3`) and the message "Hello Zeus" is displayed 4 times.
- For `i = 1`, the inner loop performs 4 iterations (for `j = 0`, `j = 1`, `j = 2`, and `j = 3`) and the message "Hello Zeus" is displayed 4 times.
- For `i = 2`, the inner loop performs 4 iterations (for `j = 0`, `j = 1`, `j = 2`, and `j = 3`) and the message "Hello Zeus" is displayed 4 times.

Therefore, the message "Hello Zeus" displays a total of 3 × 4 = 12 times.

Remember! The outer loop controls the number of complete iterations of the inner one!

Chapter 20
Doing Loops – Nested Structures

> **Notice:** An outer loop and the inner (nested) loop must not use the same var variable.

Exercise 20.1.2 – Find Out What is Displayed

For the next code fragment, find out the value that variable x contains at the end.

```
x = 1
i = 5
while i <= 7:
    for j in range(1, 5, 2):
        x = x * 2
    i += 1

print(x)
```

Solution

To find the value that variable x contains at the end, you must first find the number of times the statement x = x * 2 is executed.

The outer loop performs three iterations (for i = 5, i = 6, and i = 7) whereas the inner loop performs two iterations (for j = 1 and j = 3). Thus the statement x = x * 2 is executed 3 × 2 = 6 times.

The initial value of variable x is 1. Since the statement x = x * 2 is executed 6 times, the final value that is displayed on user's screen is 64.

Why is it 64? It is certain what you are thinking: "*It must be 12, not 64, because 6 × 2 equals to 12*".

Sorry to disappoint you but the answer still is 64. Why? Let's see why!

At the beginning, variable x contains a value of 1.

- When the statement x = x * 2 is executed for the first time, the value of variable x becomes 2.
- When the statement x = x * 2 is executed for the second time, the value of variable x becomes 4.
- So far so good. Now watch! When the statement x = x * 2 is executed for the third time, the value of variable x becomes 8.
- When it is executed for the fourth time, the value of variable x becomes 16.
- When it is executed for the fifth time, the value of variable x becomes 32.
- Finally, when the statement x = x * 2 is executed for the sixth time, the value of variable x becomes 64.

20.2 Review Questions: True/False

Choose **true** or **false** for each of the following statements.

1. A nested loop is an inner loop within an outer one.
2. The maximum number of levels of nesting in a loop structure is four.
3. When two loop structures are nested one within the other, they must not use the same variable as *var*.

4. In the following code fragment
   ```
   for i in range(1, 4):
       for j in range(1, 4):
           print("Hello")
   ```
   the word "Hello" is displayed six times.

5. In the following code fragment
   ```
   for i in range(2):
       for j in range(1, 4):
           for k in range(1, 5, 2):
               print("Hello")
   ```
   the word "Hello" is displayed 12 times.

6. In the following code fragment
   ```
   i = 1
   while i <= 4:
       for i in range(3, 0, -1):
           print("Hello")
       i += 1
   ```
   the word "Hello" is displayed an infinite number of times.

20.3 Review Questions: Multiple Choice

Select the correct answer for each of the following statements.

1. In the following code fragment
   ```
   for i in range(1, 3):
       for j in range(1, 3):
           print("Hello")
   ```
   the values of variables i and j (in order of appearance) are
   a. j = 1, i = 1, j = 1, i = 2, j = 2, i = 1, j = 2, i = 2
   b. i = 1, j = 1, i = 1, j = 2, i = 2, j = 1, i = 2, j = 2
   c. i = 1, j = 1, i = 2, j = 2
   d. j = 1, i = 1, j = 2, i = 2

2. In the following code fragment
   ```
   x = 1
   while x != 5:
       for i in range(3):
           print("Hello Artemis")
       x += 2
   ```
   the message "Hello Artemis" is displayed
   a. an infinite number of times.
   b. 15 times.

c. 6 times.
d. none of the above

3. In the following code fragment

```python
x = 1
while x == 5:
    for i in range(4):
        print("Hello Hera")
    x += 1
```

the message "Hello Hera" is displayed

a. an infinite number of times.
b. 20 times.
c. 15 times.
d. none of the above

4. In the following code fragment

```python
x = 2
while x != 5:
    for i in range(500):
        print("Hello Zeus")
    x += 2
```

the message "Hello Zeus" is displayed

a. an infinite number of times.
b. 1000 times.
c. 1500 times.
d. none of the above

5. The following code fragment

```python
for i in range(1, 4):
    for j in range(1, 3):
        print(i, ", ", j, ", ", sep = "", end = "")
    print("The End!" , end = "")
```

displays

a. 1, 1, 1, 2, The End!2, 1, 2, 2, The End!3, 1, 3, 2, The End!
b. 1, 1, 1, 2, 2, 1, 2, 2, 3, 1, 3, 2, The End!
c. 1, 1, 2, 1, 3, 1, 1, 2, 2, 2, 3, 2, The End!
d. none of the above

20.4 Review Exercises

Complete the following exercises.

1. Fill in the gaps in the following code fragments so all code fragments display the message "Hello Hephaestus" exactly 100 times.

    i. ```
        for a in range(6, ...):
            for b in range(25):
                print("Hello Hephaestus")
        ```

    ii. ```
        for a in range(0, ...... , 5):
            for b in range(10, 20):
                print("Hello Hephaestus")
        ```

    iii. ```
        for a in range(......, -17, -2):
            for b in range(150, 50, -5):
                print("Hello Hephaestus")
        ```

    iv. ```
        for a in range(-11, -16, -1):
            for b in range(100, ...... + 2, 2):
                print("Hello Hephaestus")
        ```

2. Write a Python program that displays an hours and minutes table in the following form.

    ```
    0       0
    0       1
    0       2
    0       3
    ...
    0       59
    1       0
    1       1
    1       2
    1       3
    ...
    23      59
    ```

    Please note that the output is aligned with tabs.

3. Using nested loop structures, write a Python program that displays the following output.

    5 5 5 5 5
    4 4 4 4
    3 3 3
    2 2
    1

4. Using nested loop structures, write a Python program that displays the following output.

   ```
   0
   0 1
   0 1 2
   0 1 2 3
   0 1 2 3 4
   0 1 2 3 4 5
   ```

5. Using nested loop structures, write a Python program that displays the following rectangle.

   ```
   * * * * * * * *
   * * * * * * * *
   * * * * * * * *
   ```

6. Write a Python program that prompts the user to enter an integer N between 3 and 20 and then displays a square of size N on each side. For example, if the user enters 4 for N, the program must display as shown here.

   ```
   * * * *
   * * * *
   * * * *
   * * * *
   ```

7. Using nested loop structures, write a Python program that displays the following triangle.

   ```
   *
   * *
   * * *
   * * * *
   * * * * *
   ```

8. Using nested loop structures, write a Python program that displays the following triangle.

   ```
   *
   * *
   * * *
   * * * *
   * * * * *
   * * * *
   * * *
   * *
   *
   ```

Chapter 21
Tips and Tricks with Loop Structures

21.1 Introduction

This chapter is dedicated to teaching you some useful tips and tricks that can help you write "better" code. You should always keep them in mind when you design your own Python programs!

These tips and tricks can help you increase your code's readability, help you choose which loop structure is better to use in each given problem, and help you make the code shorter or even faster. Of course there is no single perfect method because on one occasion the use of a specific tip or trick may help, but on another occasion the same tip or trick may have exactly the opposite result. Most of the time, code optimization is a matter of programming experience.

Remember! Smaller algorithms are not always the best solution to a given problem. To solve a specific problem, you might write a short algorithm that unfortunately proves to consume a lot of CPU time. On the other hand, you might solve the same problem with another algorithm that seems longer but calculates the result much faster.

21.2 Choosing a Loop Structure

The following diagram can help you choose which loop structure is better to use in each given problem, depending on the number of iterations.

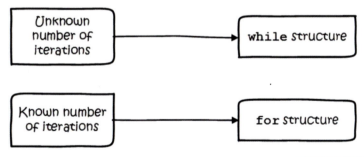

Notice: This diagram recommends the best option, not the only option. For example, when the number of iterations is known, it is not wrong to use a `while` structure instead. The proposed `for` structure, though, is more convenient.

21.3 The "Ultimate" Rule

One question that often preys on programmers' minds when using `while` structures, is how to determine which statements should be written inside the loop structure, and which outside, and in which order.

There is one simple yet powerful rule—the "Ultimate" rule! Once you follow it, the potential for making a logic error is reduced to zero!

The "Ultimate" rule states:

- The variable or variables that participate in a loop's Boolean expression must be initialized before entering the loop.
- The value of the variable or variables that participate in a loop's Boolean expression must be updated (altered) within the loop. And more specifically, the statement that does this update/alteration must be one of the **last** statements of the loop.

For example, if variable *var* is the variable that participates in a loop's Boolean expression, a `while` structure should always be in the following form:

```
initialize var
while Boolean_Expression(var) :
    #Here goes
    #a statement or block of statements

    Update/alter var
```

where

- `initialize var` is any statement that assigns an initial value to variable *var*. It can be either an input statement such as `var = input("Enter a value: ")`, or an assignment statement using the assignment operator (=).
- `Boolean_Expression(var)` can be any Boolean expression from a simple to a complex one, dependent on variable *var*.
- `Update/alter var` is any statement that alters the value of *var*, such as an input statement, an assignment statement using the assignment operator (=), or even compound assignment operators. This statement must be placed just before the point where the loop's Boolean expression is evaluated. This is why this statement must be one of the **last** statements of the loop.

Following are some examples that use the "Ultimate" rule.

Example 1

```
a = int(input())        #Initialization of a
while a > 0:            #A Boolean expression dependent on a
    print(a)
    a = a - 1           #Update/alteration of a
```

Example 2

```python
total = 0                   #Initialization of total
while total < 1000:         #A Boolean expression dependent on total
    y = int(input())
    total += y              #Update/alteration of total
```

Example 3

```python
a = int(input())            #Initialization of a
b = int(input())            #Initialization of b
while a + b > 0:            #A Boolean expression dependent on a and b
    print(a, b)
    a = int(input())        #Update/alteration of a
    b = int(input())        #Update/alteration of b
```

Now you will realize why you should always follow the "Ultimate" rule!" Let's say that the wording of an exercise was:

Write a Python program that prompts the user to enter numbers repeatedly until the total number of positives given is five.

This exercise was given to a class, and a student gave the following Python program as an answer.

```python
positives_given = 0

x = float(input("Enter a number: "))
while positives_given != 5:
    if x > 0:
        positives_given += 1
    x = float(input("Enter a number: "))

print("Positives given:", positives_given)
```

At first sight the program looks correct. It prompts the user to enter a number, it enters the loop and checks whether or not the given number is positive, it prompts the user to enter a second number, and so on. However, this program contains a logic error—and unfortunately a difficult one. Can you spot it?

If you try to follow the flow of execution, you can confirm for yourself that the program runs smoothly—so smoothly that it makes you wonder if this book is reliable or if you should throw it away!

The problem becomes clear only when you try to enter all five of the expected positive values. Suppose the user has already entered four positive values. This means the variable `positives_given` contains a value of 4. When the user enters the fifth positive value, the program doesn't directly count it, but the flow of execution goes to check the Boolean expression of the `while` structure. The value of variable `positives_given` is still 4, so the flow of execution enters the loop, and it inevitably prompts for a number again—which is, of course, wrong!

This is why you should always go by the book! Let's see how this program should be written.

Since the Boolean expression of the `while` structure is dependent on the variable `positives_given`, this is the variable that must be initialized outside of the loop. This variable must also be updated or altered within the loop. The statement that does this update or alteration must be the last statement within the loop, as shown in the code fragment (in general form) that follows.

```python
positives_given = 0       #Initialization of positives_given
while positives_given != 5: # A Boolean expression dependent on positives_given
    #Here goes
    #a statement or block of statements.
    if x > 0:
        positives_given += 1   #Update/alteration of positives_given
```

Now you can add any necessary statements to complete the program. The only statements that are missing here are the statement that prompts the user to enter a number (this must be done within the loop), and the statement that displays the result (this must be done when the loop finishes all of its iterations). So, the final program becomes

```python
positives_given = 0
while positives_given != 5:
    x = float(input("Enter a number: "))
    if x > 0:
        positives_given += 1

print("Positives given:", positives_given)
```

21.4 Breaking Out of a Loop

Loops can consume too much CPU time so you have to be very careful when you use them. There are times when you need to break out of, or end, a loop before it completes all of its iterations, usually when a specified condition is met.

Suppose there is a `for` structure that searches for a given letter within a string, as shown in the next Python program.

```python
text = "I have a dream"

letter = input("Enter a letter to search: ")

found = False
for x in text:
    if x == letter:
        found = True

if found == True:
    print("Letter", letter, "found!")
```

Now suppose that the user enters the letter "h". As you already know, the `for` structure iterates a specific number of times, and it doesn't care if the letter is actually found or not. Although the letter "h" does exist at the second position of variable `text`, unfortunately the loop continues to iterate until the end of the string, and this wastes CPU time.

Chapter 21
Tips and Tricks with Loop Structures

Someone may say *"So what? Variable* `text` *contains just 14 characters. No big deal!"* But it is a big deal, actually! In large-scale data processing everything counts, so you should be very careful when using loop structures, especially loop structures that iterate too many times.

So, what you can do to make programs like the previous one run faster is to break out of the loop when a specified condition is met—in this case, when the given letter is found.

In Python, you can use the `break` statement to break out of a loop before it completes all of its iterations. Look at the following Python program. When it finds the given letter within variable `text`, the flow of execution immediately exits the `for` structure.

file_21_4
```python
text = "I have a dream"

letter = input("Enter a letter to search: ")

found = False
for x in text:
    if x == letter:
        found = True
        break

if found == True:
    print("Letter", letter, "found!")
```

21.5 Endless Loops and How to Avoid Them

All loop structures must include a way to stop endless iterations from occurring within them. This means that there must be something inside the loop that eventually makes the flow of execution exit the loop.

The next example contains an *endless loop* (also known as an *infinite loop*). Unfortunately, the programmer forgot to increase variable `i` inside the loop; therefore, variable `i` can never reach the value 10.

```python
i = 1
while i != 10:
    print("Hello there!")
```

An endless loop continues to iterate forever, and the only way to stop it from iterating is to use magic forces! For example, when an application in a Windows operating system "hangs" (probably because the flow of execution entered an endless loop), the user must use the key combination ALT+CTRL+DEL to force the application to end.

> **Notice**: *In IDLE, when you accidentally write and execute an endless loop, you can just hit the CTRL + C key combination and the Python interpreter will immediately stop any action. In Eclipse, on the other hand, you can stop any action by clicking on the "Terminate"* ■ *toolbar icon.*

So, always remember to include at least one such statement to make the flow of execution exit the loop. But still, this is not always enough! Take a look at the following code fragment.

```
i = 1
while i != 10:
    print("Hello there!")
    i += 2
```

Even though this code fragment does contain a statement that increases variable i inside the loop (i += 2), unfortunately the flow of execution never exits the loop because the value 10 is never assigned to the variable i!

One thing that you can do to avoid this type of mistake is to never check the counter variable (here, variable i) using == and != comparison operators, especially in cases in which the counter variable increments or decrements by a value other than 1. You can use <, <=, >, and >= comparison operators instead; they guarantee that the flow of execution exits the loop when the counter variable exceeds the termination value. The previous example can be fixed by replacing the != with a <, or even a <= comparison operator.

```
i = 1
while i < 10:
    print("Hello there!")
    i += 2
```

21.6 The "From Inner to Outer" Method

This book proposes the *from inner to outer* method to help you learn "Algorithmic Thinking" from the inside out. This method first manipulates and designs the inner (nested) structures and then, as the program is developed, more and more structures are added, nesting the previous ones.

Let's try the following example.

Write a Python program that displays the following multiplication table as it is shown below.

1x1=1	1x2=2	1x3=3	1x4=4	1x5=5	1x6=6	1x7=7	1x8=8	1x9=9
2x1=2	2x2=4	2x3=6	2x4=8	2x5=10	2x6=12	2x7=14	2x8=16	2x9=18
3x1=3	3x2=6	3x3=9	3x4=12	3x5=15	3x6=18	3x7=21	3x8=24	3x9=27
4x1=4	4x2=8	4x3=12	4x4=16	4x5=20	4x6=24	4x7=28	4x8=32	4x9=36
5x1=5	5x2=10	5x3=15	5x4=20	5x5=25	5x6=30	5x7=35	5x8=40	5x9=45
6x1=6	6x2=12	6x3=18	6x4=24	6x5=30	6x6=36	6x7=42	6x8=48	6x9=54
7x1=7	7x2=14	7x3=21	7x4=28	7x5=35	7x6=42	7x7=49	7x8=56	7x9=63
8x1=8	8x2=16	8x3=24	8x4=32	8x5=40	8x6=48	8x7=56	8x8=64	8x9=72
9x1=9	9x2=18	9x3=27	9x4=36	9x5=45	9x6=54	9x7=63	9x8=72	9x9=81

According to the "from inner to outer" method, you start by writing the inner loop structure and then, when everything is tested and operates fine, you can add the outer loop structure.

So, let's try to display only the first line of the multiplication table. If you examine this line it reveals that, in each multiplication, the multiplicand is always 1. Imagine a variable i that contains the value 1. The loop structure that displays only the first line of the multiplication table is as follows.

```
for j in range(1, 10):
    print(i, "x", j, "=", i * j, end = "\t")
```

If you execute this code fragment, the result is

1x1=1   1x2=2   1x3=3   1x4=4   1x5=5   1x6=6   1x7=7   1x8=8   1x9=9

> **Remember!** The special sequence of the characters \t "displays" a tab character after each iteration. This ensures that everything is aligned properly.

The inner (nested) loop structure is ready. What you need now is a way to execute this structure nine times, but each time variable i must contain a different value, from 1 to 9. This code fragment is as follows.

```python
for i in range(1, 10):
    #Here goes the code that displays one single line
    #of the multiplication table
    print()
```

> **Notice:** The `print()` statement is used to "display" a line break between lines.

Now, you can combine both code fragments, nesting the first into the second one. The final Python program becomes

file_21_6
```python
for i in range(1, 10):
    for j in range(1, 10):
        print(i, "x", j, "=", i * j, end = "\t")
    print()
```

21.7 Review Questions: True/False

Choose **true** or **false** for each of the following statements.

1. When the number of iterations is unknown, you can use a definite loop structure.
2. When the number of iterations is known, you cannot use a `while` structure.
3. According to the "Ultimate" rule, in a `while` structure, the initialization of the variable that participates in the loop's Boolean expression must be done inside the loop.
4. According to the "Ultimate" rule, in a `while` structure, the statement that updates or alters the value of the variable that participates in the loop's Boolean expression must be the last statement within the loop.
5. In Python, you can break out of a loop before it completes all of its iterations using the `break_loop` statement.
6. When the not equal (!=) comparison operator is used in the Boolean expression of a `while` structure, the loop always iterates endlessly.

21.8 Review Questions: Multiple Choice

Select the correct answer for each of the following statements.

1. When the number of iterations is unknown, you can use
    a. the `for` structure.
    b. the `while` structure.
    c. both of the above
2. When the number of iterations is known, you can use
    a. the `for` structure.
    b. the `while` structure.
    c. both of the above
3. According to the "Ultimate" rule, in a `while` structure, the initialization of the variable that participates in the loop's Boolean expression must be done
    a. inside the loop.
    b. outside the loop.
    c. both of the above
4. According to the "Ultimate" rule, in a `while` structure, the update/alteration of the variable that participates in the loop's Boolean expression must be done
    a. inside the loop.
    b. outside the loop.
    c. both of the above
5. When this comparison operator is used in the Boolean expression of a `while` structure, the loop iterates forever.
    a. `==`
    b. `<=`
    c. `>=`
    d. it depends

21.9 Review Exercises

Complete the following exercises.

1. The following program is supposed to prompt the user to enter names repeatedly until the word "STOP" (used as a name) is entered. At the end, the program must display the total number of names entered as well as how many of these names were not "John".

```python
count_not_johns = 0
count_names = 0
name = ""
while name != "STOP":
    name = input("Enter a name: ")
    count_names += 1
    if name != "John":
        count_not_johns += 1

print("Names other than John entered", count_not_johns, "times")
```

Chapter 21
Tips and Tricks with Loop Structures

```
print(count_names, "names entered")
```

However, the program displays wrong results! Using the "Ultimate" Rule, try to modify the program so that it displays the correct results.

2. Write a Python program that prompts the user to enter some text. The text can be either a single word or a whole sentence. Then, the program must display a message stating whether the given text is one single word or a complete sentence.

    Hint: Search for a space character! If a space character is found, it means that the user entered a sentence. The program must stop searching further when it finds at least one space character.

3. Write a Python program that prompts the user to enter a sentence. The program then displays the message "The sentence contains a number" if the sentence contains at least one number. The program must stop searching further when it finds at least one digit.

4. Correct the following code fragment so that it does not iterate endlessly.

    ```
    print("Printing all integers from 1 to 100")
    i = 1
    while i < 101:
        print(i)
    ```

5. Correct the Boolean expression of the following while structure so that it does not iterate endlessly.

    ```
    print("Printing odd integers from 1 to 99")
    i = 1
    while not(i == 100):
        print(i)
        i += 2
    ```

6. Write a Python program that displays every combination of two integers as well as their resulting product, for pairs of integers between 1 and 4. The output must display as follows.

    1 x 1 = 1
    1 x 2 = 2
    1 x 3 = 3
    1 x 4 = 4
    2 x 1 = 2
    2 x 2 = 4
    2 x 3 = 6
    2 x 4 = 8
    ...
    ...
    4 x 1 = 4
    4 x 2 = 8
    4 x 3 = 12
    4 x 4 = 16

7. Write a Python program that displays the multiplication table for pairs of integers between 1 and 12, as shown next. Please note that the output is aligned with tabs.

	|	1	2	3	4	5	6	7	8	9	10	11	12
1	|	1	2	3	4	5	6	7	8	9	10	11	12
2	|	2	4	6	8	10	12	14	16	18	20	22	24
3	|	3	6	9	12	15	18	21	24	27	30	33	36
...	|	...	...	...	...	...	...	...	...	...	...	...	...
11	|	11	22	33	44	55	66	77	88	99	110	121	132
12	|	12	24	36	48	60	72	84	96	108	120	132	144

Chapter 22
More Exercises with Loop Structures

22.1 Exercises of a General Nature with Loop Structures

Exercise 22.1.1 — Finding the Sum of 1 + 2 + 3 + ... + 100

Write a Python program that calculates and displays the following sum:

$$S = 1 + 2 + 3 + ... + 100$$

Solution

This exercise can be solved using a sequence structure. Not the best option, but it's an option! Variable i increments from 1 to 100, and each time its value is accumulated in variable s.

```
s = 0
i = 1

s = s + i    #this pair of statements must be written 100 times.
i = i + 1

s = s + i
i = i + 1

...
...

s = s + i
i = i + 1

print(s)
```

Obviously, you can do the same using a `while` structure that increments variable i from 1 to 100. In each iteration, its value is accumulated in variable s.

file_22_1_1a

```
s = 0
i = 1

while i <= 100:
    s = s + i
    i = i + 1

print(s)
```

Or you can do the same using a for structure, as shown here.

file_22_1_1b

```
s = 0
for i in range(1, 101):
    s = s + i

print(s)
```

Exercise 22.1.2 — Finding the Product of 2 × 4 × 6 × 8 × 10

Write a Python program that calculates and displays the following product:

$$P = 2 \times 4 \times 6 \times 8 \times 10$$

Solution

Once again, this exercise can be solved using a sequence structure.

```
p = 1
i = 2

p = p * i
i = i + 2

p = p * i
i = i + 2

p = p * i
i = i + 2

p = p * i
i = i + 2

p = p * i
i = i + 2

print(p)
```

And once more, you can do the same using a while structure that increments variable i by 2, from 2 to 10.

file_22_1_2a

```
p = 1

i = 2
while i <= 10:
    p = p * i
```

Chapter 22
More Exercises with Loop Structures

```
        i += 2

print(p)
```

Or you can even use a `for` structure, as shown here.

file_22_1_2b
```
p = 1

for i in range(2, 12, 2):
    p = p * i

print(p)
```

Exercise 22.1.3 — Finding the Average Value of Positive Numbers

Write a Python program that prompts the user to enter 100 numbers and then calculates and displays the average value of the positive numbers.

Solution

Since you know the total number of iterations, you can use a `for` structure. Inside the loop, however, an `if` structure must check whether the given number is positive; if so, it must accumulate the given number in variable `total`. When the flow of execution exits the loop, the average value can then be calculated. The Python program is as follows.

file_22_1_3a
```
total = 0
count = 0

for i in range(100):
    x = float(input("Enter a number: "))
    if x > 0:
        total += x
        count += 1

if count != 0:
    print(total / count)
else:
    print("No positives entered!")
```

> **Notice:** The `if count != 0` statement is necessary because there is a possibility that the user may enter negative values only. By including this check, the program prevents any division-by-zero errors.

Exercise 22.1.4 — Counting the Numbers According to Which is Greater

Write a Python program that prompts the user to enter 10 pairs of numbers and then counts and displays the number of times that the first number of a given pair was greater than the second number.

Solution

Once again, a `for` structure can be used. The Python program is as follows.

file_22_1_4b
```python
count_a = 0
count_b = 0

for i in range(10):
    a = int(input("Enter number A: "))
    b = int(input("Enter number B: "))

    if a > b:
        count_a += 1
    elif b > a:
        count_b += 1

print(count_a, count_b)
```

A reasonable question that someone may ask is "*Why is an `if-elif` structure being used here? Why not use an `if-else` structure instead?*"

Suppose that an `if-else` structure such as the following is used.
```python
if a > b:
    count_a += 1
else:
    count_b += 1
```
In this decision structure, the variable count_b increments when variable b is greater than variable a (this is desirable) but also when variable b is equal to variable a (this is undesirable). Using an `if-elif` structure instead ensures that variable count_b increments only when variable b is greater than (and not when it is equal to) variable a.

Exercise 22.1.5 — Counting the Numbers According to Their Digits

Write a Python program that prompts the user to enter 20 integers. The program then counts and displays three different results: the number of one-digit integers that were given, the number of two-digit integers, and the number of three-digit integers. Assume that the user enters values between 1 and 999.

Solution

Nothing new here! The Python program is as follows.

file_22_1_5
```python
count1 = 0
count2 = 0
count3 = 0

for i in range(20):
```

```
a = int(input("Enter a number: "))

if a <= 9:
    count1 += 1
elif a <= 99:
    count2 += 1
else:
    count3 += 1

print(count1, count2, count3)
```

Exercise 22.1.6 — How Many Numbers Fit in a Sum

Write a Python program that prompts the user to enter numeric values repeatedly until their sum exceeds 1000. At the end, the program must display the total quantity of numbers entered.

Solution

In this case, you don't know the exact number of iterations, so you cannot use a `for` structure. Let's use a `while` structure instead, but, in order to make your program free of logic errors you should follow the "Ultimate" rule discussed in paragraph 21.3. According to this rule, the `while` structure that solves this problem should be as follows.

```
total = 0               #Initialization of total
while total <= 1000:    #A Boolean expression dependent on total
    #Here goes
    #a statement or block of statements

    total += x          #Update/alteration of total
```

The only statements that are missing are the statement that prompts the user to enter a number, and the statement that counts the numbers entered. The final Python program becomes

file_22_1_6
```
count = 0               #This is not here due to the Ultimate Rule!

total = 0
while total <= 1000:
    x = float(input("Enter a number: "))
    count += 1

    total += x

print(count)
```

Exercise 22.1.7 — Iterating as Many Times as the User Wants

Write a Python program that prompts the user to enter two numbers. It then calculates and displays the result of the first number raised to the power of the second one. The program must iterate as many times as the user wants. At the end of each calculation, the program must ask the user if they want to calculate the result of another pair of numbers. If the answer is "yes" the program must repeat; it must end otherwise. Make your program accept the answer in all possible forms, such as "yes", "YES", "Yes", or even "YeS".

Solution

According to the "Ultimate" rule, the `while` structure should be as follows, given in general form.

```python
answer = "yes"    #Initialization of answer

while answer.upper() == "YES":
    #Here goes the code that
    #prompts the user to enter two numbers and then
    #calculates and displays the first number
    #raised to the power of the second one.

    #Update/alteration of answer
    answer = input("Would you like to repeat? ")
```

Notice: The `upper()` method ensures that the program operates properly for any given answer: "yes", "YES", "Yes", or even "YeS" or "yEs"!

The solution to this exercise becomes

file_22_1_7

```python
answer = "yes"    #Initialization of answer

while answer.upper() == "YES":
    a = int(input("Enter number A: "))
    b = int(input("Enter number B: "))

    result = a ** b
    print("The result is:", result)

    answer = input("Would you like to repeat? ")
```

Chapter 22
More Exercises with Loop Structures

Exercise 22.1.8 — Finding Minimum Value with Loop Structures

Write a Python program that prompts the user to enter the weight of four people. It then finds and displays the lightest weight.

Solution

In Exercise 13.1.3, you learned how to find the minimum value among four values using `if` structures. Now, the following code fragment does almost the same but uses only one variable w to hold the user's given values.

```python
w = int(input("Enter a weight: "))     #User enters 1st weight
maximum = w

w = int(input("Enter a weight: "))     #User enters 2nd weight
if w > maximum:
    maximum = w

w = int(input("Enter a weight: "))     #User enters 3rd weight
if w > maximum:
    maximum = w

w = int(input("Enter a weight: "))     #User enters 4th weight
if w > maximum:
    maximum = w
```

Except for the first pair of statements, all other blocks of statements are identical; therefore, only one of those can be enclosed within a `for` structure and be executed three times, as follows.

file_22_1_8

```python
w = int(input("Enter a weight: "))     #User enters 1st weight
minimum = w

for i in range(3):
    w = int(input("Enter a weight: "))   #User enters 2nd, 3rd and 4th weight
    if w < minimum:
        minimum = w
```

Of course, if you want to allow the user to enter more values, you can simply increase the *final_value* of the `for` structure!

> **Notice:** *You can find the maximum instead of the minimum value by simply replacing the "less than" with a "greater than" operator in the `if` structure.*

> **Notice:** *Please note that the `for` structure must iterate one time less than the total number of values given.*

Exercise 22.1.9 — Fahrenheit to Kelvin, from 0 to 100

Write a Python program that displays all degrees Fahrenheit from 0 to 100 and their equivalent degrees Kelvin. Use an increment value of 0.5. It is given that

$$Kelvin = \frac{Fahrenheit + 459.67}{1.8}$$

Solution

All you need here is a variable named `fahrenheit` and a `while` structure that increments the value of the variable `fahrenheit` from 0 to 100 using an increment step of 0.5. The solution is shown next.

file_22_1_9
```
fahrenheit = 0
while fahrenheit <= 100:
    kelvin = (fahrenheit + 459.67) / 1.8
    print("Fahrenheit:", fahrenheit, "Kelvin:", kelvin)
    fahrenheit += 0.5
```

> **Notice**: You cannot use a `for` structure to solve this exercise. The `range()` function that is used along with the `for` statement supports only values of the integer type for the increment step, and in this case, the step is 0.5.

Exercise 22.1.10 — Rice on a Chessboard

There is a myth about a poor man who invented chess. The King of India was so pleased with that new game that he offered to give the poor man anything he wished for. The poor but wise man told his King that he would like one grain of rice for the first square of the board, two grains for the second, four grains for the third and so on, doubled for each of the 64 squares of the game board. This seemed to the King to be a modest request, so he ordered his servants to bring the rice.

Write a Python program that calculates how many grains of rice will be on the chessboard in the end.

Solution

Assume a chessboard of only 2 × 2 = 4 squares and a variable `grains` assigned the initial value 1 (this is the number of grains of the 1st square). A `for` structure that iterates three times can double the value of variable `grains` in each iteration, as shown in the next code fragment.

```
grains = 1
for i in range(3):
    grains = 2 * grains
```

The value of the variable `grains` at the end of each iteration is shown in the next table.

Iteration	Value of variable grains
1st	2 × 1 = 2
2nd	2 × 2 = 4
3rd	2 × 4 = 8

At the end of the 3rd iteration, the variable grains contains the value 8. This value, however, is not the total number of grains on the chessboard but only the number of grains on the 4th square. If you need to find the total number of grains on the chessboard you can sum up the grains on all squares, that is, 1 + 2 + 4 + 8 = 15.

In the real world a real chessboard contains 8 × 8 = 64 squares, thus you need to iterate for 63 times. The Python program is as follows.

file_22_1_10
```
grains = 1
total = 1
for i in range(63):
    grains = 2 * grains
    total = total + grains

print(total)
```

In case you are wondering how big this number is, here is your answer: On the chessboard there will be 18,446,744,073,709,551,615 grains of rice!

Exercise 22.1.11 — Game - Find the Secret Number

Write a Python program that assigns a random secret integer between 1 and 100 to a variable and then prompts the user to guess the number. If the integer given is greater than the secret one, a message "Your guess is bigger than my secret number. Try again." must be displayed. If the integer given is less than the secret one, a message "Your guess is smaller than my secret number. Try again." must be displayed. This must repeat until the user finally finds the secret number. Then, a message "You found it!" must be displayed, as well as the total number of the user's attempts.

Solution

According to the "Ultimate" rule, the `while` structure should be as follows, given in general form.

```
guess = int(input("Enter a guess: "))    #Initialization of guess
while guess != secret_number:

    #Here goes the rest of the code

    #Update/alteration of guess
    guess = int(input("Enter a guess: "))
```

The rest of the code that goes into the `while` structure is quite easy. More precisely, the user's guess must be compared to the secret number and proper messages must be displayed. Also, the variable that holds the user's attempts must be increased by 1.

> **Notice:** *If you don't remember how to generate random integers you may need to refresh your memory and read paragraph 10.2 again.*

The solution is as follows

file_22_1_11

```python
import random

secret_number = random.randrange(1, 101)

attempts = 1

guess = int(input("Enter a guess: "))
while guess != secret_number:
    if guess > secret_number:
        print("Your guess is bigger than my secret number. Try again.")
    else:
        print("Your guess is smaller than my secret number. Try again.")

    attempts += 1

    guess = int(input("Enter a guess: "))

print("You found it!")
print("Attempts:", attempts)
```

22.2 Review Exercises

Complete the following exercises.

1. Write a Python program that calculates and displays the following sum:
$$S = 1 + 3 + 5 + \ldots + 99$$

2. Write a Python program that prompts the user to enter an integer N and then calculates and displays the following sum:
$$S = 2 + 4 + 6 + \ldots + 2*N$$

3. Write a Python program that prompts a teacher to enter the total number of students as well as their grades and then calculates and displays the average value of those who got an "A", that is 90 to 100.

4. Write a Python program that prompts the user to repeatedly enter numeric values until their sum exceeds 3000. At the end, the program must display the total number of zeros entered.

5. The area of a circle can be calculated using the following formula:
$$\text{Area} = \pi \cdot \text{Radius}^2$$

    Write a Python program that prompts the user to enter the length of the radius of a circle and then calculates and displays its area. The program must iterate as many times as the user wishes. At the end of each area calculation, the program must ask the user if they wish to calculate the area of another circle. If the answer is "yes" the program must repeat; it must end otherwise. Make your program accept the answer in all possible forms such as "yes", "YES", "Yes", or even "YeS".

    Hint: The value of π is about 3.141.

Chapter 22
More Exercises with Loop Structures

6. Write a Python program that displays all possible RAM sizes between 1 byte and 1GByte, such as 1, 2, 4, 8, 16, 32, 64, 128, and so on.

   Hint: 1GByte equals 2^{30} bytes, or 1073741824 bytes

7. Write a Python program that displays the following sequence of numbers:

   $$-1, 1, -2, 2, -3, 3, -4, 4, \ldots -100, 100$$

8. Write a Python program that displays the following sequence of numbers:

   $$1, 11, 111, 1111, 11111, \ldots 11111111$$

9. Write a Python program that prompts the user to enter the temperatures recorded at 12:00 p.m. on each day in August and then calculates and displays the average as well as the highest temperature.

10. A scientist needs a software application to record the level of the sea in order to extract some useful information. Write a Python program that prompts the scientist to enter the hourly measured level of the sea and the corresponding hour each measure was taken, for a period of one day. Then, the program must display the highest and the lowest sea levels as well as the hour at which these levels were recorded.

11. Expand the game of exercise 22.1.11 by making it operate for two players. The player that wins is the one that finds the random secret number in fewer attempts.

12. Write a Python program that prompts a teacher to enter the total number of students, their grades, and their gender (M for Male, F for Female), and then calculates and displays all of the following:

    a. the average value of those who got an "A" (90–100)

    b. the average value of those who got a "B" (80–89)

    c. the average value of boys who got an "A" (90–100)

    d. the total number of girls that got less than "B"

    e. the average grade of the whole class

13. Write a Python program that displays the discount that a customer receives based on the amount of their order, according to the following table.

Amount	Discount
$0 < amount < $20	0%
$20 ≤ amount < $50	3%
$50 ≤ amount < $100	5%
$100 ≤ amount	10%

    At the end of each discount calculation, the program must ask the user if they wish to display the discount of another amount. If the answer is "yes," the program must repeat; it must end otherwise. Make your program accept the answer in all possible forms, such as "yes", "YES", "Yes", or even "YeS".

Chapter 23
Turtle Graphics

23.1 Introduction

"Turtle" is a Python feature which, within a window, lets you teach a virtual turtle to move around and draw shapes of your choice.

A turtle has three properties

1. a position
2. an orientation
3. a pen

You can instruct the turtle to move either forward or backward, to turn left or right, to pull its pen up or down, and so on. By using simple statements and everything you've learned so far, you can draw simple or even very complex drawings.

> **Notice**: Just for the record, Logo was the first programming language that supported turtle graphics.

23.2 The x-y Plane

Before you start learning about Python's turtle, you need to understand some things about turtle's coordinate system.

A turtle uses 2 coordinates to determine its position on the screen. The "X position" determines the horizontal and the "Y position" determines the vertical position of the turtle.

Let's assume the window in which the turtle can move is a rectangle of 400x300 pixels, as shown in **Figure 23-1**.

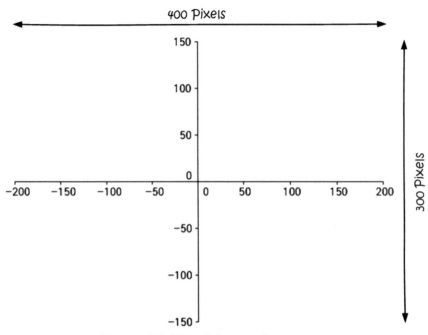

Figure 23-1 Turtle's coordinate system.

This means that:
- the X position can range from −200 to 200, where −200 is the leftmost and 200 is the rightmost position where the turtle can be.
- the Y position can range from −150 to 150, where −150 is the lowest and 150 is the highest position where the turtle can be.

By convention, coordinates are written as a pair (x, y). The center of the window is at the position (0, 0). For example, in **Figure 23-2** the turtle is located at the position (50, 100).

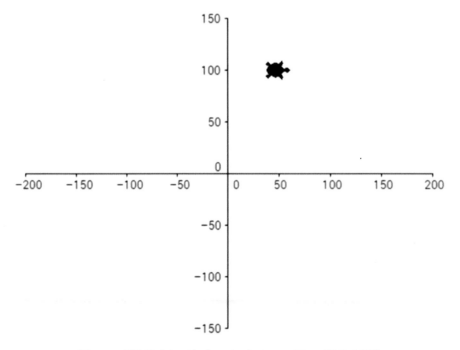

Figure 23-2 A turtle located at position (50, 100)

23.3 Where is the Turtle?

In order to start playing with turtles, you need just four lines of code, as shown in the code fragment that follows. Let's call your turtle "George".

```
import turtle              #Import turtle module

wn = turtle.Screen()       #Create a graphics window
george = turtle.Turtle()   #Create a new turtle. Let's call it "george"

wn.exitonclick()           #Wait for a user click on the graphics window
```

If you try to execute these four lines of code, you will get a window and a turtle at position (0, 0) that faces to the right as shown in **Figure 23-3**.

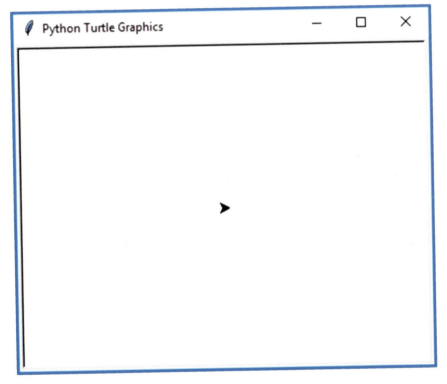

Figure 23-3 A "turtle" located at position (0, 0)

> **Notice:** *The position (0, 0) is located at the center of the window.*

It's obvious what you are thinking right now: "*This is not a turtle. This is an arrow!*" Yes, you are right! This doesn't look like a turtle!

You can alter George's default appearance by using the statement george.shape("turtle"), as shown here.

```
import turtle

wn = turtle.Screen()
george = turtle.Turtle()
```

```python
george.shape("turtle")    #Change George to a real turtle

wn.exitonclick()
```

Now, George looks like a real turtle, as shown in **Figure 23-4**.

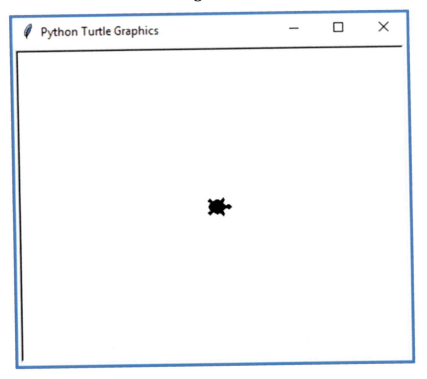

Figure 23-4 George as a real turtle

Notice! Please note that initially George faces to the right.

23.4 Moving Forward and Backward

A turtle can move forward or backward by a distance specified in pixels. The following program tells George to move forward by 50 pixels.

file_23_4a

```python
import turtle

wn = turtle.Screen()
george = turtle.Turtle()
george.shape("turtle")

george.forward(50)    #Move George forward by 50 pixels

wn.exitonclick()
```

The output result is shown in **Figure 23-5**.

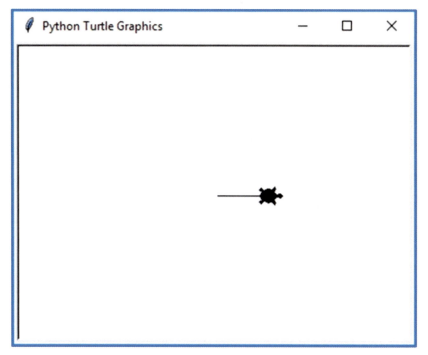

Figure 23-5 George has moved forward by 50 pixels

> **Remember!** *A turtle always moves in the direction it is facing. George initially faces to the right. So, the statement* `george.forward(50)` *instructs him to move in the direction shown in* **Figure 23-5**.

Correspondingly, the following program tells George to move backward by 100 pixels.

file_23_4b

```
import turtle

wn = turtle.Screen()
george = turtle.Turtle()
george.shape("turtle")

george.backward(100)   #Move George backward by 100 pixels

wn.exitonclick()
```

The output result is shown in **Figure 23-6**.

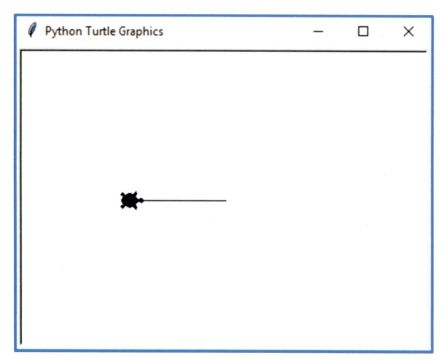

Figure 23-6 George has moved backward by 100 pixels.

23.5 Turning Left and Right

A turtle can move forward or backward but it can also turn left or right. **Figure 23-7** shows a protractor and a turtle that faces to the right.

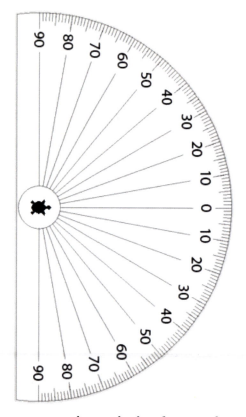

Figure 23-7 A protractor and a turtle that faces to the right

> **Remember!** Initially, when a turtle program starts, the turtle always faces to the right.

The following program tells George to turn 90 degrees to the left (rotate counterclockwise by 90 degrees).

file_23_5a
```python
import turtle

wn = turtle.Screen()
george = turtle.Turtle()
george.shape("turtle")

george.left(90)        #Rotate counterclockwise by 90 degrees

wn.exitonclick()
```

The result is shown in **Figure 23-8**

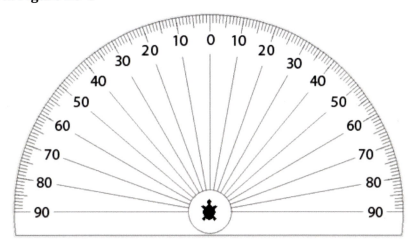

Figure 23-8 George has turned 90 degrees to the left.

Next, you can tell George to turn 45 degrees to the right (rotate clockwise by 45 degrees).

file_23_5b
```python
import turtle

wn = turtle.Screen()
george = turtle.Turtle()
george.shape("turtle")

george.left(90)         #Rotate counterclockwise by 90 degrees
george.right(45)        #Rotate clockwise by 45 degrees

wn.exitonclick()
```

The result is shown in **Figure 23-9**

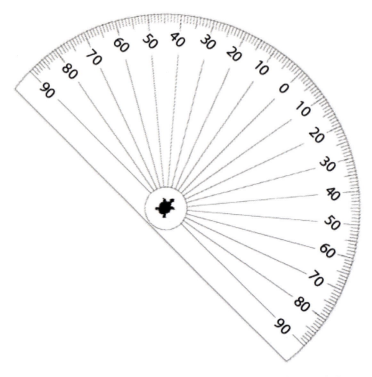

Figure 23-9 *George has turned 90 degrees to the left and then 45 degrees to the right*

Exercise 23.5.1 — Drawing a Rectangle

Write a Python program that draws a 200×100 rectangle on the screen.

Solution

This is easy. You can do this by telling your turtle to

- move forward by 200 pixels
- turn left by 90 degrees
- move forward by 100 pixels
- turn left by 90 degrees again
- move forward by 200 pixels
- turn left by 90 degrees
- move forward by 100 pixels

The corresponding Python program is shown here.

file_23_5_1

```python
import turtle

wn = turtle.Screen()
george = turtle.Turtle()
george.shape("turtle")

george.forward(200)
```

```
george.left(90)
george.forward(100)
george.left(90)
george.forward(200)
george.left(90)
george.forward(100)

wn.exitonclick()
```

The corresponding output result is shown in **Figure 23-10**.

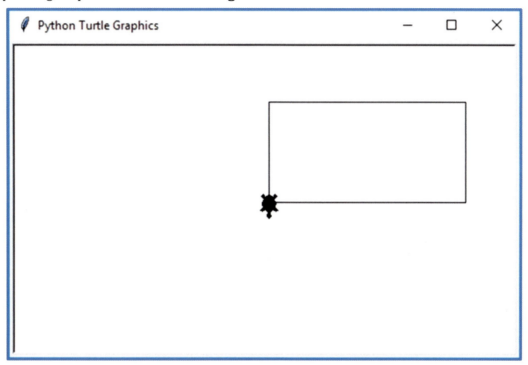

Figure 23-10 George draws a rectangle

Remember! Keep always in mind that, when a turtle program starts, the turtle always faces to the right.

Exercise 23.5.2 — Drawing a Rectangle of Custom Size

Write a Python program that prompts the user to enter the length of the base and the height of a rectangle. The program then draws the rectangle on the screen.

Solution

This is easy! The corresponding Python program is shown here.

file_23_5_2
```
import turtle

x = int(input("Enter the length of the base: "))
y = int(input("Enter the length of the height: "))
```

```
wn = turtle.Screen()
george = turtle.Turtle()
george.shape("turtle")

george.forward(x)
george.left(90)
george.forward(y)
george.left(90)
george.forward(x)
george.left(90)
george.forward(y)

wn.exitonclick()
```

23.6 Set the Orientation to a Specified Angle

There are times when you need to turn your turtle directly to a specified angle regardless of its last heading. Use the protractor shown in **Figure 23-11** to find any preferred angle.

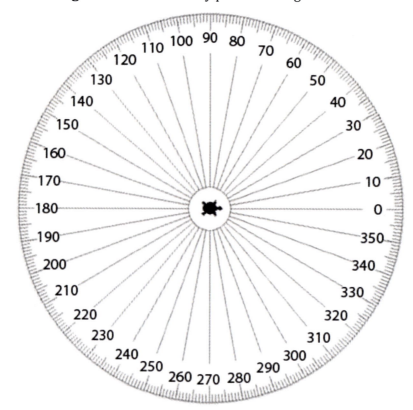

Figure 23-11 A 0–360 degree protractor

In the program that follows, George draws a right-angled triangle by setting its heading to specified angles.

file_23_6

```
import turtle

wn = turtle.Screen()
george = turtle.Turtle()
george.shape("turtle")

george.forward(100)
george.setheading(270)
george.forward(100)
george.setheading(135)
george.forward(141)

wn.exitonclick()
```

and the output result is shown in **Figure 23-12**.

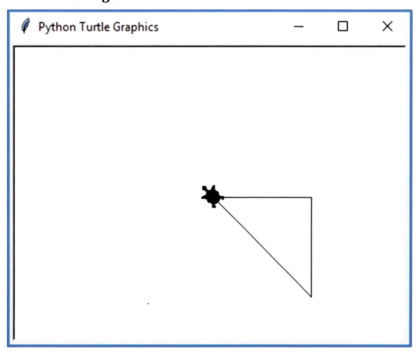

Figure 23-12 George draws a right-angled triangle

23.7 Setting the Delay

If you wish to change the speed at which your turtle moves in the drawing window, you can use the `turtle.delay()` method. In the program that follows, the turtle draws a triangle very slowly so anyone can watch it moving around.

file_23_7

```python
import turtle

wn = turtle.Screen()
george = turtle.Turtle()
george.shape("turtle")

#Set the delay to 50 milliseconds
turtle.delay(50)

#Draw a triangle
george.forward(100)
george.left(120)
george.forward(100)
george.left(120)
george.forward(100)
george.left(120)

wn.exitonclick()
```

The output result is shown in **Figure 23-13**.

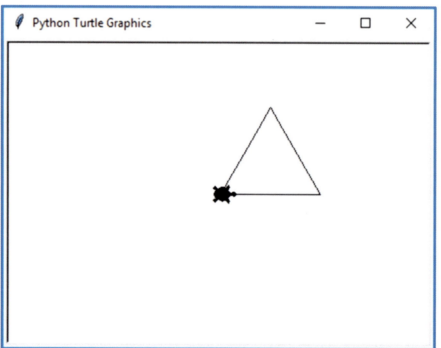

Figure 23-13 George draws a triangle slowly

Notice: *The longer the drawing delay, the slower the animation.*

23.8 Changing Pen's Color and Size

The following program changes pen's color and draws a blue line.

file_23_8a

```python
import turtle

wn = turtle.Screen()
george = turtle.Turtle()
george.shape("turtle")

#Change pen's color to blue
george.color("blue")

#Draw a blue line
george.forward(100)

wn.exitonclick()
```

> *Notice*: You can find a list of permitted color names at
> *http://www.tcl.tk/man/tcl8.4/TkCmd/colors.htm*

As well as changing the pen's color, you can also change its size (width). The following program changes the pen's size and draws a thick and a thin line.

file_23_8b

```python
import turtle

wn = turtle.Screen()
george = turtle.Turtle()
george.shape("turtle")

#Change pen's size to 5 pixels
george.pensize(5)

#Draw a thick line
george.backward(100)

#Change pen's size back to 1 pixel
george.pensize(1)

#Draw a thin line
george.backward(100)
```

```
wn.exitonclick()
```

The output result is shown in **Figure 23-14**.

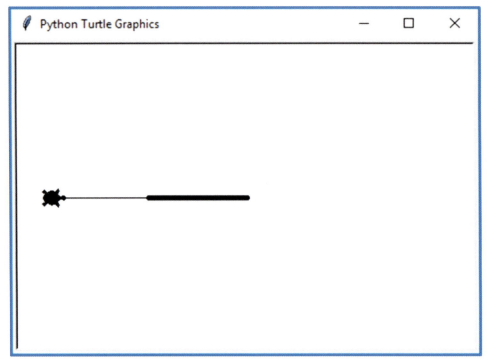

Figure 23-14 George draws a thick and a thin line

23.9 Pulling Turtle's Pen Up or Down

There are some times when you wish to move your turtle without drawing a line. This can be done easily by pulling turtle's pen up, moving the turtle to the position you wish and then pulling turtle's pen down as shown in the program that follows.

file_23_9

```python
import turtle

wn = turtle.Screen()
george = turtle.Turtle()
george.shape("turtle")

george.forward(50)
george.penup()              #Pull pen up
george.backward(200)
george.pendown()            #Pull pen down
george.forward(50)

wn.exitonclick()
```

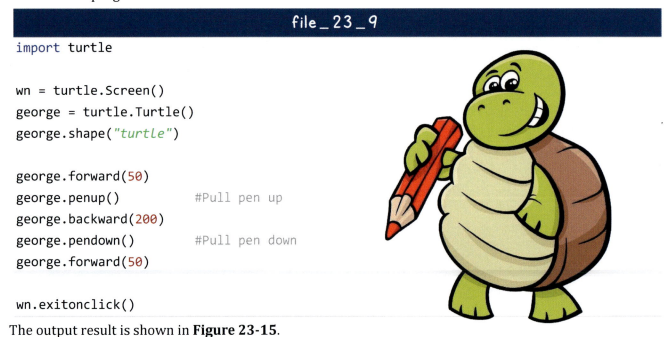

The output result is shown in **Figure 23-15**.

Chapter 23
Turtle Graphics

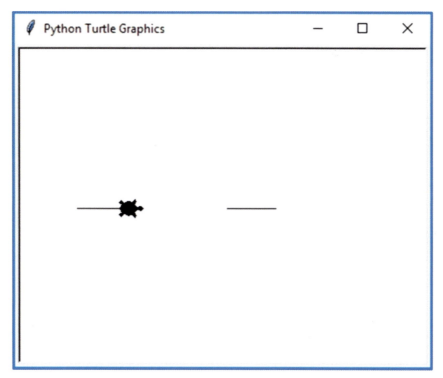

Figure 23-15 George can pull his pen up and down

Exercise 23.9.1 — Drawing a House

Write a Python program that draws the following house on the screen. Use a blue color for the rectangle and a red color for the roof. All necessary dimensions and angles are given on the drawing.

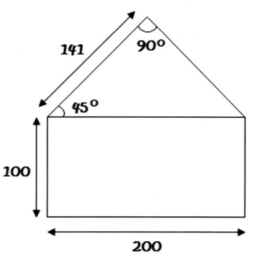

Solution

In Exercise 23.5.1, you learned how to draw the following rectangle.

At the end of the process, the turtle faces downward. To draw the roof, you have to move George to the top left corner of the rectangle without drawing a line and then set his orientation directly to 45 degrees, as shown here.

The Python program is shown here

file_23_9_1

```python
import turtle

wn = turtle.Screen()
george = turtle.Turtle()
george.shape("turtle")

#Draw a blue rectangle
george.color("blue")
george.forward(200)
george.left(90)
george.forward(100)
george.left(90)
george.forward(200)
george.left(90)
george.forward(100)

#Move George to the top left corner of the rectangle
george.penup()
george.backward(100)
george.pendown()

#Draw the red roof
george.setheading(45)
george.color("red")
```

Chapter 23
Turtle Graphics

```
george.forward(141)
george.right(90)
george.forward(141)

wn.exitonclick()
```

and the output result is shown here.

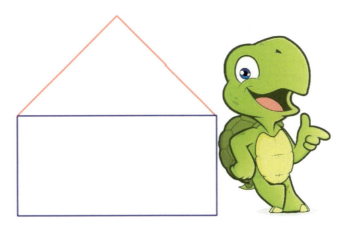

23.10 Moving a Turtle Directly to a Specified Position

You can move your turtle to specified x, y coordinates, as shown in the program that follows.

file_23_10a
```
import turtle

wn = turtle.Screen()
george = turtle.Turtle()
george.shape("turtle")

george.goto(-200, 100)

wn.exitonclick()
```

The output result is shown in **Figure 23-16**.

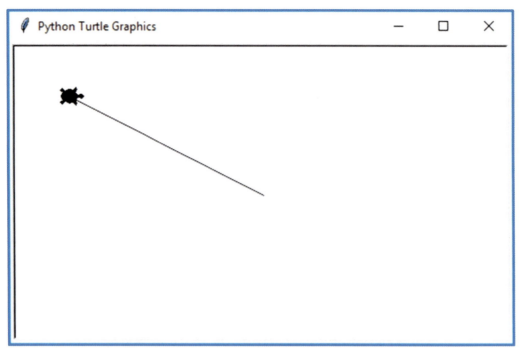

Figure 23-16 George moves directly to a specified position

Notice: The `george.goto(-200, 100)` *statement moves George to a specified position but it does not change his orientation. Moreover, if the pen is down it still draws a line.*

The following program draws an X on the screen.

file_23_10b

```python
import turtle

wn = turtle.Screen()
george = turtle.Turtle()
george.shape("turtle")

george.goto(-100, 200)
george.goto(0, 0)
george.goto(-100, -200)
george.goto(0, 0)
george.goto(100, -200)
george.goto(0, 0)
george.goto(100, 200)
george.goto(0, 0)

wn.exitonclick()
```

The output result is shown in **Figure 23-17**.

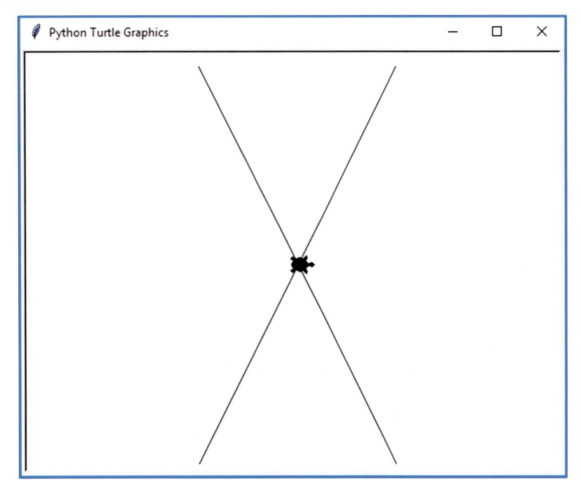

Figure 23-17 George draws an X

23.11 Using Decision and Loop Structures with Turtles

Everything you've learned about Python, from sequence to loop structures, can be used with turtles to create even more astonishing drawings. Who knows—maybe one day you will become a famous turtle painter!

Let's say you wish to draw a 50×50 square. One solution is to write the code that follows. Not a perfect solution, but it works.

```python
import turtle

wn = turtle.Screen()
george = turtle.Turtle()
george.shape("turtle")

george.forward(50)
george.left(90)
george.forward(50)
george.left(90)
george.forward(50)
george.left(90)
```

```
george.forward(50)
george.left(90)

wn.exitonclick()
```

If you look closely, however, you will notice that this pair of statements

```
george.forward(50)
george.left(90)
```

is written four times. So, it is even better if you use a for structure that iterates four times, as shown in the code that follows.

file_23_11a

```
import turtle

wn = turtle.Screen()
george = turtle.Turtle()
george.shape("turtle")

for i in range(4):
    george.forward(50)
    george.left(90)

wn.exitonclick()
```

The output result is shown in **Figure 23-18**.

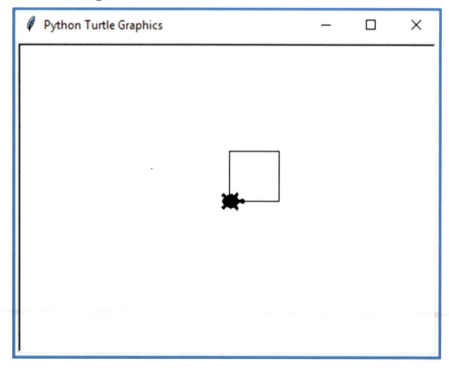

Figure 23-18 George draws a square, using a for structure

Chapter 23
Turtle Graphics

Now, let's say you wish to draw two squares, side by side. One solution would be to write the corresponding code twice, once for the first square and once for the second one, as shown in the code that follows.

```python
import turtle

wn = turtle.Screen()
george = turtle.Turtle()
george.shape("turtle")

#Move the turtle to pole position
george.penup()
george.backward(200)
george.pendown()


#############################################
# First square
#############################################
for i in range(4):
    george.forward(50)
    george.left(90)

#Move the turtle to the position
#where next square will be drawn
george.penup()
george.forward(100)
george.pendown()
#End of first square


#############################################
# Second square
#############################################
for i in range(4):
    george.forward(50)
    george.left(90)

#Move the turtle to the position
#where next square will be drawn
george.penup()
george.forward(100)
george.pendown()
#End of second square

wn.exitonclick()
```

Of course, it would be very difficult to draw 10, or even 100 squares this way! Your program could end up being huge!

The `for` structure is always the answer to all such problems! If you carefully study the previous program you will notice two groups of identical statements. The first group draws the first square, and the second one draws the second square, respectively. The following program can draw the same two 50×50 squares, side by side, using a `for` structure instead.

file_23_11b

```python
import turtle

wn = turtle.Screen()
george = turtle.Turtle()
george.shape("turtle")

#Move the turtle to pole position
george.penup()
george.backward(200)
george.pendown()

for square in range(2):
    #Draw a square
    for i in range(4):
        george.forward(50)
        george.left(90)

    #Move the turtle to the position
    #where next square will be drawn
    george.penup()
    george.forward(100)
    george.pendown()

wn.exitonclick()
```

The output result is shown in **Figure 23-19**.

Chapter 23
Turtle Graphics

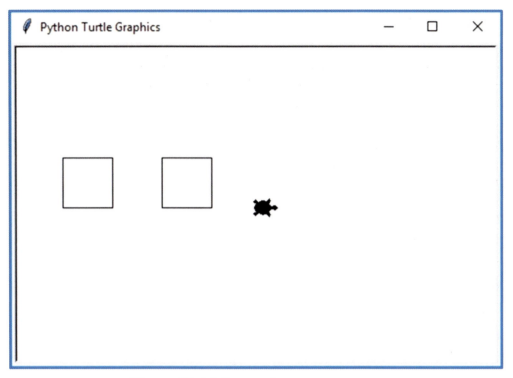

Figure 23-19 George draws two squares

Obviously, it is very easy now to draw 5 or even 10 squares this way. The only thing you have to change is the number of iterations the outer `for` structure performs. Just try it and see the output result.

Exercise 23.11.1 — Drawing Squares of Different Sizes

Write a Python program that draws three squares, side by side, on the screen. The three squares must be of different sizes so the second square is twice the size of the first one, and the third square is three times the size of the first square. The size of the first square must be 50×50 pixels.

Solution

The length of the sides of the first, second, and third squares must be 50, 100, and 150 pixels long, respectively. These values are multiples of 50, so, you can use a `for` structure and a multiplier to solve this exercise.

file_23_11_1

```python
import turtle

wn = turtle.Screen()
george = turtle.Turtle()
george.shape("turtle")

#Move the turtle to pole position
george.penup()
george.backward(330)
george.pendown()

for multiplier in range(1, 4):
```

```
#Draw a square
for i in range(4):
    george.forward(50 * multiplier)
    george.left(90)

#Move george to a position
#where next square will be drawn
george.penup()
george.forward(50 * multiplier)
george.forward(30)
george.pendown()

wn.exitonclick()
```

The output result is shown in **Figure 23-20**.

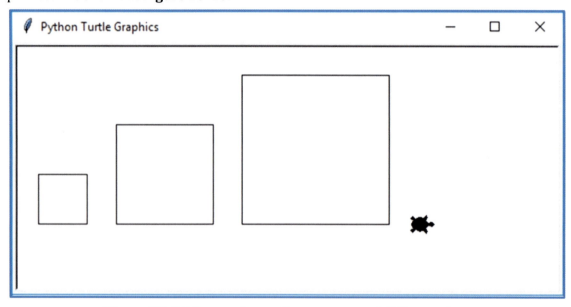

Figure 23-20 George draws three squares of different sizes

Exercise 23.11.2 — Drawing Houses of Different Sizes

Write a Python program that draws three houses, side by side, on the screen. The three houses must be of different sizes so that the second house is twice the size of the first one and the third house is three times the size of the first house, as shown in the drawing that follows. All necessary dimensions and angles are given on the drawing.

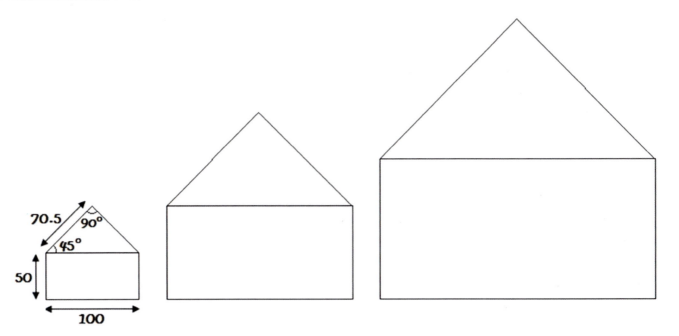

Solution

In Exercise 23.9.1, you learned how to draw one single house. Now, you can use this knowledge with a for structure and a multiplier to solve this particular exercise.

Keep in mind that when the turtle finishes one house within the loop, it must move to a position where next house will be drawn. In Exercise 23.9.1, the turtle starts drawing the house from the bottom left corner of the rectangle and finishes drawing it at the position shown in **Figure 23-21**.

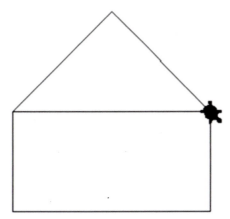

Figure 23-21 This is the position where the turtle finishes drawing the house.

So, to move the turtle to a position where the next house will be drawn, the program must

- pull the turtle's pen up
- move it to the bottom right corner of the rectangle
- turn it so as to face to the right
- move it some pixels forward
- pull its pen down

This is done by the last six statements in the program that follows.

file_23_11_2

```python
import turtle

wn = turtle.Screen()
george = turtle.Turtle()
george.shape("turtle")

#Move the turtle to pole position
george.penup()
george.backward(330)
george.pendown()

for multiplier in range(1, 4):
    #Draw a rectangle
    george.forward(100 * multiplier)
    george.left(90)
    george.forward(50 * multiplier)
    george.left(90)
    george.forward(100 * multiplier)
    george.left(90)
    george.forward(50 * multiplier)

    #Move George to the top left corner of the rectangle
    george.penup()
    george.backward(50 * multiplier)
    george.pendown()

    #Draw the roof
    george.setheading(45)
    george.forward(70.5 * multiplier)
    george.right(90)
    george.forward(70.5 * multiplier)

    #Move george to a position
    #where next house will be drawn
    george.penup()
    george.setheading(270)
    george.forward(50 * multiplier)
    george.setheading(0)
    george.forward(30)
    george.pendown()
```

```
wn.exitonclick()
```

Exercise 23.11.3 — Drawing Polygons

Write a Python program that draws a pentagon. The length of its sides must be 100 pixels and the line width must be 2 pixels.

What should you change in your program to draw a hexagon or a heptagon?

Solution

To draw a pentagon, some geometry concepts are necessary. As you can see in **Figure 23-22**, when the turtle draws one of pentagon's sides, it then must turn by a specific angle to the right. This is the exterior angle of the polygon, which is equal to 360/5 = 72 degrees, where 5 is the number of sides of the pentagon.

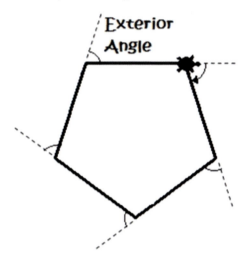

Figure 23-22 George must turn 72 degrees

The solution to this problem is shown in the program that follows.

file_23_11_3

```python
import turtle

wn = turtle.Screen()
george = turtle.Turtle()
george.shape("turtle")

george.pensize(2)

sides = 5

for i in range(sides):
    george.forward(100)
    george.right(360 / sides)

wn.exitonclick()
```

Have you figured out what to change in your program, in order to draw a hexagon or a heptagon?

Yup, it wasn't difficult! Change the value of variable `sides` and draw any polygon you wish!

Exercise 23.11.4 – Drawing a Star

Write a Python program that draws a five-point star. The length of its sides must be 150 pixels and the line width must be 3 pixels.

Solution

Using **Figure 23-23** and some simple geometry rules you can easily find that, at the end of each line, the turtle must turn 36 × 4 = 144 degrees to the right. You can easily find the value of 36 if you divide the value 180 by 5.

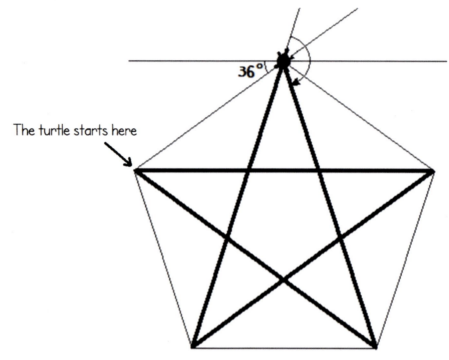

Figure 23-23 George must turn 144 degrees

The program that draws a five-point star is as follows.

```
                        file_23_11_4a
import turtle

wn = turtle.Screen()
george = turtle.Turtle()
george.shape("turtle")

george.pensize(3)

for i in range(5):
    george.forward(150)
    george.right(180 / 5 * 4)     # 180 / 5 * 4 = 36 * 4 = 144

wn.exitonclick()
```

If you wish to draw a seven-point star, you can use the following program.

file_23_11_4b

```python
import turtle

wn = turtle.Screen()
george = turtle.Turtle()
george.shape("turtle")

george.pensize(3)

points = 7

for i in range(points):
    george.forward(150)
    george.right(180 / points * (points - 1))

wn.exitonclick()
```

Notice: Obviously, you can use this program to draw any star, with any number of points. Keep in mind, though, that for the program to work properly there must be an odd number of points, such as 5, 7, 9, 11, 13, and so on.

Exercise 23.11.5 — Drawing Random Stars at Random Positions

Write a Python program that draws 10 stars of random size, with a random number of points, and at random positions.

Solution

The following statement generates a random odd integer between 5 and 21.

```python
points = random.randrange(5, 23, 2)
```

You need this integer to draw stars with a random number of points! If you don't remember how to generate random integers, you may need to refresh your knowledge and read paragraph 10.2 again.

Now, let's use the "from inner to outer" method proposed in paragraph 21.6. Let's try to draw just one star of random size, with a random number of points, at a random position. The code fragment, along with all necessary comments, is shown here.

```python
#Pick random x, y values and move the turtle to that position
x = random.randrange(-200, 200)
y = random.randrange(-200, 200)
george.penup()
george.goto(x, y)
george.pendown()

#Pick a random number of points
```

```python
points = random.randrange(5, 23, 2)

#Pick a random side length
length = random.randrange(10, 100)

#Draw a star
for i in range(points):
    george.forward(length)
    george.right(180 / points * (points - 1))
```

Now that everything has been clarified, in order to draw 10 stars you can just nest this code fragment in a for structure that iterates 10 times, as follows.

file_23_11_5

```python
import random
import turtle

wn = turtle.Screen()
george = turtle.Turtle()
george.shape("turtle")

#Draw stars as quickly as possible
turtle.delay(0)

for star in range(10):
    #Pick random x, y values and move the turtle to that position
    x = random.randrange(-200, 200)
    y = random.randrange(-200, 200)
    george.penup()
    george.goto(x, y)
    george.pendown()

    #Pick a random number of points
    points = random.randrange(5, 23, 2)

    #Pick a random side length
    length = random.randrange(10, 100)

    #Draw a star
    for i in range(points):
        george.forward(length)
        george.right(180 / points * (points - 1))
```

```
wn.exitonclick()
```

The output result can be something like the one shown in **Figure 23-24**.

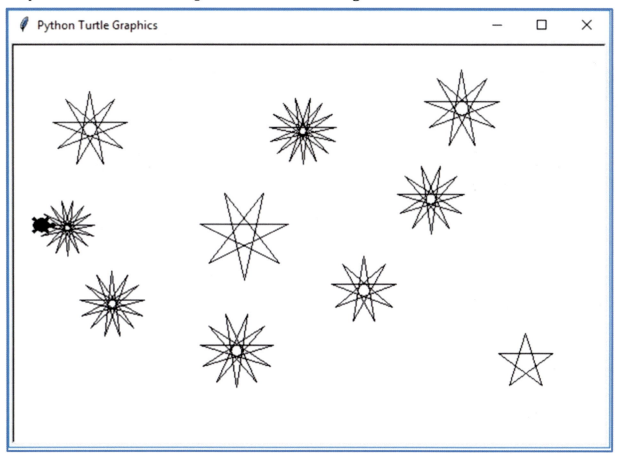

Figure 23-24 10 stars of random size, with a random number of points, and at random positions

Exercise 23.11.6 – Using Decision Structures to Draw Stars

Write a Python program that draws the star shown here. The length of its sides and the width of its lines can be of your choice. All necessary angles are given in the drawing.

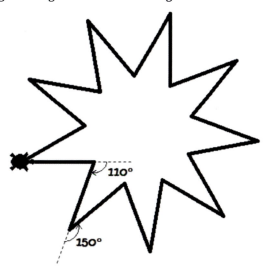

Solution

The problem in this exercise is that there are two different angles. The first time, the turtle must move forward and turn 110 degrees to the right (clockwise). The next time, however, the turtle must move forward but turn 150 degrees to the left (counterclockwise). And this process must be repeated 18 times. The solution to this exercise is shown here.

file_23_11_6

```python
import turtle

wn = turtle.Screen()
george = turtle.Turtle()
george.shape("turtle")

george.pensize(3)

flag = False
for x in range(18):
    george.forward(100)

    if flag == False:
        george.right(110)
    else:
        george.left(150)

    flag = not flag         #This statement reverses flag from True to False
                            #and vice versa

wn.exitonclick()
```

23.12 Review Exercises

Complete the following exercises.

1. Write a Python program that draws an arrow. Choose dimensions and angles of your own.
2. Write a Python program that draws a parallelogram. Choose dimensions and angles of your own.
3. Write a Python program that draws a rhombus. Choose dimensions and angles of your own.
4. Write a Python program that draws a trapezium. Choose dimensions and angles of your own.

5. Write a Python program that draws the following shape. Choose dimensions of your own.

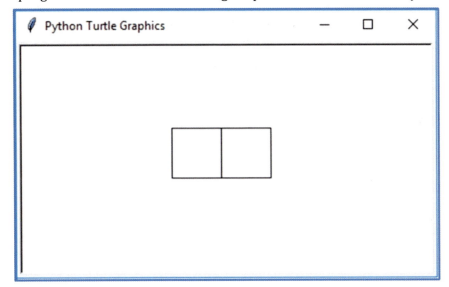

6. Write a Python program that draws four squares. The output result must look like the one that follows. Choose dimensions of your own.

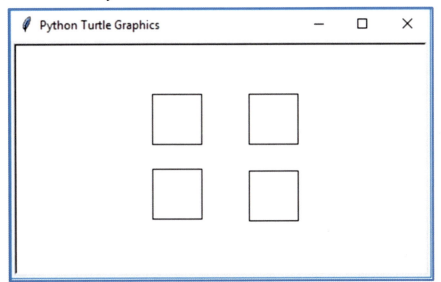

7. Write a Python program that prompts the user to enter the size of turtle's pen, as well as the length of the base and the height of a rectangle. The program then draws the rectangle on the screen.

8. Write a Python program that prompts the user to enter the length of the side of an equilateral triangle and then draws it on the screen.

Hint: In an equilateral triangle, all the angles are equal—each one measures 60 degrees.

9. Write a Python program that draws the shape that follows. Choose dimensions of your own.

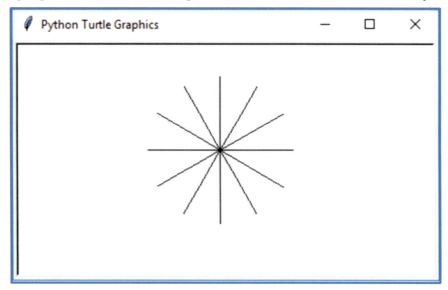

10. Write a Python program that draws three stars, one within the other, like those shown in the shape that follows. Choose dimensions of your own.

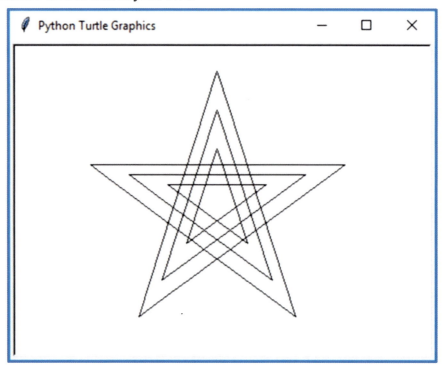

11. Write a Python program that draws three squares. The output result must look like the one that follows. Choose dimensions and angles of your own.

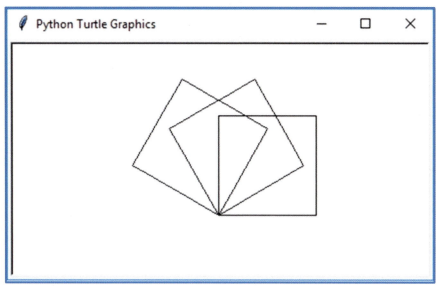

12. Modify the code of the previous exercise to draw 12 squares. See what happens!
13. Modify the code of the previous exercise to draw the shape that follows. Choose dimensions of your own.

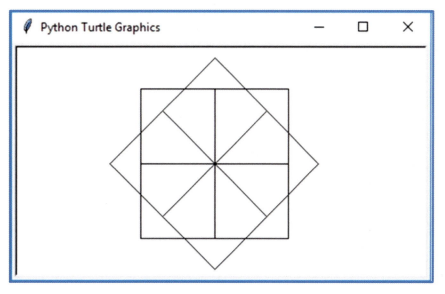

14. Write a Python program that draws the following house on the screen. Use a blue color for the walls, a red color for the roof, and a brown color for the windows and the door. All necessary dimensions and angles are given on the drawing.

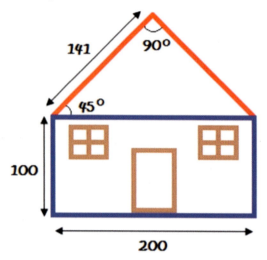

15. Modify the code of the previous exercise so as to draw three houses, side by side.

Chapter 24
Data Structures in Python

24.1 Introduction to Data Structures

Variables are a good way to store values in memory but they have one limitation—they can hold only one value at a time. For example, consider the following wording of an exercise.

Write a Python program that prompts the user to enter the names of five students. It then displays them in the exact reverse of the order in which they were given.

In the code fragment that follows

```python
for i in range(5):
    name = input("Enter a name: ")
```

when the loop finally finishes iterating, the variable name contains only that last name that was given. Unfortunately, all the previous four names have been lost! Using this code fragment, it is impossible to display them in the exact reverse of the order in which they were given.

One possible solution would be to use five individual variables, as follows.

```python
name1 = input("Enter a name: ")
name2 = input("Enter a name: ")
name3 = input("Enter a name: ")
name4 = input("Enter a name: ")
name5 = input("Enter a name: ")

print(name5)
print(name4)
print(name3)
print(name2)
print(name1)
```

Not a perfect solution, but it works! There are many cases, however, where a program needs to process large amounts of data. What if the wording of this exercise asked the user to enter 1,000 names instead of five? Think about it! Do you have the patience to write a similar Python program for each of those names? Of course not! Fortunately, there are *data structures*!

> **Notice:** In computer science, a data structure is a collection of data organized so that you can perform operations on it in the most effective way.

There are quite a few data structures available in Python, such as *lists, tuples, dictionaries, sets, frozensets*, and *strings*. Yes, you heard that right! Strings are data structures! A string is nothing more than a collection of alphanumeric characters!

Beyond strings (for which you have already learned enough), lists, tuples, and dictionaries are the most commonly used data structures in Python. The following chapters will analyze all three of these.

24.2 What is a List?

A *list* is a type of data structure that can hold multiple values under one common name. You can think of a list as a collection of items. Each item in a list is called an *element*, and each element is given a unique number known as an *index position*, or simply an *index*. Lists are *mutable* (changeable), which means that the values of their elements can be changed, and new elements can be added to or removed from the list.

> **Notice:** *Lists in computer science resemble the matrices used in mathematics. A mathematical matrix is a collection of numbers or other mathematical objects that is arranged in rows and/or columns.*

> **Notice:** *In many computer languages, such as C, and C++ (to name a few), there are no lists. These languages use another kind of data structure that is called an "array." Lists, however, are more efficient and powerful than arrays.*

The following example shows a list that holds the grades of six students. The name of the list is grades. For your convenience, the corresponding index is written above each element. In Python, index numbering always starts at zero by default.

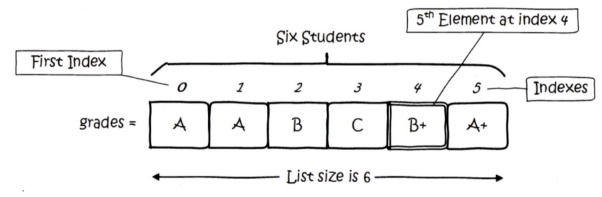

> **Remember!** *Since index numbering starts at zero, the index of the last list element is 1 less than the total number of elements in the list. In the list* grades, *the index of the last element is 5 but the total number of elements is 6.*

You can think of the list grades as if it were six individual variables—grades0, grades1, grades2, ... grades5—with each variable holding the grade of one student. The advantage of a list, however, is that it can hold multiple values under one common name.

Exercise 24.2.1 — Designing a Data Structure

Design a data structure that can hold the ages of 8 people, and then add some typical values to the structure.

Chapter 24
Data Structures in Python

Solution

All you have to do is design a list with 8 elements (indexes 0 to 7). It can be a list with either one row or one column, as follows.

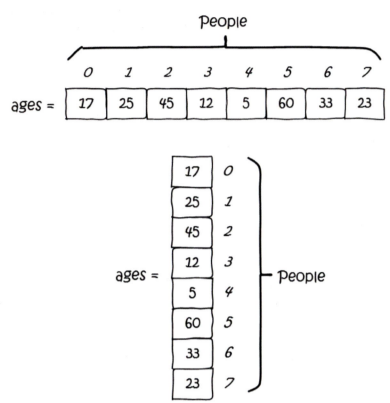

Keep in mind though, that there are no lists with one row or one column in Python. These concepts may exist in mathematical matrices (or in your imagination!) but not in Python. The lists in Python are just lists—end of story! If you want to visualize them having one row or one column, that is up to you.

Exercise 24.2.2 – Designing Data Structures

Design the necessary data structures to hold the names and the ages of seven people, and then add some typical values to the structures.

Solution

This exercise can be implemented with two lists. Let's design them with one column each.

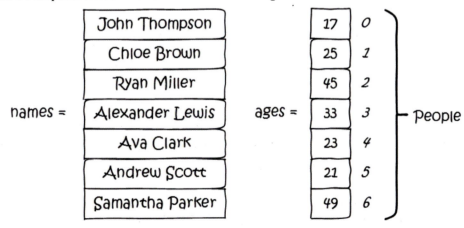

As you may have already noticed, there is a very close relationship between the elements of the two lists, meaning that there is a one-to-one match between the index positions of the elements of list names and those of list ages. In list names, at index 0, there is "John Thompson" and exactly at the same index, in the list ages, there is his age. Yep! John is 17 years old! Obviously, Chloe Brown is 25, Ryan Miller is 45, and so on.

24.3 Creating Lists in Python

Python has many ways to create a list and add values to it. Depending on the given problem, it's up to you which one to use.

Let's try to create the following list using the most common approaches.

	0	1	2	3
ages =	12	25	9	11

First Approach

To create a list and directly assign values to its elements, you can use the next Python statement, given in general form.

```
list_name = [ value0, value1, value2, …, valueM ]
```

For this approach, you can create the list ages using the following statement:

```
ages = [12, 25, 9, 11]
```

In this approach, indexes are set automatically. The value 12 is assigned to the element at index position 0, value 25 is assigned to the element at index position 1, and so on. Index numbering always starts at zero by default.

Second Approach

You can create a list of *size* empty elements in Python using the following statement given in general form:

```
list_name = [None] * size
```

where *size* can be any positive integer value, or it can even be a variable that contains any positive integer value.

The next statement creates the list ages with 4 empty elements.

```
ages = [None] * 4
```

> **Notice:** The statement ages = [None] * 4 *reserves four locations in main memory (RAM).*

You can assign a value to a list element using the following statement, given in general form:

```
list_name[index] = value
```

where *index* is the index position of the element in the list.

The next code fragment creates the list ages (reserving four locations in main memory) and then assigns values to them.

```
ages = [None] * 4
```

```
ages[0] = 12
ages[1] = 25
ages[2] = 9
ages[3] = 11
```

> **Notice:** *The size of the list* `ages` *is 4.*

> **Notice**: *In paragraph 4.3 you learned about the rules that you must follow when assigning names to Python variables. Assigning names to lists follows exactly the same rules!*

Of course, instead of using constant values for *index*, you can also use variables or expressions, as follows.

```
ages = [None] * 4
```

```
k = 0
```

```
ages[k] = 12
ages[k + 1] = 25
ages[k + 2] = 9
ages[k + 3] = 11
```

Third Approach

In this approach, you can create a totally empty list (without elements) and then add elements (and values) to it using the append() method, as shown in the following Python statements, given in general form.

```
list_name = []
```

```
list_name.append(value0)
list_name.append(value1)
list_name.append(value2)
...
list_name.append(valueM)
```

Using this approach, you can create the list `ages` using the following code fragment:

```
ages = []
ages.append(12)
ages.append(25)
ages.append(9)
ages.append(11)
```

> **Notice:** *Please note that in this approach as well,* `index` *numbering starts at zero by default.*

> **Notice**: The statement `ages = []` does not reserve any locations in main memory (RAM). It just states that the list `ages` is ready to accept new elements.

24.4 What is a Tuple?

A *tuple* is almost identical to a list. The main difference is that tuples are immutable (unchangeable), which means that the value of their elements cannot be changed once the tuple is created—and obviously you cannot add new elements to it or remove existing elements from it.

24.5 Creating Tuples in Python

To create a tuple, you must put comma-separated values within parentheses as shown in the next Python statement, given in general form.

```
tuple_name = ( value0, value1, value2, …, valueM )
```

The following example creates a tuple containing 5 elements.

```
gods = ("Zeus", "Ares", "Hera", "Aphrodite", "Hermes")
```

Indexes are set automatically. The value "Zeus" is assigned to the element at index position 0, the value "Ares" is assigned to the element at index position 1, and so on. Index numbering always starts at zero by default.

The next example creates two tuples. The first one contains the names of three students and the second one contains their ages. Obviously, there is a one-to-one match between the index positions of the elements of tuple names and those of tuple ages. Maria is 12, George is 11, and John is 13 years old.

```
names = ("Maria", "George", "John")
ages = (12, 11, 13)
```

You can also create a tuple by mixing different types of elements. In the example that follows, the tuple students contains both strings and integers.

```
students = ("Maria", 12, "George", 11, "John", 13)
```

24.6 How to Get a Value from a List or Tuple

Getting values from a list or tuple is just a matter of pointing to a specific element. Each element of a list or tuple can be uniquely identified using an index. The following code fragment creates a list and displays "A+" (without the double quotes) on the screen.

```
grades = ["B+", "A+", "A", "C-"]
print(grades[1])
```

Of course, instead of using constant values for *index*, you can also use variables or expressions. The following example creates a tuple and displays "Aphrodite and Hera" (without the double quotes) on the screen.

```
gods = ("Zeus", "Ares", "Hera", "Aphrodite", "Hermes")
k = 3
```

```python
print(gods[k], "and", gods[k - 1])
```

> **Remember!** Square brackets [ ] are used to create a list but parentheses ( ) are used to create a tuple!

> **Notice:** To access an element of either a list or a tuple, you must use square brackets for both.

A negative index accesses an element by starting to count from the end of the list or tuple. In the list grades, the position of each element (using negative indexes) is as follows.

```
              -4   -3  -2  -1
grades =    | B+ | A+ | A | C- |
```

The following example

```python
grades = ["B+", "A+", "A", "C-"]
print(grades[-1] , "and", grades[-3])
```

displays "C– and A+" (without the double quotes) on the screen.

If you want to display all the elements of a list, you can do the following

```python
grades = ["B+", "A+", "A", "C-"]
print(grades)          #It displays: ['B+', 'A+', 'A', 'C-']
```

Similarly, if you want to display all the elements of a tuple, you can do the following

```python
names = ("George", "John", "Maria")
print(names)           #It displays: ('George', 'John', 'Maria')
```

> **Remember!** In Python, you can define a string using either single or double quotes.

Just like in strings, you can get a subset of a list or tuple, called a "slice", as shown here.

```python
grades = ["B+", "A+", "A", "C-"]

print(grades[1:3])      #It displays: ["A+", "A"]
```

> **Notice:** In Python, slicing is a mechanism to select a range of elements from a list or tuple (or from a sequence, in general).

As you already know, the slicing mechanism can also have a third argument, called *step*, as shown here.

```python
grades = ["B+", "A+", "A", "C-", "A-", "B-", "C", "B", "C+"]
print(grades[1:7:2])    #It displays: ['A+', 'C-', 'B-']
```

A negative *step* returns a list or tuple in reverse order

```python
gods = ("Ares", "Hera", "Aphrodite", "Hermes")
print(gods[::-1])       #It displays: ('Hermes', 'Aphrodite', 'Hera', 'Ares')
```

Exercise 24.6.1 — Find What is Displayed

Try to determine the values that list b will contain when the following code fragment is executed.

```
b = [None] * 3

b[2] = 9
x = 0
b[x] = b[2] + 4
b[x + 1] = b[0] + 5

print(b)
```

Solution

The following steps are performed:

- A list of three empty elements is created, as shown here

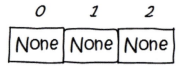

- Value 9 is assigned to the element at index 2. The list now looks like this

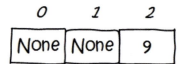

- Value 0 is assigned to variable x
- Value 13 is assigned to the element at index 0. The list now looks like this

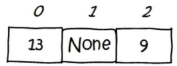

- Value 18 is assigned to the element at index 1. The list finally looks like this

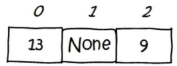

- [13, 18, 9] is displayed on the user's screen

Exercise 24.6.2 — Using a Non-Existing Index in Lists

What is wrong in the following Python program?

```
grades = ["B+", "A+", "A", "C-"]
print(grades[100])
```

Chapter 24
Data Structures in Python

Solution

Obviously, you must never refer to a non-existing list element. In this exercise, there is no element at index position 100. If you attempt to execute this program, Python displays an error message as shown in **Figure 24-1**.

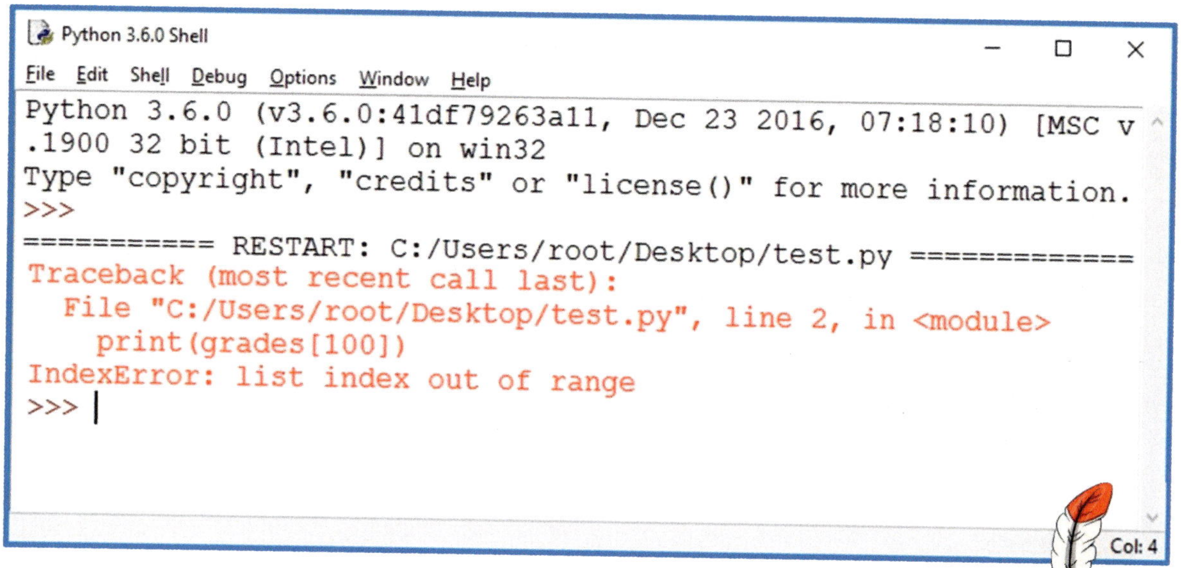

Figure 24-1 An error message indicating an invalid index

24.7 How to Alter the Value of a List Element

To alter the value of an existing list element is a piece of cake. All you need to do is use the appropriate index and assign a new value to that element. The example that follows shows exactly this.

```python
#Create a list
indian_tribes = [ "Navajo", "Cherokee", "Sioux" ]
print(indian_tribes)     #It displays: ['Navajo', 'Cherokee', 'Sioux']

#Alter the value of an existing element
indian_tribes[1] = "Apache"
print(indian_tribes)     #It displays: ['Navajo', 'Apache', 'Sioux']
```

Exercise 24.7.1 — Find the Error

What is wrong in the following Python program?

```python
names = ("George", "John", "Maria")
names[1] = "Johnathan"
print(names)
```

Solution

Before reading the answer below, can you find the error by yourself?

No? Come one, you can do better than that!

Yeah, you got it! As already stated, a tuple is immutable, which means that the value of its elements cannot be changed once the tuple is created. Since names is a tuple (not a list), the second line of this code fragment, inevitably, produces an error once the program is executed!

24.8 How to Iterate Through a List or Tuple

Now comes the interesting part. A program can iterate through the elements of a list or tuple using a loop structure (usually a `for` structure.) There are two approaches we can use to iterate through a list.

First Approach

This approach refers to each list or tuple element using its index. Following is a code fragment, written in general form

```
for index in range(size):
    process structure_name[index]
```

in which *process* is any Python statement or block of statements that processes one element of the list or tuple *structure_name* at each iteration.

The following Python program, displays all elements of the tuple gods, one at each iteration.

```
gods = ("Zeus", "Ares", "Hera", "Aphrodite", "Hermes")
for i in range(5):
    print(gods[i])
```

> *Notice:* The name of the variable i is not binding. You can use any variable name you want, such as index, ind, j, and many more.

> *Notice:* Please note that since the tuple gods contains five elements, the for structure must iterate from 0 to 4 and not from 1 to 5. This is because the indexes of the four elements are 0, 1, 2, 3, and 4, correspondingly.

Since lists are mutable, you can use a loop structure to alter all or some of its values. The following code fragment doubles the values of some elements of the list b.

```
b = [80, 65, 60, 72, 30, 40]
for i in range(3):
    b[i] = b[i] * 2
```

Second Approach

This approach is very simple but not as flexible as the previous one. There are cases where it cannot be used, as you will see below. Following is a code fragment, written in general form

```
for element in structure_name:
    process element
```

in which *process* is any Python statement or block of statements that processes one element of the list or tuple *structure_name* at each iteration.

The following Python program, displays all elements of the list grades, one at each iteration.

Chapter 24
Data Structures in Python

```python
grades = ["B+", "A+", "A", "C-"]

for x in grades:
    print(x)
```

> **Notice:** In the first iteration, the value of the first element is assigned to variable x. In the second iteration, the value of the second element is assigned to variable x and so on!

The following Python program displays all elements of the tuple gods, one at each iteration, in reverse order.

```python
gods = ("Hera", "Zeus", "Ares", "Aphrodite", "Hermes")
for god in gods[::-1]:
    print(god)
```

Unfortunately, this approach cannot be used to alter the values of the elements of a list. For example, if you want to double the values of all elements of the list numbers, you can**not** do the following:

```python
numbers = [5, 10, 3, 2]

for number in numbers:
    number *= 2
```

> **Notice:** number is a simple variable where, at each iteration, each successive value of the list numbers is assigned to. However, the opposite never happens! The value of number is never assigned back to any element!

> **Remember!** If you want to alter the values of the elements of a list, you should use the first approach.

Exercise 24.8.1 — Finding the Sum

Write a Python program that creates a tuple with the following values

56, 12, 33, 8, 3, 2, 98

and then calculates and displays their sum.

Solution

You have learned two ways to iterate through the tuple elements. Let's use both ways and see the differences. You will find an extra third approach below, which is the Pythonic way to calculate the sum of the elements of a list or tuple.

First approach

The solution is as follows.

file_24_8_1a
```python
values = (56, 12, 33, 8, 3, 2, 98)

total = 0
```

```
for i in range(7):
    total = total + values[i]

print(total)
```

Second approach

The solution is as follows.

file_24_8_1b
```
values = (56, 12, 33, 8, 3, 2, 98)

total = 0
for value in values:
    total = total + value

print(total)
```

Third approach

This approach uses no loop structures. It just uses the `fsum()` function of the `math` module.

file_24_8_1c
```
import math

values = (56, 12, 33, 8, 3, 2, 98)

total = math.fsum(values)

print(total)
```

Notice: If you don't remember anything about the `fsum()` function, refresh your memory by re-reading paragraph 10.2.

24.9 How to Add User-Entered Values to a List

There is nothing new here. Instead of reading a value from the keyboard and assigning that value to a variable, you can directly assign that value to a specific list element. The next code fragment prompts the user to enter the names of three people, and assigns them to the elements at index positions 0, 1, and 2, of the list names.

```
names = [None] * 3     #Pre-reserve 3 locations in main memory (RAM)

names[0] = input("Enter name No 1: ")
names[1] = input("Enter name No 2: ")
names[2] = input("Enter name No 3: ")
```

You can, of course, do the same, using the `append()` method instead, as shown in the code fragment that follows.

```python
names = []   #Create a totally empty list

names.append(input("Enter name No 1: "))
names.append(input("Enter name No 2: "))
names.append(input("Enter name No 3: "))
```

Exercise 24.9.1 — Displaying Words in Reverse Order

Write a Python program that lets the user enter 20 words. The program then displays them in the exact reverse of the order in which they were given.

Solution

Lists are perfect for problems like this one. The following is an appropriate solution.

file_24_9_1a
```python
words = [None] * 20

for i in range(20):
    words[i] = input()

for i in range(19, -1, -1):
    print(words[i])
```

Remember! Since index numbering starts at zero, the index of the last list element is 1 less than the total number of elements in the list.

Keep in mind that in Python you can iterate in reverse order through the list elements using the slicing mechanism and a value of −1 for *step*. The following program creates a totally empty list and then uses the `append()` method to add elements to the list. Finally, the slicing mechanism is used to display them in the exact reverse of the order in which they were given.

file_24_9_1b
```python
words = []
for i in range(20):
    words.append(input())

for word in words[::-1]:
    print(word)
```

Notice: Sometimes the wording of an exercise may say nothing about using a data structure. However, this doesn't mean that you can't use one. Use lists, tuples, and dictionaries whenever you think they are necessary.

> **Remember!** When the append() method is used, elements are appended to a list (added at the end of the list).

Exercise 24.9.2 — Displaying Positive Numbers in Reverse Order

Write a Python program that lets the user enter 100 numbers and then displays only the positive ones in the reverse of the order in which they were given.

Solution

In this exercise, the program must accept all values from the user and store them in a list. However, within the for structure that is responsible for displaying the list elements, a nested decision structure must check for and display only the positive values. The solution is as follows.

file_24_9_2

```python
ELEMENTS = 100

values = []
for i in range(ELEMENTS):
    values.append(float(input()))

for value in values[::-1]:
    if value > 0:
        print(value)
```

Exercise 24.9.3 — Finding the Sum

Write a Python program that prompts the user to enter 50 numbers into a list and then calculates and displays their sum.

Solution

The solution is as follows.

file_24_9_3a

```python
ELEMENTS = 50

values = [None] * ELEMENTS
for i in range(ELEMENTS):
    values[i] = float(input("Enter a value: "))

total = 0
for i in range(ELEMENTS):
    total = total + values[i]

print(total)
```

Chapter 24
Data Structures in Python

If you are wondering whether or not this exercise could have been solved using just one `for` structure, the answer is "yes." An alternative solution is presented next.

file_24_9_3b

```python
ELEMENTS = 50

values = [None] * ELEMENTS

total = 0
for i in range(ELEMENTS):
    values[i] = float(input("Enter a value: "))
    total = total + values[i]

print(total)
```

But let's clarify something! Even though many processes can be performed inside just one `for` structure, it is simpler to <u>carry out each individual process in a separate `for` structure</u>. This is probably not so efficient but, since you are still a novice programmer, try to adopt this programming style just for now. Later, when you have the experience and become a Python guru, you will be able to "merge" many processes in just one `for` structure!

Now, let's see a more Pythonic approach using the `fsum()` function.

file_24_9_3c

```python
import math
ELEMENTS = 50

values = []
for i in range(ELEMENTS):
    values.append(float(input("Enter a value: ")))

total = math.fsum(values)

print(total)
```

Exercise 24.9.4 — Finding the Average Value

Write a Python program that prompts the user to enter 20 numbers into a list. It then displays a message only when their average value is less than 10.

Solution

To find the average value of the given numbers the program must first find their sum and then divide that sum by 20. Just like in the previous exercise, to find the sum, you can accumulate the given numbers into that variable `total` or you can just use the `fsum()` function. Once the average value is found, the program must check whether to display the corresponding message.

First approach

file_24_9_4a

```python
ELEMENTS = 20

values = []
for i in range(ELEMENTS):
    values.append(float(input("Enter a value: ")))

#Accumulate values in total
total = 0
for i in range(ELEMENTS):
    total = total + values[i]

average = total / ELEMENTS

if average < 10:
    print("Average value is less than 10")
```

Second approach

file_24_9_4b

```python
import math
ELEMENTS = 20

values = []
for i in range(ELEMENTS):
    values.append(float(input("Enter a value: ")))

if math.fsum(values) / ELEMENTS < 10:
    print("Average value is less than 10")
```

Exercise 24.9.5 — Displaying Reals Only

Write a Python program that prompts the user to enter 10 numeric values in a list. The program then displays the indexes of the elements that contain reals.

Solution

To check whether or not, a number is a real (float), you can use the Boolean expression

$$element\ !=\ int(element)$$

The function `int()` returns the integer portion of a real. So, when `element` contains a real, such as a value of 7.5, this Boolean expression evaluates to `True`. On the other hand, when `element` contains an integer, such as a value of 3, the Boolean expression evaluates to `False`. The solution is as follows.

file_24_9_5

```
ELEMENTS = 10

b = []
for i in range(ELEMENTS):
    b.append(float(input("Enter a value for element " + str(i) + ": ")))

for i in range(ELEMENTS):
    if b[i] != int(b[i]):
        print("A real found at index:", i)
```

Exercise 24.9.6 — Displaying Odd Indexes Only

Write a Python program that prompts the user to enter 8 numeric values in a list and then displays the elements with odd-numbered indexes (that is, indexes 1, 3, 5, and 7).

Solution

To display the elements with odd-numbered indexes, you need a `for` structure that starts from 1 and increments by 2. The Python program is presented next.

file_24_9_6a

```
ELEMENTS = 8

values = []
for i in range(ELEMENTS):
    values.append(float(input("Enter a value for element " + str(i) + ": ")))

#Display the elements with odd-numbered indexes
for i in range(1, ELEMENTS, 2):          #Start from 1 and increment by 2
    print(values[i])
```

As already stated, in Python you can iterate through the list elements using the slicing mechanism. In the following program the slicing mechanism is used to display only the elements with odd-numbered indexes.

file_24_9_6b

```
ELEMENTS = 8

values = []
for i in range(ELEMENTS):
    values.append(float(input("Enter a value for element " + str(i) + ": ")))

#Display the elements with odd-numbered indexes
for value in values[1:ELEMENTS:2]:       #Start from 1 and increment by 2
    print(value)
```

24.10 What is a Dictionary?

The main difference between a *dictionary* and a list or tuple is that the dictionary elements can be uniquely identified using a key and not necessarily an integer value. Each key of a dictionary is associated (or mapped, if you prefer) to an element. The keys of a dictionary must be of an immutable data type (such as strings, integers, floats, or tuples)

The following example presents a dictionary that holds the names of a family. The name of the dictionary is family and the corresponding keys are written above each element.

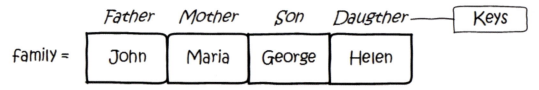

Notice: *The keys of dictionary elements must be unique within the dictionary. This means that in the dictionary* family, *for example, you cannot have two keys named* Father.

Notice: *The values of dictionary elements can be of any type.*

24.11 Creating Dictionaries in Python

Let's try to create the following dictionary using the most common approaches.

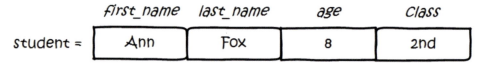

First Approach

To create a dictionary and directly assign values to its elements, you can use the next Python statement, given in general form.

dict_name = {key0: value0, key1: value1, key2: value2, ..., keyM: valueM }

Using this approach, the dictionary student can be created using the following statement:

student = {"first_name": "Ann", "last_name": "Fox", "age": 8, "class": "2nd"}

Notice: *Each key is separated from its value by a colon (:), the elements are separated by commas, and everything is enclosed within curly brackets { }.*

Second Approach

In this approach, you can create a totally empty dictionary and then add elements (key-value pairs), as shown in the following Python statements, given in general form.

dict_name = {}

dict_name[key0] = value0

Chapter 24
Data Structures in Python

```
dict_name[key1] = value1
dict_name[key2] = value2
…
dict_name[keyM] = valueM
```

Using this approach, the dictionary `student` can be created using the following code fragment:

```
student = {}

student["first_name"] = "Ann"
student["last_name"] = "Fox"
student["age"] = 8
student["class"] = "2nd"
```

24.12 How to Get a Value from a Dictionary

To get the value of a specific dictionary element, you must point to that element using its corresponding key. The following code fragment creates a dictionary, and then displays "Ares is the God of War", without the double quotes, on the screen.

```
olympians = {"Zeus": "King of the Gods", \
             "Hera": "Goddess of Marriage", \
             "Ares": "God of War", \
             "Poseidon": "God of the Sea", \
             "Demeter": "Goddess of the Harvest", \
             "Artemis": "Goddess of the Hunt", \
             "Apollo": "God of Music and Medicine", \
             "Aphrodite": "Goddess of Love and Beauty", \
             "Hermes": "Messenger of the Gods", \
             "Athena": "Goddess of Wisdom", \
             "Hephaistos": "God of Fire and the Forge", \
             "Dionysus": "God of the Wine" \
            }

print("Ares is the", olympians["Ares"])
```

Notice: In Python, you can break up a long line among multiple lines using the backslash (\) character at the end of each line (except the last one).

Notice: Only keys can be used to access an element. This means that `olympians["Ares"]` correctly returns "God of War" but `olympians["God of War"]` cannot return "Ares".

Exercise 24.12.1 — Using a Non-Existing Key in Dictionaries

What is wrong in the following Python program?

```
family = { "Father": "John", "Mother": "Maria", "Son": "George"}
```

```python
print(family["daughter"])
```

Solution

Similar to lists and tuples, you must never refer to a non-existing dictionary element. In this exercise, there is no key "daughter," therefore the second statement will produce an error!

24.13 How to Alter the Value of a Dictionary Element

To alter the value of an existing dictionary element you need to use the appropriate key and assign a new value to that element. The example that follows shows exactly this.

```python
#Create a dictionary
tribes = {"Indian": "Navajo", "African": "Zulu"}
print(tribes) #It displays: {'Indian': 'Navajo', 'African': 'Zulu'}

#Alter the value of an existing element
tribes["Indian"] = "Apache"
print(tribes) #It displays: {'Indian': 'Apache', 'African': 'Zulu'}
```

Exercise 24.13.1 — Assigning a Value to a Non-Existing Key

Is there anything wrong in the following code fragment?

```python
indian_tribes = {0: "Navajo", 1: "Cherokee", 2: "Sioux"}
indian_tribes[3] = "Apache"
```

Solution

No, this time there is absolutely nothing wrong in this code fragment. At first glance, you might have thought that the second statement tries to alter the value of a non-existing key and it will produce an error. This is **not** true for Python's dictionaries, though. Since `indian_tribes` is a dictionary and key "3" does not exist, the second statement **adds** a brand new fourth element to the dictionary!

> *Notice: The keys of a dictionary can be of any immutable data type, including integers.*

Keep in mind though, if `indian_tribes` were actually a list, the second statement would certainly produce an error. Take a look at the following code fragment

```python
indian_tribes_list = ["Navajo", "Cherokee", "Sioux"]
indian_tribes_list[3] = "Apache"
```

In this example, since `indian_tribes` is a list and index 3 does not exist, the second statement tries to **alter** the value of a non-existing element and obviously produces an error!

24.14 How to Iterate Through a Dictionary

To iterate through the elements of a dictionary you can use a `for` structure. There are two approaches actually. Let's study them both!

First Approach

Following is a code fragment, written in general form

```
for key in structure_name:
    process structure_name[key]
```

in which *process* is any Python statement or block of statements that processes one element of the dictionary *structure_name* at each iteration.

The following Python program displays the letters A, B, C, and D, and their corresponding Morse[1] code.

```
morse_code = {"A": ".-", "B": "-...", "C": "-.-.", "D": "-.."}

for letter in morse_code:
    print(letter, morse_code[letter])
```

The next example gives a bonus of $2000 to each employee of a computer software company!

```
salaries = { "Project Manager": 83000, \
             "Software Engineer": 81000, \
             "Network Engineer": 64000, \
             "Systems Administrator": 61000, \
             "Software Developer": 70000
           }

for title in salaries:
    salaries[title] += 2000
```

Second Approach

Following is a code fragment, written in general form

```
for key, value in structure_name.items():
    process key, value
```

in which *process* is any Python statement or block of statements that processes one element of the dictionary *structure_name* at each iteration.

The following Python program displays all elements of the list grades, one at each iteration.

```
grades = {"John": "B+", "George": "A+", "Maria":"A", "Helen": "A-"}

for name, grade in grades.items():
    print(name, "got", grade)
```

Unfortunately, this approach cannot be used to alter the values of the elements of a dictionary. For example, if you want to double the values of all elements of the dictionary salaries, you can**not** do the following:

---

1. Samuel Finley Breese Morse (1791–1872) was an American painter and inventor. Morse contributed to the invention of a single-wire telegraph system and he was a co-developer of the Morse code.

```
salaries = { "Project Manager": 83000, \
             "Software Engineer": 81000, \
             "Network Engineer": 64000,\
             "Systems Administrator": 61000,\
             "Software Developer": 70000
           }

for title, salary in salaries.items():
    salary += 2000
```

> *Notice:* salary *is a simple variable that, at each iteration, each successive value of the dictionary* salaries *is assigned to. However, the opposite never happens! The value of* salary *is never assigned back to any element!*

> *Remember!* *If you want to alter the values of the elements of a dictionary, you should use the first approach.*

24.15 Useful Statements, Functions and Methods

Deleting elements from a list

```
del list_name[index]
```

The del statement is used to remove an element from a list (when given its index), to remove slices from a list or to clear the entire list.

Example

file_24_15a

```python
a = [3, 60, 15]
print(a[1])              #It displays: 60
del a[1]
print(a)                 #It displays: [3, 15]
print(a[1])              #It displays: 15


b = [5, 2, 10, 12, 23, 6]
del b[2:5]
print(b)                 #It displays: [5, 2, 6]


#Clear the list
del b[:]
print(b)                 #It displays: []
```

Chapter 24
Data Structures in Python

Deleting elements from a dictionary

```
del dict_name[key]
```

The del statement can also be used to remove an element from a dictionary given its key.

Example

file_24_15b

```python
fruits = {"O": "Orange", "A": "Apple", "W": "Watermelon"}

del fruits["A"]

print(fruits)    #It displays: {'O': 'Orange', 'W': 'Watermelon'}
```

Counting the number of elements

```
len(structure_name)
```

You already know this function! In paragraph 11.4 you learned that the len() function returns the number of characters in a string. Now it's time to learn that the function len() returns the number of elements of any data structure such as list, a tuple, or even a dictionary.

Example

file_24_15c

```python
a = [3, 6, 10, 12, 4, 2, 1]

print(len(a))                #It displays: 7

length = len(a[2:4])
print(length)                #It displays: 2

for i in range(len(a)):
    print(a[i], end = " ")   #It displays: 3 6 10 12 4 2 1
```

Finding the maximum value

```
max(structure_name)
```

This function returns the greatest value of a list or tuple. In the case of a dictionary, it returns the greatest key.

Example

file_24_15d

```python
a = [3, 6, 10, 2, 1, 12, 4]

print(max(a))                #It displays: 12

maximum = max(a[1:4])
print(maximum)               #It displays: 10
```

```python
c = ("Apollo", "Hermes", "Athena", "Aphrodite", "Dionysus")
print(max(c))                   #It displays: Hermes
```

Finding the minimum value

```
min(structure_name)
```

This function returns the smallest value of a list or a tuple. In the case of a dictionary, it returns the smallest key.

Example

file_24_15e

```python
a = [3, 6, 10, 2, 1, 12, 4]

print(min(a))                   #It displays: 1

minimum = min(a[1:4])
print(minimum)                  #It displays: 2

c = ("Apollo", "Hermes", "Athena", "Aphrodite", "Dionysus")
print(min(c))                   #It displays: Aphrodite
```

Sorting a list

Sorting is the process of putting the list elements in a certain order. Here you have two options: you can sort a list using the `sort()` method, or you can get a new sorted list from an initial list using the `sorted()` function, leaving the initial list untouched.

Using the sort() method

```
list_name.sort([reverse = True])
```

This method sorts a list in ascending or in descending order.

Example

file_24_15f

```python
a = [3, 6, 10, 2, 1, 12, 4]
a.sort()
print(a)    #It displays: [1  2  3  4  6  10  12]


#sort in reverse order
a.sort(reverse = True)
print(a)    #It displays: [12  10  6  4  3  2  1]


c = ["Hermes", "Apollo", "Dionysus"]
c.sort()
print(c)    #It displays: [Apollo  Dionysus  Hermes]
```

Chapter 24
Data Structures in Python

> **Notice:** The `sort()` method cannot be used with immutable data types, such as tuples.

Using the sorted() function

`sorted(`*structure_name*` [, reverse = True])`

This function returns a new sorted list or a tuple, either in ascending or in descending order, leaving the initial structure untouched.

Example

file_24_15g

```
a = [3, 6, 10, 2, 1, 12, 4]
b = sorted(a)

print(a)    #It displays: [3, 6, 10, 2, 1, 12, 4]
print(b)    #It displays: [1  2  3  4  6  10  12]

#sorted() function can be used with tuples as well
c = ("Hermes", "Apollo", "Dionysus")
d = sorted(c, reverse = True)
for element in d:
    print(element, end = " ")    #It displays: Hermes Dionysus Apollo


#sorted() function can be used directly in a for statement
for element in sorted(c):
    print(element, end = " ")    #It displays: Apollo Dionysus Hermes
```

24.16 Review Questions: True/False

Choose **true** or **false** for each of the following statements.

1. Lists and tuples are structures that can hold multiple values.
2. List elements are located in main memory (RAM).
3. Each tuple element has a unique index.
4. There can be two identical keys within a dictionary.
5. In tuples, index numbering always starts at zero by default.
6. The index of the last tuple element is equal to the total number of its elements.
7. The next statement contains a syntax error.
   ```
   student names = [None] * 10
   ```
8. In a Python program, two lists cannot have the same name.
9. The next statement is syntactically correct.
   ```
   student = {"first_name": "Ann" - "last_name": "Fox" - "age": 8}
   ```
10. In a Python program, two tuples cannot have the same number of elements.

11. You cannot use a variable as an index in a list.
12. You can use a mathematical expression as an index in a tuple.
13. You cannot use a variable as a key in a dictionary.
14. The following code fragment produces no errors.
    ```
    a = "a"
    fruits = {"o": "Orange", "a": "Apple", "w": "Watermelon"}
    print(fruits[a])
    ```
15. In order to calculate the sum of 20 numeric values given by a user, you must use a list.
16. You can let the user enter a value into list b using the statement b[k] = input()
17. The following statement creates a list of two empty elements.
    ```
    names = [None] * 3
    ```
18. The following code fragment assigns the value 10 to the list element at index 7.
    ```
    values[5] = 7
    values[values[5]] = 10
    ```
19. The following code fragment assigns the value "Sally" without the double quotes to the list element at index 3.
    ```
    names = [None] * 3
    names[2] = "John"
    names[1] = "George"
    names[0] = "Sally"
    ```
20. The following statement assigns the value "Sally" without the double quotes to the list element at index 2.
    ```
    names = ["John", "George", "Sally"]
    ```
21. The following code fragment displays "Sally" without the double quotes on the screen.
    ```
    names = [None] * 3
    k = 0
    names[k] = "John"
    k += 1
    names[k] = "George"
    k += 1
    names[k] = "Sally"
    k -= 1
    print(names[k])
    ```
22. The following code fragment is syntactically correct.
    ```
    names = [None] * 3
    names[0] = "John"
    names[1] = "George"
    names[2] = "Sally"
    print(names[])
    ```

Chapter 24
Data Structures in Python

23. The following code fragment displays "Maria", without the double quotes, on the screen.
    ```
    names = ("John", "George", "Sally", "Maria")
    print(names[int(3.5)])
    ```

24. The following code fragment produces no errors.
    ```
    grades = ("B+", "A+", "A")
    print(grades[3])
    ```

25. The following code fragment produces no errors.
    ```
    values = (1, 3, 2, 9)
    print(values[values[0]])
    ```

26. The following code fragment displays the value of 1 on the screen.
    ```
    values = [1, 3, 2, 0]
    print(values[values[values[values[0]]]])
    ```

27. The following code fragment displays all the elements of the tuple names.
    ```
    names = ("John", "George", "Sally", "Maria")
    for i in range(1, 5):
        print(names[i])
    ```

28. The following code fragment produces no errors.
    ```
    names = ["John", "George", "Sally", "Maria"]
    for i in range(2, 5):
        print(names[i])
    ```

29. The following code fragment lets the user enter 100 values to list b.
    ```
    for i in range(100):
        b[i] = input()
    ```

30. If list b contains 30 elements, the following code fragment doubles the values of all of its elements.
    ```
    for i in range(29, -1, -1):
        b[i] = b[i] * 2
    ```

31. It is possible to use a for structure to double the values of some of the elements of a tuple.

32. If list b contains 30 elements, the following code fragment displays all of them.
    ```
    for element in b[0:29]:
        print(element)
    ```

33. If b is a dictionary, the following code fragment displays all of its elements.
    ```
    for key, element in b:
        print(element)
    ```

34. The following two code fragments display the same value.

    ```
    a = [1, 6, 12, 2, 1]
    print(len(a))
    ```

    ```
    a = "Hello"
    print(len(a))
    ```

35. The following code fragment displays three values.

    ```
    a = [10, 20, 30, 40, 50]
    for i in range(3, len(a)):
        print(a[i])
    ```

36. The following code fragment displays the values of all elements of the list b.

    ```
    b = [10, 20, 30, 40, 50]
    for i in range(len(b)):
        print(i)
    ```

37. The following code fragment doubles the values of all elements of the list b.

    ```
    for i in range(len(b)):
        b[i] *= 2
    ```

38. The following code fragment displays the value of 30 on the screen.

    ```
    a = [20, 50, 10, 30, 15]
    print(max(a[2:len(a)]))
    ```

39. The following code fragment displays the value of 50 on the screen.

    ```
    a = [20, 50, 10, 30, 15]
    b = [-1, -3, -2, -4, -1]
    print(a[min(b)])
    ```

40. The following code fragment displays the smallest value of list b.

    ```
    b = [3, 6, 10, 2, 1, 12, 4]
    b.sort()
    print(b[0])
    ```

41. The following code fragment displays the smallest value of list b.

    ```
    b = [3, 1, 2, 10, 4, 12, 6]
    print(sorted(b, reverse = True)[-1])
    ```

42. The following code fragment produces an error.

    ```
    b = (3, 1, 2)
    print(sorted(b))
    ```

43. The following code fragment produces an error.

    ```
    b = (3, 1, 2)
    b.sort()
    print(b)
    ```

44. The following code fragment produces an error.
    ```
    b = (3, 1, 2)
    del b[1]
    print(b)
    ```

45. The following code fragment produces an error.
    ```
    fruits = {"O": "Orange", "A": "Apple", "W": "Watermelon"}
    del fruits["Orange"]
    print(fruits)
    ```

24.17 Review Questions: Multiple Choice

Select the correct answer for each of the following statements.

1. The following statement
   ```
   last_names = [None] * 5
   ```
   a. contains a logic error.
   b. contains a syntax error.
   c. contains two syntax errors.
   d. contains three syntax errors.

2. If variable x contains the value 4, the following statement
   ```
   values[x + 1] = 5
   ```
   a. assigns the value 4 to the list element at index 5.
   b. assigns the value 5 to the list element at index 4.
   c. assigns the value 5 to the list element at index 5.
   d. none of the above

3. The following statement
   ```
   values = [5, 6, 9, 1, 1, 1]
   ```
   a. assigns the value 5 to the element at index 1.
   b. assigns the value 5 to the element at index 0.
   c. produces an error.
   d. none of the above

4. The following code fragment
   ```
   values[0] = 1
   values[values[0]] = 2
   values[values[1]] = 3
   values[values[2]] = 4
   ```
   a. assigns the value 4 to the list element at index 3.
   b. assigns the value 3 to the list element at index 2.
   c. assigns the value 2 to the list element at index 1.
   d. all of the above

e. none of the above

5. You can iterate through a list with a `for` structure that uses
   a. variable i as a counter.
   b. variable j as a counter.
   c. variable k as a counter.
   d. any variable name as a counter.

6. The following code fragment
   ```
   names = ("George", "John", "Maria", "Sally")
   for i in range(3, 0, -1):
       print(names[i])
   ```
   a. displays all names in ascending order.
   b. displays some names in ascending order.
   c. displays all names in descending order.
   d. displays some names in descending order.
   e. none of the above

7. If tuple b contains 30 elements, the following code fragment
   ```
   for i in range(29, 0, -1):
       b[i] = b[i] * 2
   ```
   a. doubles the values of some of its elements.
   b. doubles the values of all of its elements.
   c. none of the above

8. The following code fragment
   ```
   struct = {"first_name": "George", "last_name": "Miles", "age": 28}
   for a, b in struct.items():
       print(b)
   ```
   a. displays all the keys of the dictionary elements.
   b. displays all the values of the dictionary elements.
   c. displays all the key-value pairs of the dictionary elements.
   d. none of the above

9. The following code fragment
   ```
   indian_tribes = {0: "Navajo", 1: "Cherokee", 2: "Sioux", 3: "Apache"}

   for i in range(4):
       print(indian_tribes[i])
   ```
   a. displays all the keys of the dictionary elements.
   b. displays all the values of the dictionary elements.
   c. displays all the key-value pairs of the dictionary elements.
   d. none of the above

10. The following code fragment
    ```
    tribes = {"tribeA": "Navajo", "tribeB": "Cherokee", "tribeC": "Sioux"}

    for x in tribes:
        tribes[x] = tribes[x].upper()

    print(tribes)
    ```
    a. converts all the keys of the dictionary elements to uppercase.
    b. converts all the values of the dictionary elements to uppercase.
    c. convert all the key-value pairs of the dictionary elements to uppercase.
    d. none of the above

11. The following code fragment
    ```
    struct = {"first_name": "George", "Last_name": "Miles", "age": 28}
    for x in struct:
        print(x)
    ```
    a. displays all the keys of the dictionary elements.
    b. displays all the values of the dictionary elements.
    c. displays all the key-value pairs of the dictionary elements.
    d. none of the above

12. The following two code fragments
    ```
    a = [3, 6, 10, 2, 4, 12, 1]         a = (3, 6, 10, 2, 4, 12, 1)
    for i in range(7):                  for i in range(len(a)):
        print(a[i])                         print(a[i])
    ```
    a. produce the same results.
    b. do not produce the same results.
    c. none of the above

13. The following two code fragments
    ```
    a = [3, 6, 10, 2, 4, 12, 1]         a = [3, 6, 10, 2, 4, 12, 1]
    for i in range(len(a)):             for element in a:
        print(a[i])                         print(element)
    ```
    a. produce the same results.
    b. do not produce the same results.
    c. none of the above

14. The statement `min(a[1:len(a)])`
    a. returns the lowest value of a portion of list a.
    b. returns the lowest value of list a.
    c. none of the above

15. The following code fragment

    ```
    a = [3, 6, 10, 1, 4, 12, 2]
    print(a[-min(a)])
    ```

    a. displays the value of 1 on the screen.
    b. displays the value of 6 on the screen.
    c. displays the value of 2 on the screen.
    d. none of the above

16. The following two code fragments

    ```
    a = (3, 6, 10, 2, 4, 12, 1)
    for i in range(len(a)):
        print(sorted(a)[i])
    ```

    ```
    a = (3, 6, 10, 2, 4, 12, 1)
    for element in sorted(a):
        print(element)
    ```

    a. produce the same results.
    b. do not produce the same results.
    c. none of the above

17. The following three code fragments

    ```
    b.sort(reverse = True)
    print(b[0])
    ```

    ```
    print(sorted(b)[-1])
    ```

    ```
    print(max(b))
    ```

    a. display the greatest value of the list b on the screen.
    b. display the smallest value of the list b on the screen.
    c. none of the above

24.18 Review Exercises

Complete the following exercises.

1. Design a data structure to hold the weights (in pounds) of five people, and then add some typical values to the structure.
2. Design the necessary data structures to hold the names and the weights (in pounds) of seven people, and then add some typical values to the structures.
3. Design the necessary data structures to hold the names of eight lakes as well as the average area (in square miles) and maximum depth (in feet) of each lake. Then add some typical values to the structures.
4. Design the necessary data structures to hold the names of five lakes as well as the average area (in square miles) of each lake in June, July, and August. Then add some typical values to the structures.
5. Design the necessary data structures to hold the three dimensions (width, height, and depth in inches) of 10 boxes. Then add some typical values to the data structures.
6. Try to determine the values that list b will contain when the following code fragment is executed.

    ```
    b = [None] * 3
    b[2] = 1
    x = 0
    b[x + b[2]] = 4
    ```

Chapter 24
Data Structures in Python

```
       b[x] = b[x + 1] * 4
```

7. Try to determine the values that list b will contain when the following code fragment is executed.

    ```
    b = [None] * 5
    b[1] = 5
    x = 0
    b[x] = 4
    b[b[0]] = b[x + 1] * 2
    b[b[0] - 2] = 10
    x += 2
    b[x + 1] = b[x] + 9
    ```

8. Try to determine the values that list b will contain when the following code fragment is executed.

    ```
    b = [17, 12, 45, 12, 12, 49]

    for i in range(6):
        if b[i] == 12:
            b[i] -= 1
        else:
            b[i] += 1
    ```

9. Try to determine the values that list b will contain when the following code fragment is executed.

    ```
    b = [10, 15, 12, 23, 22, 19]

    for i in range(1, 5):
        b[i] = b[i + 1] + b[i - 1]
    ```

10. Try to determine the values that are displayed when the following code fragment is executed.

    ```
    tribes = {"Indian-1": "Navajo", "Indian-2": "Cherokee", \
              "Indian-3" : "Sioux", "African-1": "Zulu", \
              "African-2": "Maasai", "African-3": "Yoruba"}

    for x, y in tribes.items():
        if x[:6] == "Indian":
            print(y)
    ```

11. Write a Python program that prompts the user to enter 100 numbers in a list and then displays these values raised to the power of three.

12. Write a Python program that prompts the user to enter 80 numbers in a list. Then, the program must raise the list values to the power of two, and finally display them in the exact reverse of the order in which they were given.

13. Write a Python program that prompts the user to enter 50 integers in a list and then displays those that are equal to or greater than 10.

14. Write a Python program that prompts the user to enter 30 numbers in a list and then calculates and displays the sum of those that are positive.

15. Write a Python program that prompts the user to enter 50 integers in a list and then calculates and displays the sum of those that have two digits.

    Hint: All two-digit integers are between 10 and 99.

16. Write a Python program that prompts the user to enter 40 numbers in a list. It then calculates and displays the sum of the positive numbers and the sum of the negative ones.

17. Write a Python program that prompts the user to enter 20 numbers in a list. It then calculates and displays their average value.

18. Write a Python program that prompts the user to enter 50 integer values in a list. It then displays the indexes of the elements that contain values lower than 20.

19. Write a Python program that prompts the user to enter 60 numeric values in a list. It then displays the elements with even-numbered indexes (that is, indexes 0, 2, 4, 6, and so on).

20. Write a Python program that prompts the user to enter 20 numeric values in a list. It then calculates and displays the sum of the elements that have even indexes.

21. Write code fragment in Python that creates the following list of 100 elements.

    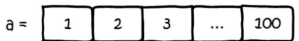

22. Write code fragment in Python that creates the following list of 100 elements.

    a = | 2 | 4 | 6 | ... | 200 |

23. Write a Python program that prompts the user to enter an integer N and then creates and displays the following list of N elements. Assume that the user enters an integer greater than 1.

    a = | 1 | 4 | 9 | ... | N^2 |

24. Write a Python program that prompts the user to enter 10 numeric values in a list and then displays the indexes of the elements that contain integers.

25. Write a Python program that prompts the user to enter 50 numeric values in a list and then counts and displays the total number of negative elements.

26. Write a Python program that prompts the user to enter 20 words in a list and then displays those that have less than five characters.

    Hint: Use the len() function.

27. Write a Python program that lets the user enter 30 words in a list. It then displays those words that have less than 5 characters, then those that have less than 10 characters, and finally those that have less than 20 characters. Assume that the user enters only words with less than 20 characters.

    Hint: Try to display the words using two for structures nested one within the other.

28. Write a Python program that prompts the user to enter 40 words and then displays those that contain the letter "w" at least twice.

Chapter 24
Data Structures in Python

24.19 Review Questions

Answer the following questions.

1. What limitation do variables have that data structures don't?
2. What is a list in Python?
3. What is a tuple in Python?
4. What is a dictionary in Python?
5. What is each item of a data structure called?
6. In a list of 100 elements, what is the index of the last element?
7. Name six known data structures that Python supports.
8. What happens when a statement tries to display the value of a non-existing tuple element?
9. What happens when a statement tries to assign a value to a non-existing list element?
10. What happens when a statement tries to assign a value to a non-existing dictionary element?

Chapter 25
More Exercises with Data Structures

25.1 Simple Exercises with Data Structures

Exercise 25.1.1 — Creating a List with the Greatest Values

Write a Python program that lets the user enter numerical values into lists a and b of 20 elements each. Then the program, must create a new list new_arr of 20 elements. The new list must contain in each position the greatest value of lists a and b of the corresponding position.

Solution

Nothing new here! You need one for structure to read the values for lists a and b, one for creating the list new_arr, and one to display list new_arr on the screen. The Python program is shown here.

file_25_1_1

```python
ELEMENTS = 20

#Read lists a and b
a = [None] * ELEMENTS
b = [None] * ELEMENTS
for i in range(ELEMENTS):
    a[i] = float(input())
for i in range(ELEMENTS):
    b[i] = float(input())

#Create list new_arr
new_arr = [None] * ELEMENTS
for i in range(ELEMENTS):
    if a[i] > b[i]:
        new_arr[i] = a[i]
    else:
        new_arr[i] = b[i]

#Display list new_arr
for element in new_arr:
    print(element)
```

Exercise 25.1.2 — On Which Days Was There a Possibility of Snow?

Write a Python program that lets the user enter the temperatures (in degrees Fahrenheit) recorded at 12:00 p.m. each day for the 31 days of January. The Python program must then display the numbers of those days (1,

2, ..., 31) on which there was a possibility of snow, that is, those days on which temperatures were below 36 degrees Fahrenheit (about 2 degrees Celsius).

Solution

The list for this exercise is shown next.

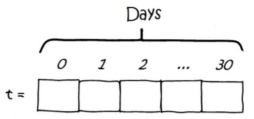

and the Python program is as follows.

file_25_1_2

```
DAYS = 31

t = [None] * DAYS

for i in range(DAYS):
    t[i] = int(input())

for i in range(DAYS):
    if t[i] < 36:
        print(i + 1, end = "\t")
```

Exercise 25.1.3 — Was There Any Possibility of Snow?

Write a Python program that lets the user enter the temperatures (in degrees Fahrenheit) recorded at 12:00 p.m. each day for the 31 days of January. The Python program must then display a message indicating if there was a possibility of snow in January, that is, if there were any temperatures below 36 degrees Fahrenheit (about 2 degrees Celsius).

Solution

The code fragment that follows is **incorrect.** You **cannot** do what you did in the previous exercise.

```
for i in range(DAYS):
    if t[i] < 36:
        print("There was a possibility of snow in January!")
```

If January had more than one day with a temperature below 36 degrees Fahrenheit, the same message would be displayed multiple times—and obviously you do not want this! You actually want to display a message once, regardless of whether January had one, two, or even more days below 36 degrees Fahrenheit.

There are two approaches, actually. Let's study them both.

First approach - Counting all temperatures below 36 degrees Fahrenheit

In this approach, you can use a variable in the program to count all the days on which the temperature was below 36 degrees Fahrenheit. After all of the days have been examined, the program can check the value of this variable. If the value is not zero, it means that there was at least one day where there was a possibility of snow.

file_25_1_3a

```
DAYS = 31

t = [None] * DAYS

for i in range(DAYS):
    t[i] = int(input())

count = 0
for i in range(DAYS):
    if t[i] < 36:
        count += 1

if count != 0:
    print("There was a possibility of snow in January!")
```

Second approach - Using a flag

In this approach, instead of counting all those days that had a temperature below 36 degrees Fahrenheit, you can use a Boolean variable (a flag). The solution is presented next.

file_25_1_3b

```
DAYS = 31

t = [None] * DAYS

for i in range(DAYS):
    t[i] = int(input())

found = False
for i in range(DAYS):
    if t[i] < 36:
        found = True

if found == True:
    print("There was a possibility of snow in January!")
```

Notice: Imagine the variable found as if it's a real flag. Initially, the flag is not hoisted (found = False). Within the for structure, however, when a temperature below 36 degrees Fahrenheit is found, the flag is hoisted (the value True is assigned to the variable found) and it is never lowered again.

> **Notice:** If the loop performs all of its iterations and no temperature below 36 degrees Fahrenheit is found, the variable `found` will still contain its initial value (`False`) since the flow of execution never entered the decision structure.

25.2 How to Use More Than One Data Structures in a Program

So far, every example or exercise has used just one list or one tuple or one dictionary. But what if a problem requires you to use two lists, or one list and one tuple, or one list and two dictionaries? Next you will find some exercises that show you how various data structures can be used together to solve a particular problem.

Exercise 25.2.1 — Finding the Average Value

There are 20 students and each one of them has received his or her grades for three lessons. Write a Python program that prompts the user to enter the name and the grades of each student for all lessons. It then calculates and displays the names of all students who have an average grade greater than 89.

Solution

The required lists are as follows

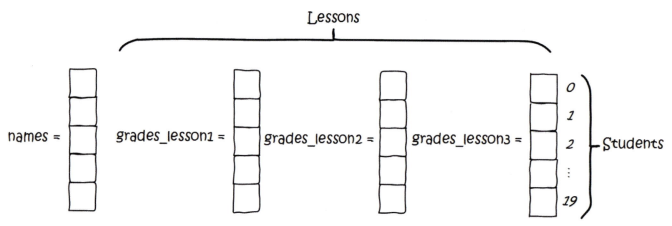

As you can see, there is a one-to-one match between the index positions of the elements of list `names` and those of lists `grades_lesson1`, `grades_lesson2`, and `grades_lesson3`. Suppose that the first of the twenty students is George and the grades he received for the three lessons are 90, 95, and 92. The name "George" will be stored at index 0 of the list `names`, and exactly at the same index, in the lists `grades_lesson1`, `grades_lesson2`, and `grades_lesson3`, there will be stored his grades for the three lessons. The next student and his or her grades will be stored at index 1 of the lists `names`, `grades_lesson1`, `grades_lesson2`, and `grades_lesson3` correspondingly, and so on.

The Python program is as follows.

file_25_2_1

```
STUDENTS = 20

names = [None] * STUDENTS
grades_lesson1 = [None] * STUDENTS
grades_lesson2 = [None] * STUDENTS
```

Chapter 25
More Exercises with Data Structures

```python
grades_lesson3 = [None] * STUDENTS

for i in range(STUDENTS):
    names[i] = input("Enter student name No" + str(i + 1) + ": ")
    grades_lesson1[i] = int(input("Enter grade for lesson 1: "))
    grades_lesson2[i] = int(input("Enter grade for lesson 2: "))
    grades_lesson3[i] = int(input("Enter grade for lesson 3: "))

#Calculate the average grade for each student
#and display the names of those who are greater than 89
for i in range(STUDENTS):
    total = grades_lesson1[i] + grades_lesson2[i] + grades_lesson3[i]
    average = total / 3.0
    if average > 89:
        print(names[i])
```

Exercise 25.2.2 — Using a List Along with a Dictionary

There are 30 students and each one of them has received his or her grades for a test. Write a Python program that prompts the user to enter the grades (as a letter) for each student. It then displays, for each student, the grade as a percentage according to the following table.

Grade	Percentage
A	90 – 100
B	80 – 89
C	70 – 79
D	60 – 69
E / F	0 – 59

Solution

A dictionary that holds the given table can be used. The solution is as follows.

file_25_2_2

```python
STUDENTS = 30
grades_table = {"A": "90-100", "B": "80-89", "C": "70-79", \
                "D": "60-69", "E": "0-59", "F": "0-59"}

names = [None] * STUDENTS
grades = [None] * STUDENTS

for i in range(STUDENTS):
    names[i] = input("Enter student name No" + str(i + 1) + ": ")
    grades[i] = input("Enter his or her grade: ")
```

```
for i in range(STUDENTS):
    grade = grades[i]
    grade_as_percentage = grades_table[grade]

    print(names[i], grade_as_percentage)
```

Now, if you fully understood how the last for structure works, then take a look in the code fragment that follows. It is equivalent to that last for structure, but it performs more efficiently, since it uses fewer variables!

```
for i in range(STUDENTS):
    print(names[i], grades_table[grades[i]])
```

25.3 Finding Minimum and Maximum Values in Lists

In exercise 22.1.8 you learned how to find the maximum value among four given values using a loop structure and without using any data structures. But when values are stored in a data structure, things become much easier!

Exercise 25.3.1 — Which Depth is the Greatest?

Write a Python program that lets the user enter the depths of 20 lakes and then displays the depth of the deepest one.

Solution

After the user enters the depths of the 20 lakes in the list depths, the initial value of the variable maximum can be the value of the first element of the list depths: that is, depths[0]. The program can then search thereafter (starting from index 1) for any value greater than this. The final solution is quite simple and is presented next, without further explanation.

file_25_3_1a

```
LAKES = 20

depths = [None] * LAKES
for i in range(LAKES):
    depths[i] = float(input())

#initial value
maximum = depths[0]
#Search furthermore, starting from index 1
for i in range(1, LAKES):
    if depths[i] > maximum:
        maximum = depths[i]

print(maximum)
```

Chapter 25
More Exercises with Data Structures

> **Notice**: It wouldn't be wrong to start iterating from index 0 instead of 1, though the program would perform one useless iteration.

Keep in mind though, that a more Pythonic way to find the greatest value of a list is to use the `max()` function, as shown here.

file_25_3_1b

```
LAKES = 20

depths = [None] * LAKES
for i in range(LAKES):
    depths[i] = float(input())

maximum = max(depths)

print(maximum)
```

> **Notice**: Correspondingly, if you want to find the smallest value of a list you can use the `min()` function.

Exercise 25.3.2 — Which Lake is the Deepest?

Write a Python program that lets the user enter the names and the depths of 20 lakes and then displays the name of the deepest one.

Solution

In this exercise, you need two lists: one to hold the names, and one to hold the depths of the lakes. The solution is presented next.

file_25_3_2

```
LAKES = 20

names = [None] * LAKES
depths = [None] * LAKES

#Read names and depths
for i in range(LAKES):
    names[i] = input()
    depths[i] = float(input())

#Find maximum depth
maximum = depths[0]
m_name = names[0]
for i in range(1, LAKES):
    if depths[i] > maximum:
```

```
        maximum = depths[i]
        m_name = names[i]

print(m_name)
```

> **Notice**: You cannot use the function `max()` in this exercise! It would return the greatest depth, not the name of the lake with that greatest depth!

Exercise 25.3.3 — Which Lake, in Which Country, Having Which Average Area, is the Deepest?

Write a Python program that lets the user enter the names and the depths of 20 lakes as well as the country in which they belong, and their average area. The program must then display all available information about the deepest lake.

Solution

In this exercise, you need four lists: one to hold the names, one to hold the depths, one to hold the names of the countries, and one to hold the lakes' average areas. There are two approaches, actually. The first one is pretty much the same as the one used in the previous exercise. The second one is more efficient since it uses fewer variables. Let's study them both!

First approach - One variable for each

This is pretty much the same as the one used in the previous exercise. The solution is presented next.

file_25_3_3a

```
LAKES = 20

names = [None] * LAKES
depths = [None] * LAKES
countries = [None] * LAKES
areas = [None] * LAKES

for i in range(LAKES):
    names[i] = input()
    depths[i] = float(input())
    countries[i] = input()
    areas[i] = float(input())

#Find the maximum depth and all available information about it
maximum = depths[0]
m_name = names[0]
m_country = countries[0]
m_area = areas[0]
for i in range(1, LAKES):
    if depths[i] > maximum:
        maximum = depths[i]
```

Chapter 25
More Exercises with Data Structures

```
        m_name = names[i]
        m_country = countries[i]
        m_area = areas[i]

print(maximum, m_name, m_country, m_area)
```

Second approach - One index for everything

In this approach fewer variables are used. Instead of using all those variables (m_name, m_country, and m_area), you can use just one variable, a variable that holds the index in which the maximum value exists!

Confused? Let's look at the next example of six lakes. The depths are expressed in feet and the average areas in square miles.

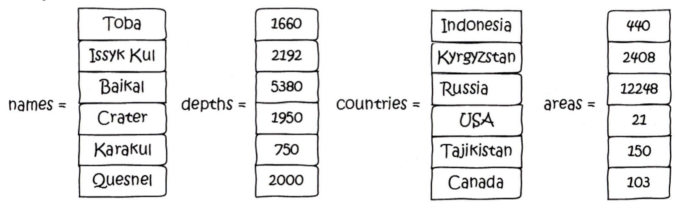

Obviously the deepest lake is Lake Baikal at position 2. However, instead of holding the name "Baikal" in variable m_name, the country "Russia" in variable m_country, and the area "12248" in variable m_area as in the previous approach, you can use just one variable to hold the index position in which these values actually exist (in this case, this is value 2). The solution is presented next.

file_25_3_3b

```
LAKES = 20

names = [None] * LAKES
depths = [None] * LAKES
countries = [None] * LAKES
areas = [None] * LAKES

for i in range(LAKES):
    names[i] = input()
    depths[i] = float(input())
    countries[i] = input()
    areas[i] = float(input())

#Find the maximum depth and
#the index in which this maximum depth exists
maximum = depths[0]
index_of_max = 0
```

```
for i in range(1, LAKES):
    if depths[i] > maximum:
        maximum = depths[i]
        index_of_max = i

#Display information using index_of_max as index
print(depths[index_of_max], names[index_of_max])
print(countries[index_of_max], areas[index_of_max])
```

> **Remember!** Assigning an initial value of 0 to variable `index_of_max` is necessary since there is always a possibility that the maximum value does exist in position 0.

Exercise 25.3.4 — Which Students are the Shortest?

Write a Python program that prompts the user to enter the names and the heights of 100 students. The program then displays the names of all those who share the one shortest height.

Solution

In this exercise, the shortest height is found using the `min()` function. Then, a `for` structure searches the list for all values that are equal to that shortest height.

The solution in presented next.

file_25_3_4

```
STUDENTS = 100

names = [None] * STUDENTS
heights = [None] * STUDENTS
for i in range(STUDENTS):
    names[i] = input("Enter name for student No " + str(i + 1) + ": ")
    heights[i] = float(input("Enter his or her height: "))

minimum = min(heights)

print("The following students have got the shortest height:")
for i in range(STUDENTS):
    if heights[i] == minimum:
        print(names[i])
```

Chapter 25
More Exercises with Data Structures

> **Notice**: *Keep in mind that the following code fragment is also correct but very inefficient.*
> ```
> print("The following students have got the shortest height:")
> for i in range(STUDENTS):
>     if heights[i] == min(heights):
>         print(names[i])
> ```
> *The reason is that function* `min()` *is called each time the loop iterates—that is, 100 times!*

25.4 Searching Elements in Data Structures

A search algorithm searches in a data structure to find the element, or elements, that equal a given value.

When searching in a data structure, there can be two situations.

- You want to search for a given value in a data structure that may contain the same value multiple times. Therefore, you need to find **all** the elements (or their corresponding indexes) that are equal to that given value.

- You want to search for a given value in a data structure where each value is unique. Therefore, you need to find **just one** element (or its corresponding index), the one that is equal to that given value, and then stop searching any further!

Exercise 25.4.1 — Searching in a List That May Contain the Same Value Multiple Times

Write a code fragment that searches a list for a given value. Assume that the list contains numerical values and may contain the same value multiple times.

Solution

The proposed program checks all the elements sequentially. It checks if the first list element is equal to a given value, then checks the second element, then the third, and so on until the end of the list.

The code fragment is shown next. It looks for a given value `needle` in the list `haystack`!

```
needle = float(input("Enter a value to search: "))

found = False
for i in range(ELEMENTS):
    if haystack[i] == needle:
        print(needle, "found at position:", i)
        found = True

if found == False:
    print("nothing found!")
```

Exercise 25.4.2 — Display the Last Names of All Those People Who Have the Same First Name

Write a Python program that prompts the user to enter the names of 20 people: their first names in the list first_names, *and their last names in the list* last_names. *The program must then ask the user for a first name, upon which it will search and display the last names of all those whose first name equals the given one.*

Solution

The solution is as follows.

```
file_25_4_2
```
```python
PEOPLE = 20

first_names = [None] * PEOPLE
last_names = [None] * PEOPLE

for i in range(PEOPLE):
    first_names[i] = input("Enter first name: ")
    last_names[i] = input("Enter last name: ")

needle = input("Enter a first name to search: ")

found = False
for i in range(PEOPLE):
    if first_names[i] == needle:
        print(last_names[i])
        found = True

if found == False:
    print("No one found!")
```

Exercise 25.4.3 — Searching in a Data Structure that Contains Unique Values

Write a code fragment that searches a list for a given value. Assume that the list contains numerical values and each value in the list is unique.

Solution

Since each value in the list is unique, once the given value is found there is no need to iterate without reason until the end of the list, which wastes CPU time. So when the given value is found, a break statement is used to break out of the for structure. The solution is as follows.

```python
needle = float(input("Enter a value to search: "))

found = False
for i in range(ELEMENTS):
    if haystack[i] == needle:
        print(needle, "found at position:", i)
        found = True
```

Chapter 25
More Exercises with Data Structures

```
            break

if found == False:
    print("nothing found!")
```

Exercise 25.4.4 — Searching for a Given Social Security Number

In the United States, the Social Security Number (SSN) is a nine-digit identity number applied to all U.S. citizens in order to identify them for the purposes of Social Security. Write a Python program that prompts the user to enter the SSNs and the first and last names of 100 people. The program must then ask the user for an SSN, upon which it will search and display the first and last name of the person who holds that SSN.

Solution

According to everything you learned so far, the solution to this exercise is as follows.

file_25_4_4
```
PEOPLE = 100

SSNs = [None] * PEOPLE
first_names = [None] * PEOPLE
last_names = [None] * PEOPLE

for i in range(PEOPLE):
    SSNs[i] = input("Enter SSN: ")
    first_names[i] = input("Enter first name: ")
    last_names[i] = input("Enter last name: ")

needle = input("Enter an SSN to search: ")

found = False
for i in range(PEOPLE):
    if SSNs[i] == needle:
        print(first_names[i], last_names[i])
        found = True
        break

if found == False:
    print("nothing found!")
```

> **Notice**: In the United States, there is no possibility that two or more people will have the same SSN. Therefore, even though it is not very clear in the wording of the exercise, each value in list **SSNs** is unique!

25.5 Review Questions: True/False

Choose **true** or **false** for each of the following statements.
1. In a list sorted in ascending order, the first element is the greatest of all.
2. A search algorithm can be used only on lists that contain arithmetic values.
3. A search algorithm can work as follows: it can check if the last list element is equal to a given value, then it can check the last but one element, and so on, until the beginning of the list or until the given value is found.
4. When using search algorithms, if a list contains unique values and the element that you are looking for is found, there is no need to check any further.

25.6 Review Exercises

Complete the following exercises.
1. Write a Python program that prompts the user to enter 50 positive numerical values into a list. The program must then create a new list of 48 elements. In this new list, each position must contain the average value of three elements: the values that exist in the current and the next two positions of the given list.
2. Write a Python program that prompts the user to enter numerical values into lists a, b, and c, of 15 elements each. The program must then create a new list new_arr of 15 elements. In this new list, each position must contain the lowest value of lists a, b, and c, of the corresponding position.
3. Write a Python program that lets the user enter the names and the heights of 30 mountains, as well as the country in which each one belongs. The program must then display all available information about the highest and the lowest mountain.
4. In a high school, there are two classes, with 20 and 25 students respectively. Write a Python program that prompts the user to enter the names of the students in two separate lists. Then, the program must prompt the user to enter a name and it must search for that given name in both lists. If the student's name is found, the program must display the message "Student found in class No..."; otherwise the message "Student not found in either class" must be displayed. Assume that both lists contain unique names.
5. Suppose there are two lists, usernames and passwords, that contain the login information of 100 employees of a company. Write a code fragment that prompts the user to enter a username and a password and then displays the message "Login OK!" when the combination of username and password is valid; the message "Login Failed!" must be displayed otherwise. Assume that usernames are unique but passwords are not.
6. Suppose there are two lists, names and SSNs, that contain the names and the Social Security Numbers of 1000 U.S. citizens. Write a code fragment that prompts the user to enter a value (it can be either a name or an SSN) and then searches for and displays the names and the SSNs of all the people that have this name or this SSN. If the given value is not found, the message "This value does not exist" must be displayed.

Chapter 25
More Exercises with Data Structures

7. There are 12 students and each one of them has received his or her grades for three lessons. Write a Python program that lets the user enter the grades for all lessons and then displays a message indicating whether or not there is at least one student that has an average value below 70.

8. There are 15 students and each one of them has received his or her grades for two tests. Write a Python program that lets the user enter the grades (as a percentage) for each student for both tests. It then calculates and displays, for each student, the average grade as a letter grade according to the following table.

Grade	Percentage
A	90 – 100
B	80 – 89
C	70 – 79
D	60 – 69
E / F	0 – 59

9. A basketball team with 15 players plays 4 matches. Write a Python program that lets the user enter, for each player, the number of points scored in each match. The program must then display, for each player, the total number of points scored

10. Write a Python program that lets the user enter the hourly measured temperatures of 3 cities for a period of one day, and then displays the hours in which the average temperature of all cities was below 10 degrees Fahrenheit.

11. There are 12 students and each one of them has received his or her grades for two lessons. Write a Python program that lets the user enter the name of the student as well as his or her grades in both lessons and then displays

    a. for each student, his or her name and average grade

    b. the names of the students who have an average grade less than 60

    c. the names of the students who have an average grade greater than 89, and the message "Bravo!" next to it

12. In a song contest, each artist sings a song of his or her choice. There are three judges and 15 artists, each of whom is scored for his or her performance. However, according to the rules of this contest, the total score is calculated after excluding the minimum score. Write a Python program that prompts the user to enter the names of the artists, the title of the song that each artist sings, and the score they get from each judge. The program must then display, for each artist, his or her name, the title of the song, and his or her total score.

13. A public opinion polling company asks 20 citizens to each rate two consumer products. Write a Python program that prompts the user to enter the name of each product and the score each citizen gave (A, B, C, or D). The program must then calculate and display, for each product, the name of the product and the number of citizens that gave it an "A".

14. Write a Python program that prompts the user to enter an English word, and then, using the table that follows, displays the corresponding Morse code using dots and dashes.

Morse Code			
A	.-	N	-.
B	-...	O	---
C	-.-.	P	.--.
D	-..	Q	--.-
E	.	R	.-.
F	..-.	S	...
G	--.	T	-
H	....	U	..-
I	..	V	...-
J	.---	W	.--
K	-.-	X	-..-
L	.-..	Y	-.--
M	--	Z	--..

Hint: Use a dictionary to hold the Morse code.

Chapter 26
Introduction to Subprograms

26.1 What is a Subprogram?

In computer science, a subprogram is a block of statements packaged as a unit that performs a specific task. A subprogram can be *called* (executed) within a program several times, whenever that specific task needs to be performed.

The built-in Python functions len(), str(), int(), float(), min(), and max() are examples of such subprograms. Each one performs a specific task!

Generally speaking, there are two kinds of subprograms: *functions* and *procedures*. The difference between a function and a procedure is that a function returns a result, whereas a procedure doesn't. However, in some computer languages, this distinction may not quite be apparent. There are languages in which a function can behave as a procedure and return no result, and there are languages in which a procedure can return one or even more than one result.

Notice: *Depending on the computer language being used, the meaning of the terms "function" and "procedure" may vary. For example, in Visual Basic you can find them as "functions" and "subprocedures," whereas in FORTRAN you would find them as "functions" and "subroutines." On the other hand, Python supports only functions that can play both roles; they can behave either as a function or as a procedure depending on the way they are written.*

26.2 What is Procedural Programming?

Suppose you were assigned a project to solve the drug abuse problem in your area. One possible approach (which could prove very difficult or even impossible) would be to try to solve this problem by yourself!

A better approach, however, would be to subdivide the large problem into smaller subproblems such as prevention, treatment, and rehabilitation, each of which could be further subdivided into even smaller subproblems, as shown in **Figure 26-1**.

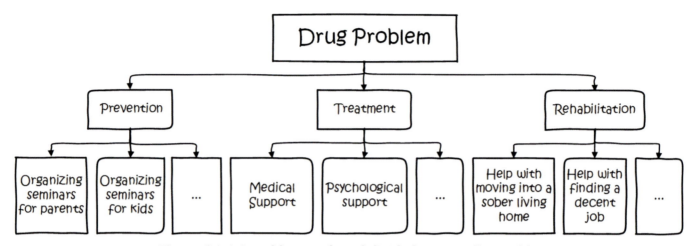

Figure 26-1 A problem can be subdivided into smaller problems

Then, as the supervisor of this project, you could rent a building and establish within it three departments: the prevention department, with all of its subdepartments; the treatment department, with all of its subdepartments; and the rehabilitation department with all of its subdepartments. Finally, you would hire staff (specialists from a variety of fields) and employ them to do different parts of the job for you!

Procedural programming does exactly the same thing. It subdivides an initial problem into smaller subproblems, and each subproblem is further subdivided into smaller subproblems. Finally, for each subproblem a small subprogram is written, and the main program (as does the supervisor), calls (employs) each of them to do a different part of the job.

Procedural programming has several advantages:

- It enables programmers to reuse the same code whenever it is necessary without having to copy it.
- It is relatively easy to implement.
- It helps programmers follow the flow of execution more easily.

Notice: A very large program can prove very difficult to debug and maintain when it is all in one piece. For this reason, it is often easier to subdivide it into smaller subprograms, each of which performs a clearly defined process.

Notice: Writing large programs without subdividing them into smaller subprograms results in a code referred to as "spaghetti code"!

26.3 What is Modular Programming?

In *modular programming*, subprograms of common functionality can be grouped together into separate modules, and each module can have its own set of data. Therefore, a program can consist of more than one part, and each of those parts (modules) can contain one or more smaller parts (subprograms).

If you were to use modular programming in the previous drug problem example, then you could have three separate buildings—one to host the prevention department and all of its subdepartments, a second one to host the treatment department and all of its subdepartments, and a third one to host the rehabilitation department and all of its subdepartments (as shown in **Figure 26-2**). These three buildings could be thought of as three different modules in modular programming, each of which contains subprograms of common functionality.

Figure 26-2 Subprograms of common functionality can be grouped together into separate modules.

Notice: The built-in `math` module of Python is such an example. It contains subprograms of common functionality such as `fsum()`, `sqrt()`, `sin()`, `cos()`, `tan()`, and many more.

26.4 Review Questions: True/False

Choose **true** or **false** for each of the following statements.

1. A subprogram is a block of statements packaged as a unit that performs a specific task.
2. In many computer languages, there are two kinds of subprograms.
3. In many computer languages, the difference between a function and a procedure is that a procedure returns a result, whereas a function does not.
4. Python supports only procedures.
5. Procedural programming helps you write "spaghetti code."
6. Procedural programming subdivides the initial problem into smaller subproblems.
7. An advantage of procedural programming is the ability to reuse the same code whenever it is necessary without having to copy it.
8. Procedural programming helps programmers follow the flow of execution more easily.
9. In modular programming, subprograms of common functionality are grouped together into separate modules.
10. In modular programming, each module can have its own set of data.
11. Modular programming uses different structures than structured programming does.
12. A program can consist of more than one module.

26.5 Review Questions

Answer the following questions.

1. What is a subprogram? Name some built-in subprograms of Python.
2. What is procedural programming?
3. What are the advantages of procedural programming?
4. What is meant by the term "spaghetti code"?
5. What is modular programming? Name some built-in modules of Python.

Chapter 27
User-Defined Subprograms

27.1 Subprograms that Return Values

In Python and many other computer languages, a subprogram that returns values is called a *function*. There are two kinds of functions in Python. There are the *built-in functions*, such as `int()`, `float()`, and there are the *user-defined functions*, those that you actually write and use in your own programs.

The general form of a Python function that returns one or more values is shown here.

```
def name([arg1, arg2, arg3, …]):
    #Here goes
    #a statement or block of statements

    return value1 [, value2, value3, … ]
```

where

- *name* is the name of the function. It follows the same rules as those used for variable names.
- *arg1, arg2, arg3, …* is a list of arguments (variables, lists etc.) used to pass values from the caller to the function. There can be as many arguments as you need.
- *value1, value2, value3, …* are the values returned to the caller. They can be a constant value, a variable, an expression, or even a data structure.

Notice: *Please note that arguments are optional; that is, a function may contain no arguments.*

For example, the next function calculates the sum of two numbers and returns the result.

```
def get_sum(num1, num2):
    result = num1 + num2
    return result
```

Of course, this can also be written as

```
def get_sum(num1, num2):
    return num1 + num2
```

The next function calculates the sum and the difference of two numbers, and returns the results.

```
def get_sum_dif(num1, num2):
    s = num1 + num2
    d = num1 - num2
    return s, d
```

27.2 How to Call a Function that Returns Values

Every call to a function that returns values is made as follows: you write the name of the function followed by a list of arguments (if required), either within a statement that assigns the function's returned value to a variable or directly within an expression.

Let's see some examples. The following function accepts an argument (a numeric value) and returns the result of that value raised to the power of three.

```python
def cube(num):
    result = num ** 3
    return result
```

Now, suppose that you want to calculate a result using the following expression

$$y = x^3 + \frac{1}{x}$$

You can either assign the returned value from the function cube() to a variable, as shown here

```python
x = float(input())

cb = cube(x)        #Assign the returned value to a variable
y = cb + 1 / x      #and use that variable

print(y)
```

or you can call the function directly in an expression,

```python
x = float(input())

y = cube(x) + 1 / x    #Call the function directly in an expression

print(y)
```

or you can even call the function directly in an print() statement.

```python
x = float(input())

print(cube(x) + 1 / x)  #Call the function directly in a print() statement
```

> **Notice:** *User-defined functions can be called just like the built-in functions of Python.*

Now let's see another example. The next Python program defines the function `get_message()` and then the main code calls it. The returned value is assigned to variable a.

file_27_2a

```python
#Define the function
def get_message():
    msg = "Hello Zeus"
    return msg
```

```
#Main code starts here
print("Hi there!")
a = get_message()
print(a)
```

If you run this program, the following messages are displayed.

Notice: *Please note that a function does not execute immediately when a program starts running. The first statement that actually executes in this example is the statement* `print("Hi there!")`.

You can pass values to a function, as long as at least one argument exists within the function's parentheses. In the next example, the function `display()` is called three times but each time a different value is passed through the argument color.

file_27_2b

```
#Define the function
def display(color):
    msg = "There is " + color + " in the rainbow"
    return msg


#Main code starts here
print(display("red"))
print(display("yellow"))
print(display("blue"))
```

If you run this program, the following messages are displayed.

In the next example, two values must be passed to function `display()`.

file_27_2c

```python
#Define the function
def display(color, exists):
    neg = ""
    if exists == False:
        neg = "n't any"

    return "There is" + neg + " " + color + " in the rainbow"

#Main code starts here
print(display("red", True))
print(display("yellow", True))
print(display("black", False))
```

If you run this program the following messages are displayed.

```
There is red in the rainbow
There is yellow in the rainbow
There isn't any black in the rainbow
```

Notice: In Python, you must place your subprograms above your main code. In other computer languages, such as Java or PHP, you can place your subprograms either above or below your main code. Even then, however, most programmers prefer to have all subprograms on the top for better observation.

As already mentioned, a function in Python can return more than one value. The next example prompts the user to enter his or her first and last name, and it then displays them.

file_27_2d

```python
#Define the function
def get_fullname():
    first_name = input("Enter first name: ")
    last_name = input("Enter last name: ")
    return first_name, last_name

#Main code starts here
fname, lname = get_fullname()
print("First name:", fname)
```

```
print("Last name:", lname)
```

27.3 Subprograms that Return no Values

Many computer languages, such as Visual Basic and Delphi to name a few, when a subprogram returns no values, they call this subprogram a *procedure*. In C, as well as in other similar computer languages such as C++, a subprogram that returns no values is known as a *void function*. In Python however, there aren't any procedures or void functions. There are just functions!

The general form of a Python function that returns no values is shown here

```
def name([arg1, arg2, arg3, …]):
    #Here goes
    #a statement or block of statements
```

where

- *name* is the name of the function. It follows the same rules as those used for variable names.
- *arg1, arg2, arg3, …* is a list of arguments (variables, lists, etc.) used to pass values from the caller to the function. There can be as many arguments as you want.

> **Notice:** *Please note that arguments are optional; that is, a function may contain no arguments.*

For example, the next function calculates the sum of two numbers and displays the result. It doesn't return anything to the caller!

```
def display_sum(num1, num2):
    result = num1 + num2
    print(result)
```

27.4 How to Call a Function that Returns no Values

You can call a function that returns no values by just writing its name. The next example defines the function display_line() and the main code calls the function whenever it needs to display a horizontal line.

file_27_4a

```
#Define the function
def display_line():
    print("------------------------------")

#Main code starts here
print("Hello there!")
display_line()

print("How do you do?")
display_line()

print("What is your name?")
```

```
display_line()
```

You can also pass values to a function, as long as at least one argument exists within function's parentheses. In the next example, the function `display_line()` is called three times but each time a different value is passed through the argument `length`, resulting in three printed lines of different lengths.

file _ 27 _ 4b

```
#Define the function
def display_line(length):
    for i in range(length):
        print("-", end = "")
    print()


#Main code starts here
print("Hello there!")
display_line(12)


print("How do you do?")
display_line(14)


print("What is your name?")
display_line(18)
```

> **Remember!** Since the function `display_line()` returns no value, you **cannot** assign the returned value to a variable. The following line of code is **wrong**.
>
> ```
> y = display_line(12)
> ```
>
> Also, you **cannot** call it within a statement. The following line of code is also **wrong**.
>
> ```
> print( "Hello there!", display_line(12) )
> ```

27.5 Formal and Actual Arguments

Each subprogram contains an argument list called a *formal argument list*. As already stated, arguments in this list are optional; the formal argument list may contain no arguments, one argument, or more than one argument.

When the subprogram is called, an argument list is passed to the subprogram. This list is called an *actual argument list*.

In the next example, variables `n1` and `n2` constitute the formal argument list, whereas variables `x` and `y` constitute the actual argument list.

Chapter 27
User-Defined Subprograms

file_27_5

```
#Define the function divide().
#The arguments n1 and n2 are called formal arguments
def divide(n1, n2):
    result = n1 / n2
    return result

#Main code starts here
x = float(input())
y = float(input())

#Call the function divide().
#The arguments x and y are called actual arguments
w = divide(x, y)

print(w)
```

Please note that there is a one-to-one match between the formal and the actual arguments. The value of argument x is passed (assigned) to argument n1 and the value of argument y is passed to argument n2.

27.6 How Does a Subprogram Execute?

When the main code calls a subprogram the following steps are performed:
- The execution of the statements of the main code is interrupted.
- The values of the variables or the result of the expressions that exist in the actual argument list are passed (assigned) to the corresponding arguments (variables) in the formal argument list, and the flow of execution goes to where the subprogram is written.
- The statements of the subprogram are executed.
- When the flow of execution reaches the end of the subprogram,
  - in the case of a function that returns a value, that value is returned from the function to the main code and the flow of execution continues from where it was before calling the function.
  - in the case of a function that returns no value, the flow of execution simply continues from where it was before calling the function.

In the next Python program, the function `maximum()` accepts two arguments (numeric values) and returns the greater of the two values.

file_27_6

```
def maximum(val1, val2):
    m = val1
    if val2 > m:
        m = val2
    return m

#Main code starts here
a = float(input())
```

```
b = float(input())

maxim = maximum(a, b)

print(maxim)
```

When the Python program starts running, the first statement executed is the statement a = float(input()) (this is considered the first statement of the program). Suppose the user enters the values 3 and 8. When the call to the function maximum() is made, the execution of the statements of the main code is interrupted and the values of the variables a and b are passed (assigned, if you prefer) to the corresponding arguments (variables) val1 and val2 and the statements of the function are executed. Finally, when the flow of execution reaches the end of the function, the value 8 is returned from the function to the main code (and assigned to the variable maxim) and the flow of execution continues from where it was before calling the function. The main code prints the value of 8 on the user's screen.

27.7 Can Two Subprograms Use Variables of the Same Name?

Each subprogram uses its own memory space to hold the values of its variables. Even the main code has its own memory space! This means that you can have a variable named test in main code, another variable named test in a subprogram, and yet another variable named test in another subprogram. Pay attention though! Those three variables are three completely different variables, in different memory locations, and they can hold completely different values.

As you can see in the program that follows, there are three variables named test in three different memory locations and each one of them holds a completely different value. The comments within the program can help you understand what really goes on.

file_27_7a
```
def f1():
    test = 22
    print(test)


def f2(test):
    print(test)


#Main code starts here
test = 5
print(test)      #It displays: 5
f1()             #It displays: 22
f2(10)           #It displays: 10
print(test)      #It displays: 5
```

Now, let's see something else. In the next Python program, the variable test of the main code is passed to function f1() through an argument (variable) that also happens to be named test. As already stated, even though both variables have the same name, they are actually two different variables in two different locations in main memory! In reality, this means that although f1() alters the value of its variable test, when the flow of execution returns to the main code, this change does not affect the value of the variable test of the main code.

file_27_7b
```python
def f1(test):
    test += 1
    print(test)         #This is the variable of
                        #function f1(). Value 6 is displayed


#Main code starts here
test = 5
f1(test)
print(test)             #This is the variable of
                        #the main code. Value 5 is displayed
```

Notice: Please note that variables used in a subprogram "live" as long as the subprogram is being executed. This means that before calling the subprogram, none of its variables (including those in the formal argument list) exists in main memory (RAM). They are all created in the main memory when the subprogram is called, and they are all removed from the main memory when the subprogram finishes and the flow of execution returns to the caller. The only variables that "live" forever, or at least for as long as the Python program is being executed, are the variables of the main code and the global variables!

27.8 Can a Subprogram Call Another Subprogram?

All the time you've been reading this chapter, you may have had the impression that only the main code can call a subprogram. Of course, this is not true!

A subprogram can call any other subprogram, which in turn can call another subprogram, and so on. The next example presents exactly this situation. The main code calls the subprogram display_sum(), which in turn calls the subprogram add().

file_27_8
```python
def add(number1, number2):
    result = number1 + number2
    return result


def display_sum(num1, num2):
    print(add(num1, num2))


#Main code starts here
a = int(input())
b = int(input())

display_sum(a, b)
```

> *Notice: Please note that there is no restriction on the order in which the two subprograms should be written. It would have been exactly the same if the function* `display_sum()` *had been written before the function* `add()`.

27.9 Default Argument Values and Keyword Arguments

If you use a default value for an argument within the formal argument list, it means that if no value is passed for that argument then the default value is used. In the next example, the function `prepend_title()` is designed to prepend (add a prefix to) a title before the name. However, if no value for argument `title` is passed, the function uses the default value "Mr."

file_27_9a
```python
def prepend_title(name, title = "Mr"):
    return title + " " + name

#Main code starts here
print(prepend_title("John King"))          #It displays: Mr John King
print(prepend_title("Maria Miller", "Ms")) #It displays: Ms Maria Miller
```

> *Notice: When a default value is assigned to an argument within the formal argument list, this argument is called an "optional argument."*

> *Notice: Within the formal argument list, any optional arguments must be on the right side of any non-optional arguments; to do the opposite of this would be incorrect.*

Moreover, in Python, subprograms can be **called** using keyword arguments with the form

argument_name = value

Python assumes that keyword arguments are optional. If no argument is given in a function call, the default value is used.

file_27_9b
```python
def prepend_title(first_name, last_name, title = "Mr", reverse = False):
    if reverse == False:
        return title + " " + first_name + " " + last_name
    else:
        return title + " " + last_name + " " + first_name

#Main code starts here
print(prepend_title("John", "King"))               #It displays: Mr John King
print(prepend_title("Maria", "Myles", "Ms"))       #It displays: Ms Maria Myles
print(prepend_title("Maria", "Myles", "Ms", True)) #It displays: Ms Miller Myles

#Using keyword argument
```

```
print(prepend_title("John", "King", reverse = True))  #it displays: Mr King John
```

> *Notice: Instead of using the term "keyword arguments," many computer languages such as PHP, C#, and Visual Basic (to name a few), prefer to use the term "named arguments."*

27.10 The Scope of a Variable

The *scope* of a variable refers to the range of effect of that variable. In Python, a variable can have a *local* or *global* scope. A variable declared within a subprogram has a local scope and can be accessed only from within that subprogram. On the other hand, a variable declared outside of a subprogram has a global scope and can be accessed from within **any** subprogram, as well as from the main code.

Let's see some examples. The next example declares a global variable `test`. The value of this global variable, though, is accessed and displayed within the function.

file_27_10a

```
def display_value():
    print(test)        #It displays: 10


#Main code starts here
test = 10
display_value()
print(test)            #It displays: 10
```

The question now is, "*What happens, if you change the value of the variable* `test` *within the function* `display_value()`*? Will it affect the global variable* `test` *as well?*" In the next example the values 20 and 10 are displayed.

file_27_10b

```
def display_value():
    test = 20
    print(test)


#Main code starts here
test = 10
display_value()        #It displays: 20
print(test)            #It displays: 10
```

This happens because Python declares two variables in main memory (RAM); that is, a global variable `test` and a local variable `test`.

Now let's combine the first example with the second one and see what happens. First the program will access the variable `test`, and then it will assign a value to it, as shown in the code that follows.

file_27_10c

```
def display_value():
    print(test)     #This statement throws an error
    test = 20
    print(test)


#Main code starts here
test = 10
display_value()
print(test)
```

Unfortunately, this example throws the error message *"local variable 'test' referenced before assignment"*. This happens because Python "assumes" that you want a local variable due to the assignment statement `test = 20` within function `display_value()`. Therefore, the first `print(test)` statement inevitably throws this error message. Any variable that is defined or altered within a function is local, unless it has been forced to be a global variable. To force Python to use the global variable you have to use the keyword `global`, as you can see in the following example.

file_27_10d

```
def display_value():
    global test
    print(test)     #It displays: 10
    test = 20
    print(test)     #It displays: 20


#Main code starts here
test = 10
display_value()
print(test)         #It displays: 20
```

> **Notice:** *If the value of a global variable is altered within a subprogram, this change is also reflected outside of the subprogram. Please note that the last* `print(test)` *statement of the main code displays the value of 20.*

> **Remember**! *Any variable that is defined or altered within a function is local unless it is declared as a global variable using the keyword* `global`.

The next code fragment declares a global variable x, two local variables x and y within the function `display_values()`, and one local variable y within the function `display_other_values()`. Keep in mind that the global variable x and the local variable x are two different variables!

```
                        file_27_10e
def display_values():
    x = 7
    y = 3
    print(x, y)     #It displays: 7  3

def display_other_values():
    y = 2
    print(x, y)     #It displays: 10  2

#Main code starts here
x = 10              #x is global
print(x)            #It displays: 10
display_values()
display_other_values()
print(x)            #It displays: 10
```

> **Remember!** You can have variables of local scope of the same name within different subprograms, because they are recognized only by the subprogram in which they are declared.

27.11 Review Questions: True/False

Choose **true** or **false** for each of the following statements.

1. In some computer languages, such as C and C++, a subprogram that returns no result is known as a *void function*.
2. The variables that are used to pass values to a function are called arguments.
3. The function `int()` is a user-defined function.
4. Every call to a user-defined function that returns a value is made in the same way as a call to the built-in functions of Python.
5. A call to a function that returns a value is made differently from a call to a function that returns no value.
6. There can be as many arguments as you want in a function's formal argument list.
7. In a function, the formal argument list must contain at least one argument.
8. In a function, the formal argument list is optional.
9. In a subprogram, all formal arguments must have different names.
10. There is a one-to-one match between the formal and the actual arguments.
11. You can call a function that returns no values within a statement.
12. When the flow of execution reaches the end of a subprogram, the flow of execution continues from where it was before calling the subprogram.

13. The statement

    ```
    return x + 1
    ```

    is a valid Python statement.

14. A function can have no arguments in the actual argument list.

15. The next statement calls the function cube() three times.

    ```
    cb = cube(x) + cube(x) / 2 + cube(x) / 3
    ```

16. The following code fragment

    ```
    cb = cube(x)
    y = cb + 5
    print(y)
    ```

    displays exactly the same value as the statement

    ```
    print(cube(x) + 5)
    ```

17. The following code fragment

    ```
    y += test(x)
    y += 5
    ```

    is equivalent to the statement

    ```
    y = 5 + test(x)
    ```

18. In Python, a function must always include a return statement.

19. The name play-the-guitar can be a valid function name.

20. In Python, you can place your functions either above or below your main code.

21. When the main code calls a function, the execution of the statements of the main code is interrupted.

22. The function float() is a built-in function of Python.

23. The following code fragment

    ```
    def add(a, b):
        return a / b


    a = 10
    b = 5
    print(add(a, b))
    ```

    displays the value 15.

24. In the following Python program

    ```
    def message():
        print("Hello Aphrodite!")


    print("Hi there!")
    message()
    ```

    the first statement that executes is the statement print("Hello Aphrodite!").

Chapter 27
User-Defined Subprograms

27.12 Review Exercises

Complete the following exercises.

1. The following subprogram contains two errors. Can you spot them?

    ```
    def find_max(a, b)
        if a > b:
            maximum = a
        else:
            maximum = b
    ```

2. Try to determine the values of the variables in each step of the following Python program when the values 3, –7, –9, 0, and 4 are entered and find what is displayed on the user's screen.

    ```
    def display(a):
        if a > 0:
            print(a, "is positive")
        else:
            print(a, "is negative or zero")

    for i in range(5):
        x = int(input())
        display(x)
    ```

3. Write a subprogram that accepts three numbers through its formal argument list and then returns their sum.

4. Write a subprogram that accepts four numbers through its formal argument list and then returns their average.

5. Write a subprogram that accepts three values through its formal argument list and then displays the greatest value.

6. Do the following:
    i. Write a subprogram named `find_min` that accepts two numbers through its formal argument list and returns the lowest one. Try not to use Python's built-in function `min()`.
    ii. Using the subprogram cited above, write a Python program that prompts the user to enter four numbers and then displays the lowest one.

7. Do the following:
    i. Write a subprogram named `get_input` that prompts the user to enter an answer "yes" or "no" and then returns the value `True` or `False` correspondingly to the caller. Make the subprogram accept the answer in all possible forms such as "yes", "YES", "Yes", "No", "NO", "nO", and so on.
    ii. Write a subprogram named `find_area` that accepts the base and the height of a parallelogram through its formal argument list and then returns its area.
    iii. Using the subprograms cited above, write a Python program that prompts the user to enter the base and the height of a parallelogram and then displays its area. The program must iterate as many times as the user wishes. At the end of each calculation, the program must

ask the user whether he or she wishes to calculate the area of another parallelogram. If the answer is "yes" the program must repeat.

27.13 Review Questions

Answer the following questions.
1. What is the general form of a Python function that returns values?
2. What is the general form of a Python function that returns no values?
3. How do you make a call to a function that returns a value?
4. How do you make a call to a function that returns no value?
5. Describe the steps that are performed when the main code makes a call to a function that returns a value.
6. Describe the steps that are performed when the main code makes a call to a function that returns no value.
7. What is the formal argument list?
8. What is the actual argument list?
9. Can two subprograms use variables of the same name?
10. How long does a subprogram's variable "live" in main memory?
11. How long does a main code's variable "live" in main memory?
12. Can a subprogram call another subprogram? If yes, give some examples.
13. What is an optional argument?
14. What is meant by the term "scope" of a variable?
15. What happens when a variable has a local scope?
16. What happens when a variable has a global scope?
17. What is the difference between a local and a global variable?

Chapter 28
More Exercises with Subprograms

28.1 Some More Exercises for Extra Practice

Exercise 28.1.1 — Back to Basics - Calculating the Sum of Two Numbers

Do the following:

    i.   Write a subprogram named `total` that accepts two numeric values through its formal argument list and then calculates and returns their sum.

    ii.   Using the subprogram cited above, write a Python program that lets the user enter two numbers and then displays their sum.

Solution

In this exercise you need to write a function that accepts two values from the caller and then calculates and returns their sum. The solution is very simple and is shown here.

file_28_1_1

```python
def total(a, b):
    s = a + b
    return s


#Main code starts here
num1 = float(input())
num2 = float(input())

result = total(num1, num2)

print("The sum of", num1, "+", num2, "is", result)
```

Exercise 28.1.2 — Calculating the Sum of Two Numbers Using Fewer Lines of Code!

Rewrite the Python program of the previous exercise using fewer lines of code.

Solution

Let's try to solve the previous exercise using fewer lines of code. The solution is shown here.

file_28_1_2

```python
def total(a, b):
    return a + b


#Main code starts here
num1 = float(input())
num2 = float(input())
```

```python
print("The sum of", num1, "+", num2, "is", total(num1, num2))
```

Contrary to the solution of the previous exercise, in this one, in function `total()` the sum is not assigned to variable s but it is directly calculated and returned. Furthermore, in this main code the returned value is not assigned to a variable but it is directly displayed.

> **Remember!** *User-defined functions can be called just like the built-in functions of Python.*

Exercise 28.1.3 — A Simple Currency Converter

Do the following:

1. Write a subprogram named `display_menu` that displays the following menu.
    1. Convert USD to Euro (EUR)
    2. Convert Euro (EUR) to USD
    3. Exit

2. Using the subprogram cited above, write a Python program that displays the previously mentioned menu and prompts the user to enter a choice (of 1, 2, or 3). If choice 1 or 2 is selected, the program must prompt the user to enter an amount of money and then it must calculate and display the corresponding converted value. The process must repeat as many times as the user wishes. It is given that $1 = 0.94 EUR (€).

Solution

The solution is very simple and needs no further explanation.

file_28_1_3
```python
def display_menu():
    print("1. Convert USD to Euro (EUR)")
    print("2. Convert Euro (EUR) to USD")
    print("3. Exit")
    print("----------------------------")
    print("Enter a choice: ", end = "")

#Main code starts here
while True:
    display_menu()
    choice = int(input())

    if choice == 3:
        print("Bye!")
        break
    else:
        amount = float(input("Enter an amount: "))
        if choice == 1:
```

> The statement `while True` defines an endless loop. The `break` statement within the loop, however, ensures that the loop will eventually stop iterating.

```
            print(amount, "USD =", amount * 0.94, "Euro")
        else:
            print(amount, "Euro =", amount / 0.94, "USD")
```

Exercise 28.1.4 — A More Complete Currency Converter

Do the following:

i. Write a subprogram named `display_menu` that displays the following menu.

   1. Convert USD to Euro (EUR)
   2. Convert USD to British Pound Sterling (GBP)
   3. Convert USD to Japanese Yen (JPY)
   4. Convert USD to Canadian Dollar (CAD)
   5. Exit

ii. Write four different subprograms named `USD_to_EU`, `USD_to_GBP`, `USD_to_JPY`, and `USD_to_CAD`, that accept a currency through their formal argument list and then return the corresponding converted value.

iii. Using the subprograms cited above, write a Python program that displays the menu previously mentioned and then prompts the user to enter a choice (of 1, 2, 3, 4, or 5) and an amount in US dollars. The program must then display the required value. The process must repeat as many times as the user wishes. It is given that:

   - $1 = 0.94 EUR (€)
   - $1 = 0.79 GBP (£)
   - $1 = ¥ 113 JPY
   - $1 = 1.33 CAD ($)

Solution

According to the wording of this exercise, the function `display_menu()` should not return any value. It should just display the menu. On the other hand, the four functions that convert currencies accept a value through an argument and they must return the corresponding converted value. The solution is shown here.

file_28_1_4

```python
def display_menu():
    print("1. Convert USD to Euro (EUR)")
    print("2. Convert USD to British Pound Sterling (GBP)")
    print("3. Convert USD to Japanese Yen (JPY)")
    print("4. Convert USD to Canadian Dollar (CAD)")
    print("5. Exit")
    print("-------------------------------------------")
    print("Enter a choice: ", end = "")

def USD_to_EU(value):
    return value * 0.94
```

```python
def USD_to_GBP(value):
    return value * 0.79


def USD_to_JPY(value):
    return value * 113


def USD_to_CAD(value):
    return value * 1.33


#Main code starts here
while True:
    display_menu()
    choice = int(input())

    if choice == 5:
        print("Bye!")
        break
    else:
        amount = float(input("Enter an amount in US dollars: "))
        if choice == 1:
            print(amount, "USD =", USD_to_EU(amount), "Euro")
        elif choice == 2:
            print(amount, "USD =", USD_to_GBP(amount), "GBP")
        elif choice == 3:
            print(amount, "USD =", USD_to_JPY(amount), "JPY")
        elif choice == 4:
            print(amount, "USD =", USD_to_CAD(amount), "CAD")
```

Exercise 28.1.5 — Finding the Average Values of Positive Integers

Do the following:

i. Write a subprogram named `test_integer` that accepts a number through its formal argument list and returns `True` when the passed number is an integer; it must return `False` otherwise.

ii. Using the subprogram cited above, write a Python program that lets the user enter integer values repeatedly until a real one is entered. At the end, the program must display the average value of positive integers entered.

Solution

A `while` structure will be used, but, in order to make your program free of logic errors you should follow the "Ultimate" rule discussed in paragraph 21.3. According to this rule, the `while` structure that solves this problem should be as follows.

```
x = float(input())              #Initialization of x
while test_integer(x) == True:  #A Boolean expression dependent on x

    #Here goes
    #a statement or block of statements

    x = float(input())          #Update/alteration of x
```

The final solution is presented next.

file_28_1_5

```
def test_integer(number):
    if number == int(number):
        return True
    else:
        return False


#Main code starts here
total = 0
count = 0
x = float(input())
while test_integer(x) == True:
    if x > 0:
        total += x
        count += 1
    x = float(input())

if count > 0:
    print(total / count)
```

Notice: Please note the last decision structure, `if count > 0`. If the user enters a real right from the beginning, the variable `count`, in the end, will contain a value of zero. So, you need this to avoid any division-by-zero errors!

Exercise 28.1.6 — Roll, Roll, Roll the... Dice!

Do the following:

i. Write a subprogram named `dice` that returns a random integer between 1 and 6.

ii. Write a subprogram named `search_and_count` that accepts an integer and a list through its formal argument list and returns the number of times the integer exists in the list.

iii. Using the subprograms cited above, write a Python program that fills a list with 100 random integers (between 1 and 6) and then lets the user enter an integer. The program must find and display how many times that given integer exists in the list.

Solution

Both subprograms return one value each. Function `dice()` returns a random integer between 1 and 6, and function `search_and_count()` returns a number that indicates the number of times an integer exists in a list. The solution is presented here.

file_28_1_6

```python
import random
ELEMENTS = 100

def dice():
    return random.randrange(1, 7)


def search_and_count(x, a):
    count = 0
    for i in range(ELEMENTS):
        if a[i] == x:
            count += 1
    return count


#Main code starts here
a = [None] * ELEMENTS

#Fill the list with random values
for i in range(ELEMENTS):
    a[i] = dice()

x = int(input())
print("Given value exists in the list")
print(search_and_count(x, a), "times")
```

28.2 Review Exercises

Complete the following exercises.

1. Do the following:

    i. Write a subprogram named `Kelvin_to_Fahrenheit` that accepts a temperature in degrees Kelvin through its formal argument list and then returns its degrees Fahrenheit equivalent.

    ii. Write a subprogram named `Kelvin_to_Celsius` that accepts a temperature in degrees Kelvin through its formal argument list and then returns its degrees Celsius equivalent.

    iii. Using the subprograms cited above, write a Python program that prompts the user to enter a temperature in degrees Kelvin and then displays its degrees Fahrenheit and its degrees Celsius equivalent.

It is given that
$$Fahrenheit = 1.8 \times Kelvin - 459.67$$
and
$$Celsius = Kelvin - 273.15$$

2. Do the following:
   i. Write a subprogram named num_of_days that accepts a month (numbered 1 – 12) through its formal argument list and then returns the number of days in that month. Do not take into consideration leap years, just assume that February has 28 days.

   ii. Using the subprogram cited above, write a Python program that prompts the user to enter two months (numbered 1 – 12). The program then calculates and displays the total number of days that occur between the first day of the first month, and the last day of the second month.

3. In a computer game, players roll two dice. The player who gets the greatest sum of dice gets one point. After ten rolls, the player that wins is the one with the greatest sum of points. Do the following:
   i. Write a subprogram named dice that returns a random integer between 1 and 6.

   ii. Using the subprogram cited above, write a Python program that prompts two players to enter their names and then each player consecutively "rolls" two dice. This process repeats ten times and the player that wins is the one with the greatest sum of points.

4. The Body Mass Index (BMI) is often used to determine whether a person is overweight or underweight for his or her height. The formula used to calculate the BMI is
$$BMI = \frac{weight \cdot 703}{height^2}$$

Do the following:
   i. Write a subprogram named bmi that accepts a weight and a height through its formal argument list and then displays a message according to the following table.

BMI	Action
BMI < 16	You must add weight.
16 ≤ BMI < 18.5	You should add some weight.
18.5 ≤ BMI < 25	Maintain your weight.
25 ≤ BMI < 30	You should lose some weight.
30 ≤ BMI	You must lose weight.

   ii. Using the subprogram cited above, write a Python program that prompts the user to enter his or her weight (in pounds), age (in years), and height (in inches), and then displays the corresponding message. Moreover, the program must display an error message when the user enters a value less than 18 for age.

5. The LAV Car Rental Company has rented 40 cars, which are divided into three categories: hybrid, gas, and diesel. The company charges for a car according to the following table.

Days	Car Type		
	Gas	Diesel	Hybrid
1 – 5	$24 per day	$28 per day	$30 per day
6 and above	$22 per day	$25 per day	$28 per day

Do the following:

i. Write a subprogram named get_choice that displays the following menu.
   1. Gas
   2. Diesel
   3. Hybrid

   The subprogram must then prompt the user to enter the type of the car (1, 2, or 3) and returns it to the caller.

ii. Write a subprogram named get_days that prompts the user to enter the total number of rental days and returns it to the caller.

iii. Write a subprogram named get_charge that accepts the type of the car (1, 2, or 3) and the total number of rental days through its formal argument list and then returns the amount of money to pay according to the previous table.

iv. Using the subprograms cited above, write a Python program that prompts the user to enter all necessary information about the rented cars and then displays the following:
   1. for each car, the total amount to pay
   2. the total number of hybrid cars rented
   3. the total profit the company gets

Chapter 29
Object-Oriented Programming

29.1 What is Object-Oriented Programming?

In Chapter 27 all the programs that you read or even wrote, were using subprograms (functions). This programming style is called procedural programming and most of the time it is just fine! But when it comes to writing large programs, or working in a big company such as Microsoft, Facebook, or Google, object-oriented programming is a must use programming style!

Object-oriented programming, usually referred as OOP, is a style of programming that focuses on *objects*. In OOP, you can combine data and functionality and enclose them inside something called an object. Using object-oriented programming techniques enables you to maintain your code more easily, and write code that can be easily used by others.

But what does the phrase "OOP focuses on objects" really mean? Let's take a look at an example from the real world. Imagine a car. How can you describe a specific car? It has some attributes, such as the brand, the model, the color, and the license plate. Also, there are some actions this car can perform, or can have performed on it. For example, someone can turn it on or off, accelerate or brake, or park.

In OOP, this car can be an object with specific attributes (usually called fields) that performs specific actions (called methods.)

Obviously, you may now be asking yourself, "How can I create objects in the first place?" The answer is simple! All you need is a *class*. A class resembles a "rubber inkpad stamp!" In **Figure 29-2** there is a stamp (this is the class) with four empty fields.

Figure 29-1 A class resembles a "rubber inkpad stamp"

Someone who uses this stamp can stamp-out many cars (these are the objects). In **Figure 29-2**, for example, a little boy stamped-out those two cars and then he colored them and filled out each car's fields with specific attributes.

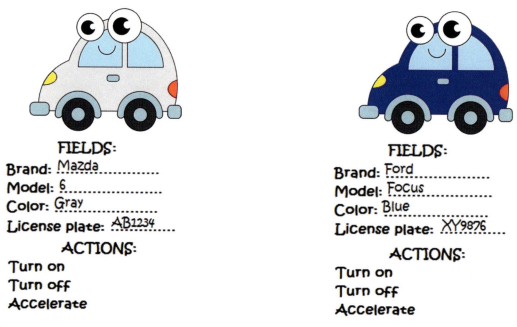

Figure 29-2 You can use the same rubber stamp as a template to stamp-out many cars

Notice: The process of creating a new object (*a new instance of a class*) is called "instantiation."

Notice: A class is a template and every object is created from a class. Each class should be designed to carry out one, and only one, task! This is why, most of the time, more than one class is used to build an entire application!

Notice: In OOP, the rubber stamp is the class. You can use the same class as a template to create (*instantiate*) many objects!

29.2 Classes and Objects in Python

Now that you know some theoretical stuff about classes and objects let's see how to write a real class in Python! The following code fragment creates the class `Car`. There are four fields and three methods within the class.

```python
class Car:
    #Define four fields
    brand = ""
    model = ""
    color = ""
    license_plate = ""

    #Define method turn_on()
```

Chapter 29
Object-Oriented Programming

```python
    def turn_on(self):
        print("The car turns on")

    #Define method turn_off()
    def turn_off(self):
        print("The car turns off")

    #Define method accelerate()
    def accelerate(self):
        print("The car accelerates")
```

Yes, it's true. Fields and methods within classes are just ordinary variables and subprograms (here functions) respectively!

> **Notice:** The class `Car` is just a template. No objects are created yet!

> **Notice:** An object is nothing more than an instance of a class, and this is why, many times, it may be called a "class instance" or "class object."

> **Notice:** No need to wonder what this `self` keyword is, yet! It will be explained thoroughly in paragraph 29.3.

To create two objects (or in other words to create two instances of the class `Car`), you need the following two lines of code.

```python
car1 = Car()
car2 = Car()
```

> **Remember!** When you create a new object (a new instance of a class) the process is called "instantiation."

Now, that you have created (instantiated) two objects, you can assign values to their fields. To do that, you have to use the dot notation, which means that you have to write the name of the object, followed by a dot and then the name of the field or the method you want to access. The next code fragment creates two objects, `car1` and `car2`, and assigns values to their fields.

```python
car1 = Car()
car2 = Car()

car1.brand = "Mazda"
car1.model = "6"
car1.color = "Gray"
car1.license_plate = "AB1234"

car2.brand = "Ford"
```

```
car2.model = "Focus"
car2.color = "Blue"
car2.license_plate = "XY9876"

print(car1.brand)      #It displays: Mazda
print(car2.brand)      #It displays: Ford
```

> **Notice:** In the previous example, `car1` and `car2` are two instances of the same class. Using `car1` and `car2` with dot notation allows you to refer to only one instance at a time. If you make any changes to one instance they will not affect any other instances!

The next code fragment calls the methods `turn_off()` and `accelerate()` of the objects `car1` and `car2` respectively.

```
car1.turn_off()
car2.accelerate()
```

> **Remember!** A class is a template that cannot be executed, whereas an object is an instance of a class that can be executed!

> **Remember!** One class can be used to create (instantiate) as many objects as you want!

29.3 The Constructor and the Keyword `self`

In Python, there is a method name that has a special role, and that is the `__init__()` method. The `__init__()` method (which is called "the constructor") is executed automatically whenever an instance of a class (an object) is created. Any initialization that you want to do with your object can be done within this method.

> **Notice:** Please note that there is a double underscore at the beginning of the name and another double underscore at the end of the name `__init__()`.

Take a look at the following example. The method `__init__()` is called twice automatically, once when the object p1 is created and once when the object p2 is created.

file_29_3a
```
class Person:
    def __init__(self):
        print("An object was created")

p1 = Person()      #Create object p1
p2 = Person()      #Create object p2
```

As you may have noticed, in the formal argument list of the `__init__()` method, there is an argument named `self`. So, what is that keyword `self` anyway? The keyword `self` is nothing more than a reference to the object itself! Take a look at the following example.

file_29_3b

```python
class Person:
    name = None
    age = None

    def say_info(self):
        print("I am", self.name)
        print("I am", self.age, "years old")

#Main code starts here
person1 = Person()
person1.name = "John"
person1.age = 14

person1.say_info()   #Call the method say_info() of the object person1
```

Even though there is no actual argument in the statement `person1.say_info()` where the method is called, a formal argument (the keyword `self`) does exist in the statement `def say_info(self)` where the method is defined. Obviously, it would be more correct if that call were made as `person1.say_info(person1)`. Written this way, it would make better sense! This actual argument `person1` would be passed (assigned) to the formal argument `self`! Yes, this is probably more correct, but always keep in mind that Python is a "write less, do more" language! So there is no need for you to pass the object itself. Python will do it for you!

> **Notice:** If you don't remember what a formal or actual argument is, please re-read paragraph 27.5

> **Notice:** Please note that when declaring the fields `name` and `age` outside of a method (but within the class), you need to write the field name without dot notation. To access the fields, however, from within a method, you must use dot notation (for example, `self.name` and `self.age`).

A question that is probably spinning around in your head right now is "*Why is it necessary to refer to these fields* `name` *and* `age` *within the method* `say_info()` *as* `self.name` *and* `self.age` *correspondingly? Is it really necessary to use the keyword* `self` *in front of them?*" A simple answer is that there is always a possibility that you could have two extra local variables of the same name (`name` and `age`) within the method. So you need a way to distinguish among those local variables and the object's fields. If you are confused, try to understand the following example. There is a field `b` within the class `MyClass` and a local variable `b` within the method `myMethod()` of the class. The `self` keyword is used to distinguish among the local variable and the field.

file_29_3c

```python
class MyClass:
    b = None    #This is a field

    def myMethod(self):
        b = "***"    #This is a local variable
        print(b, self.b, b)

#Main code starts here
x = MyClass()

x.b = "Hello!"
x.myMethod()    #It displays: *** Hello! ***
```

> **Notice:** *The keyword* `self` *can be used to refer to any member (field or method) of a class from within a method of the class.*

29.4 Passing Initial Values to the Constructor

Any method, including the constructor method `__init__()`, can have formal arguments within its formal argument list. For example, you can use these arguments to pass some initial values to the constructor of an object during creation. The example that follows creates four objects, each of which represents a Titan[1] from Greek mythology.

file_29_4a

```python
class Titan:
    name = None
    gender  = None

    def __init__(self, n, g):
        self.name = n
        self.gender = g

#Main code starts here
titan1 = Titan("Cronus", "male")
titan2 = Titan("Oceanus", "male")
```

---

1. In Greek mythology, the Titans and Titanesses were the children of Uranus and Gaea. They were giant gods who ruled during the legendary Golden Age (immediately preceding the Olympian gods). The male Titans were Coeus, Oceanus, Crius, Cronus, Hyperion, and Iapetus whereas the female Titanesses were Tethys, Mnemosyne, Themis, Theia, Rhea, and Phoebe. In a battle, known as *the Titanomachy*, fought to decide which generation of gods would rule the Universe, the Olympians won over the Titans!

Chapter 29
Object-Oriented Programming

```python
titan3 = Titan("Rhea", "female")
titan4 = Titan("Phoebe", "female")
```

> **Notice:** Please note that, even though there are three formal arguments in the constructor, there are only two actual arguments in the statements that call the constructor. Since Python is a "do more, write less" computer language, there is no need to pass the object itself. Python will do it for you!

In Python, it is legal to have one field and one local variable (or even a method argument) with the same name. So, the class Titan can also be written as follows

file_29_4b

```python
class Titan:
    name = None
    gender = None
    def __init__(self, name, gender ):
        self.name = name    #fields and arguments can have the same name
        self.gender = gender
```

The variables name and gender are arguments used to pass values to the constructor whereas `self.name` and `self.gender` are fields used to store values within the object.

Last but not least, in Python, you can simplify class Titan even more. The example that follows uses a simplified version of the class Titan.

file_29_4c

```python
class Titan:
    def __init__(self, name, gender):
        self.name = name
        self.gender = gender

#Main code starts here
titan1 = Titan("Cronus", "male")
titan2 = Titan("Oceanus", "male")
titan3 = Titan("Rhea", "female")
titan4 = Titan("Phoebe", "female")

print(titan1.name, "-", titan1.gender)
print(titan2.name, "-", titan2.gender)
print(titan3.name, "-", titan3.gender)
print(titan4.name, "-", titan4.gender)
```

29.5 Class Variables vs Instance Variables

Until this point, what you've learned is that it is not too bad to have fields declared outside of the constructor, as shown in the program that follows.

```python
class HistoryEvents:
```

```python
        day = None      #This field is declared outside of the constructor
                        #It is called "class field"

    def __init__(self):
        print("Object Instantiation")

#Main code starts here
h1 = HistoryEvents()
h1.day = "4th of July"

h2 = HistoryEvents()
h2.day = "28th of October"

print(h1.day)
print(h2.day)
```

You also learned that you can rewrite this code and declare the field day inside the constructor, as shown here.

```python
class HistoryEvents:
    def __init__(self, day):
        print("Object Intantiation")
        self.day = day  #This field is declared inside the constructor
                        #It is called "instance field"

#Main code starts here
h1 = HistoryEvents("4th of July")
h2 = HistoryEvents("28th of October")

print(h1.day)
print(h2.day)
```

> **Notice:** When a field is declared outside of the constructor, it is called a "class field" but when it is declared inside the constructor, it is called an "instance field."

> **Notice:** A class field is shared by all instances of the class whereas an instance field is unique to each instance.

So, which programming style is better? They both seem to be okay! Well, the second one is not just better—you can say that this is the right way to write a class! Why? Because, in some cases, when mutable data types (such as lists and dictionaries) are used as class fields, they may produce undesirable results. Take a look at the following example.

```python
class HistoryEvents:
    events = []            #Class field shared by all instances

    def __init__(self, day):
        self.day = day     #Instance field unique to each instance

#Main code starts here
h1 = HistoryEvents("4th of July")
h1.events.append("1776: Declaration of Independence in United States ")
h1.events.append("1810: French troops occupy Amsterdam")

h2 = HistoryEvents("28th of October")
h2.events.append("969: Byzantine troops occupy Antioch")
h2.events.append("1940: Ohi Day in Greece")

print(h1.events)
```

You may expect that the last print() statement displays only the two events of the 4th of July. Your thinking is correct, but the output result proves you wrong! The last print() statement displays four events, as shown in **Figure 29-3**.

```
Python 3.6.0 Shell
File Edit Shell Debug Options Window Help
Python 3.6.0 (v3.6.0:41df79263a11, Dec 23 2016, 07:18:10) [MSC v
.1900 32 bit (Intel)] on win32
Type "copyright", "credits" or "license()" for more information.
>>>
=========== RESTART: C:/Users/root/Desktop/test.py =============
['1776: Declaration of Independence in United States ', '1810: F
rench troops occupy Amsterdam', '969: Byzantine troops occupy An
tioch', '1940: Ohi Day in Greece']
>>>
```

Figure 29-3 When mutable data types are used as class fields, they may produce undesirable results

List events is a mutable data type. In Python, a mutable data type should never be used as a class field, since it produces undesirable results.

> **Notice:** *In general, you must use as few class fields as possible! The less the number of class fields the better.*

The next example, is the correct version of the previous one.

file_29_5

```python
class HistoryEvents:
    def __init__(self, day):
        self.day = day       #Instance field unique to each instance
        self.events = []     #Instance field unique to each instance

#Main code starts here
h1 = HistoryEvents("4th of July")
h1.events.append("1776: Declaration of Independence in United States ")
h1.events.append("1810: French troops occupy Amsterdam")

h2 = HistoryEvents("28th of October")
h2.events.append("969: Byzantine troops occupy Antioch")
h2.events.append("1940: Ohi Day in Greece")

print(h1.events)
```

29.6 Getter and Setter Methods vs Properties

A field is a variable declared directly in a class. The principles of the object-oriented programming, though, state that the data of a class should be hidden and safe from accidental alteration. Think that one day you will probably be writing classes that other programmers will use in their programs. So, you don't want them to know what is inside your classes! The internal operation of your classes should be kept hidden from the outside world. By not exposing a field, you manage to hide the internal implementation of your class. Fields should be kept private to a class and accessed through *get* and *set* methods.

> **Notice:** Generally speaking, programmers should use fields only for data that have private or protected accessibility. In Java, or C# you can set a field as private or protected using special keywords.

Let's try to understand all of this new stuff through an example. Suppose you write the following class that converts a degrees Fahrenheit temperature into its degrees Celsius equivalent.

file_29_6a

```python
class FahrenheitToCelsius:
    def __init__(self, value):
        self.temperature = value

    def get_temperature(self):
        return 5.0 / 9.0 * (self.temperature - 32.0)
```

```
#Main code starts here
x = FahrenheitToCelsius(-68)
print(x.get_temperature())
```

This class is almost perfect but has a main disadvantage. It doesn't take into consideration that a temperature cannot go below −459.67 degrees Fahrenheit (−273.15 degrees Celsius). This temperature is called *absolute zero*. So a novice programmer who knows absolutely nothing about physics, might pass a value of −500 degrees Fahrenheit to the constructor, as shown in the code fragment that follows

```
x = FahrenheitToCelsius(-500)
print(x.get_temperature())
```

Even though the program can run perfectly well and display a value of −295.55 degrees Celsius, unfortunately this temperature cannot exist in the entire universe! So a slightly different version of this class might partially solve the problem.

file_29_6b

```python
class FahrenheitToCelsius:
    def __init__(self, value):
        self.set_temperature(value)

    def get_temperature(self):
        return 5.0 / 9.0 * (self.temperature - 32.0)

    def set_temperature(self, value):
        if value >= -459.67:
            self.temperature = value
        else:
            raise ValueError("There is no temperature below -459.67")


#Main code starts here
x = FahrenheitToCelsius(-50)
print(x.get_temperature())
```

This time, a method called `set_temperature()` is used to set the value of the field `temperature`. This is better, but not exactly perfect, because the programmer must be careful and always remember to use the method `set_temperature()` each time he or she wishes to change the value of the field `temperature`. The problem is that the value of the field `temperature` can still be directly changed using its name, as shown in the code fragment that follows.

```
x = FahrenheitToCelsius(-50)
print(x.get_temperature())

x.set_temperature(-50)   #This is okay!
print(x.get_temperature())
```

```
x.temperature = -500     #Unfortunately, this is still permitted!
print(x.get_temperature())
```

This is where a property should be used! A *property* is a class member that provides a flexible mechanism to read, write, or compute the value of a field that you want to keep private. Properties expose fields, but hide implementation!

file_29_6c

```
class FahrenheitToCelsius:
    def __init__(self, value):
        self.set_temperature(value)

    def get_temperature(self):
        return 5.0 / 9 * (self._temperature - 32)

    def set_temperature(self, value):
        if value >= -459.67:
            self._temperature = value
        else:
            raise ValueError("There is no temperature below -459.67")

    #Define a property
    temperature = property(get_temperature, set_temperature)

#Main code starts here
x = FahrenheitToCelsius(-50)

print(x.temperature)          #This calls the method get_temperature()

x.temperature = -500          #This calls the method set_temperature()
                              #and throws an error

print(x.temperature)          #This calls the method get_temperature()
```

> **Notice:** Please note the underscore (_) at the beginning of the field temperature. In Python, an underscore at the beginning of a variable name can be used to denote a "private variable".

So, what does the statement temperature = property(get_temperature, set_temperature) do anyway? When a statement tries to access the value of the field temperature, the get_temperature() method is called automatically and similarly, when a statement tries to assign a value to the field temperature the set_temperature() method is called automatically! So, everything seems to be okay now! But is it, really?

One last thing can be done to make things even better! You can completely get rid of the methods get_temperature() and set_temperature(). And why do you need to do this? The answer is simple—you

Chapter 29
Object-Oriented Programming

don't want to have two ways to access the value of the field temperature, as shown in the code fragment that follows

```python
x = FahrenheitToCelsius(0)

#There are still two ways to access the value of the field temperature
x.set_temperature(-100)
x.temperature = -100
```

In order to completely get rid of the methods get_temperature() and set_temperature() you can use some of the *decorators* that Python supports.

file_29_6d

```python
class FahrenheitToCelsius:
    def __init__(self, value):
        self.temperature = value    #This calls the setter

    #Use a decorator to define the getter
    @property
    def temperature(self):
        return 5.0 / 9 * (self._temperature - 32)

    #Use a decorator to define the setter
    @temperature.setter
    def temperature(self, value):
        if value >= -459.67:
            self._temperature = value
        else:
            raise ValueError("There is no temperature below -459.67")

#Main code starts here
x = FahrenheitToCelsius(-50)     #This calls the constructor which, in turn,
                                 #calls the setter.
print(x.temperature)             #This calls the getter.

x.temperature = -60              #This calls the setter.
print(x.temperature)             #This calls the getter.

x.temperature = -500             #This calls the setter and throws an error

print(x.temperature)             #This is never executed. The flow of execution
                                 #is stopped due to the previous statement.
```

> **Notice:** *Please note that the two methods and the field share the same name,* temperature.

Notice: *A decorator is a function that takes another function as an argument and returns a new, prettier version of that function. Decorators allow you to change the behavior or extend the functionality of a function without changing the function's body.*

Exercise 29.6.1 — The Roman Numerals

Roman numerals are shown in the following table.

Number	Roman Numeral
1	I
2	II
3	III
4	IV
5	V

Do the following:

i. Write a class named **Romans** which includes

    a. a constructor and a private field named number.

    b. a property named number. It will be used to get and set the value of the private field number in integer format. The setter must throw an error when the number is not recognized.

    c. a property named roman. It will be used to get and set the value of the private field number in Roman numeral format. The setter must throw an error when the Roman numeral is not recognized.

ii. Using the class cited above, write a Python program that displays the Roman numeral that corresponds to the value of 3 as well as the number that corresponds to the Roman numeral value of "V".

Solution

The getter and the setter of the property number are very simple so there is nothing special to explain. The getter and the setter of the property roman, however, need some explanation.

The getter of the property roman can be written as follows

```python
#Define the getter
@property
def roman(self):
    if self._number == 1:
        return "I"
    elif self._number == 2:
        return "II"
    elif self._number == 3:
        return "III"
    elif self._number == 4:
        return "IV"
    elif self._number == 5:
        return "V"
```

However, even though this approach is quite simple, it is quite long and it could get even longer, if you want to expand your program so it can work with more Roman numerals. So, since you now know many about dictionaries, you can use a better approach, as shown in the code fragment that follows.

```python
#Define the getter
@property
def roman(self):
    number2roman = {1:"I", 2:"II", 3:"III", 4:"IV", 5:"V"}
    return number2roman[self._number]
```

Accordingly, the setter can be as follows

```python
#Define the setter
@roman.setter
def roman(self, value):
    roman2number = {"I":1, "II":2, "III":3, "IV":4, "V":5}
    if value in roman2number:
        self._number = roman2number[value]
    else:
        raise ValueError("Roman numeral not recognized")
```

The final Python program is as follows

file_29_6_1

```python
class Romans:

    def __init__(self):
        self._number = None   #Private field. It does not call the setter!

    #Define the getter
    @property
    def number(self):
        return self._number

    #Define the setter
    @number.setter
    def number(self, value):
        if value >=1 and value <= 5:
            self._number = value
        else:
            raise ValueError("Number not recognized")

    #Define the getter
    @property
    def roman(self):
        number2roman = {1:"I", 2:"II", 3:"III", 4:"IV", 5:"V"}
```

```python
        return number2roman[self._number]

    #Define the setter
    @roman.setter
    def roman(self, value):
        roman2number = {"I":1, "II":2, "III":3, "IV":4, "V":5}
        if value in roman2number:
            self._number = roman2number[value]
        else:
            raise ValueError("Roman numeral not recognized")

#Main code starts here
x = Romans()

x.number = 3
print(x.number)     #It displays: 3
print(x.roman)      #It displays: III

x.roman = "V"
print(x.number)     #It displays: 5
print(x.roman)      #It displays: V
```

29.7 Can a Method Call Another Method of the Same Class?

In paragraph 27.8 you learned that a subprogram can call another subprogram. Obviously, the same applies when it comes to methods—a method can call another method of the same class! Methods are nothing more than subprograms after all! So, if you want a method to call another method of the same class you should use the keyword self in front of the method that you want to call (using dot notation) as shown in the example that follows.

file_29_7

```python
class JustAClass:
    def foo1(self):
        print("foo1 was called")
        self.foo2()     #Call foo2() using dot notation

    def foo2(self):
        print("foo2 was called")

#Main code starts here
x = JustAClass()
x.foo1()     #Call foo1() which, in turn, will call foo2()
```

Chapter 29
Object-Oriented Programming

Exercise 29.7.1 – Doing Math

Do the following:

i. Write a class named DoingMath which includes

   a. a method named square that accepts a number through its formal argument list and then calculates its square and displays the message "The square of …. is …"

   b. a method named square_root that accepts a number through its formal argument list and then calculates its square root and displays the message "The square root of …. is …". However, if the number is less than zero, the method must display an error message.

   c. a method named display_results that accepts a number through its formal argument list and then calls the methods square() and square_root() to display the results.

ii. Using the class cited above, write a Python program that prompts the user to enter a number. The program then displays the root and the square root of that number.

Solution

This exercise is quite simple. The methods square(), square_root(), and display_results() must have a formal argument within their formal argument list so as to accept a passed value. The solution is as follows.

file_29_7_1

```python
import math

class DoingMath:
    def square(self, x):                #argument x accepts passed value
        print("The square of", x, "is", x * x)

    def square_root(self, x):           #argument x accepts passed value
        if x < 0:
            print("Cannot calculate square root")
        else:
            print("Square root of", x, "is", math.sqrt(x))

    def display_results(self, x):       #argument x accepts passed value
        self.square(x)
        self.square_root(x)

#Main code starts here
dm = DoingMath()

b = float(input("Enter a number: "))
dm.display_results(b)
```

29.8 Class Inheritance

Class inheritance is one of the main concepts of OOP. It lets you write a class using another class as a base. When a class is based on another class, the programmers use to say "it inherits the other class." The class that is inherited is called the *parent class*, the *base class*, or the *superclass*. The class that does the inheriting is called the *child class*, the *derived class*, or the *subclass*.

A child class automatically inherits all the methods and fields of the parent class. The best part, however, is that you can add additional characteristics (methods or fields) to the child class. Therefore, you use inheritance when you need several classes that aren't exactly identical but have many characteristics in common. To do this, you work as follows. First, you write a parent class that contains all the common characteristics. Second, you write child classes that inherit all those common characteristics from the parent class. Finally, you add additional characteristics to each child class. After all, these additional characteristics are what distinguishes a child class from its parent class!

Let's say that you want to write a program that keeps track of the teachers and students in a school. They have some characteristics in common, such as name and age, but they also have specific characteristics such as salary for teachers and grades for students that are not in common. What you can do here is write a parent class named SchoolMember that contains all those characteristics that both teachers and students have in common. Then you can write two child classes named Teacher and Student, one for teachers and one for students. Both child classes can inherit the class SchoolMember but additional fields, named salary and grades, must be added to the child classes Teacher and Student correspondingly.

The parent class SchoolMember is shown here

```python
class SchoolMember:
    def __init__(self, name, age):
        self.name = name
        self.age = age
        print("A school member was initialized")
```

If you want a class to inherit the class SchoolMember, it must be defined as follows

```python
class Name(SchoolMember):
    def __init__(self, name, age [, …]):
        SchoolMember.__init__(self, name, age)   #It calls the constructor of
                                                 #the class SchoolMember
        # A statement or block of statements
```

where *Name* is the name of the child class.

So, the class Teacher can be as follows

```python
class Teacher(SchoolMember):
    def __init__(self, name, age, salary):
        SchoolMember.__init__(self, name, age)   #It calls the constructor of
                                                 #the class SchoolMember

        self.salary = salary    #This is a specific field for class Teacher
        print("A teacher was initialized")
```

Chapter 29
Object-Oriented Programming

Similarly, the class `Student` can be as follows

```python
class Student(SchoolMember):
    def __init__(self, name, age, grades):
        SchoolMember.__init__(self, name, age)   #It calls the constructor of
                                                 #the class SchoolMember

        self.grades = grades    #This is a specific field for class Student
        print("A student was initialized")
```

> **Notice**: The statement `SchoolMember.__init__(self, name, age)` *calls the constructor of the class* `SchoolMember` *and initializes the fields* `name` *and* `age` *of the class* `Student`.

The complete Python program is as follows. Please note that getter and setter methods are included for each field.

file_29_8

```python
class SchoolMember:
    def __init__(self, name, age):
        self.name = name
        self.age = age
        print("A school member was initialized")

    @property
    def name(self):
        return self._name

    @name.setter
    def name(self, value):
        if value != "":
            self._name = value
        else:
            raise ValueError("Name cannot be empty")

    @property
    def age(self):
        return self._age

    @age.setter
    def age(self, value):
        if value > 0:
            self._age = value
        else:
```

```python
            raise ValueError("Age cannot be negative or zero")

class Teacher(SchoolMember):
    def __init__(self, name, age, salary):
        SchoolMember.__init__(self, name, age)
        self.salary = salary
        print("A teacher was initialized")

    @property
    def salary(self):
        return self._salary

    @salary.setter
    def salary(self, value):
        if value >= 0:
            self._salary = value
        else:
            raise ValueError("Salary cannot be negative")

class Student(SchoolMember):
    def __init__(self, name, age, grades):
        SchoolMember.__init__(self, name, age)
        self.grades = grades
        print("A student was initialized")

    @property
    def grades(self):
        return self._grades

    @grades.setter
    def grades(self, values):
        #values is a list.
        #Check if negative grade exists in values
        negative_found = False
        for value in values:
            if value < 0:
                negative_found = True

        if negative_found == False:
            self._grades = values
        else:
            raise ValueError("Grades cannot be negative")
```

```
#Main code starts here
teacher1 = Teacher("Mr. John Scott", 43, 35000)
teacher2 = Teacher("Mrs. Ann Carter", 5, 32000)

student1 = Student("Peter Nelson", 14, [90, 95, 92])
student2 = Student("Helen Morgan", 13, [92, 97, 94])

print(teacher1.name)
print(teacher1.age)
print(teacher1.salary)

print(student1.name)
print(student1.age)
print(student1.grades)
```

29.9 Review Questions: True/False

Choose **true** or **false** for each of the following statements.

1. Procedural programming is better than object-oriented programming when it comes to writing large programs.
2. Object-oriented programming focuses on objects.
3. An object combines data and functionality.
4. Object-oriented programming enables you to maintain your code more easily but your code cannot be used easily by others.
5. You can create an object without using a class.
6. The process of creating a new instance of a class is called "installation".
7. In OOP, you always have to create at least two instances of the same class.
8. The __init__() method is executed when an object is instantiated.
9. When you create two instances of the same class, the __init__() method of the class will be executed twice.
10. When a field is declared outside of the constructor, it is called an "instance field".
11. A class field is shared by all instances of the class.
12. The principles of the object-oriented programming state that the data of a class should be hidden and safe from accidental alteration.
13. A property is a class member that provides a flexible mechanism to read, write, or compute the value of a field.
14. A property exposes the internal implementation of a class.
15. Class inheritance is one of the main concepts of OOP.
16. When a class is inherited, it is called the "derived class".
17. A parent class automatically inherits all the methods and fields of the child class.

29.10 Review Exercises

Complete the following exercises.

1. Do the following
    i. Write a class named `Trigonometry` that includes
        a. a method named `square_area` that accepts the side of a square through its formal argument list and then calculates and returns its area.
        b. a method named `rectangle_area` that accepts the base and the height of a rectangle through its formal argument list and then calculates and returns its area.
        c. a method named `triangle_area` that accepts the base and the height of a triangle through its formal argument list and then calculates and returns its area. It is given that
        $$area = \frac{base \times height}{2}$$
    ii. Using the class cited above, write a Python program that prompts the user to enter the side of a rectangle, the base and the height of a parallelogram, and the base and the height of a triangle, and then displays the area for each one of them.

2. Do the following
    i. Write a class named `Pet` which includes
        a. a constructor
        b. an instance field named `kind`
        c. an instance field named `legs_number`
        d. a method named `start_running` that displays the message "Pet is running"
        e. a method named `stop_running` that displays the message "Pet stopped"
    ii. Write a Python program that creates two instances of the class `Pets` (for example, a dog and a monkey) and then calls some of their methods.

3. Do the following
    i. In the class `Pet` of the previous exercise
        a. alter the constructor to accept initial values for the instance fields `kind` and `legs_number` through its formal argument list.
        b. add a property named `kind`. It will be used to get and set the value of the private field `kind`. The setter must throw an error when the field is set to an empty value.
        c. add a property named `legs_number`. It will be used to get and set the value of the private field `legs_number`. The setter must throw an error when the field is set to a negative value.
    ii. Write a Python program that creates one instance of the class `Pets` (for example, a dog) and then calls both of its methods. Then try to set erroneous values for fields `kind` and `legs_number` and see what happens.

4. Do the following
    i. Write a class named Box that includes
        a. a constructor that accepts initial values for three instance fields named width, length, and height through its formal argument list.
        b. a method named display_volume that calculates and displays the volume of a box whose dimensions are width, length, and height. It is given that
        $$volume = width \times length \times height$$
        c. a method named display_dimensions that displays box's dimensions.
    ii. Using the class cited above, write a Python program that prompts the user to enter the dimensions of three boxes, and then displays their dimensions and their volume.
5. In the class Box of the previous exercise add three properties named width, length, and height. They will be used to get and set the values of the private fields width, length, and height. The setters must throw an error when the corresponding field is set to a negative value or zero.
6. Do the following
    i. Write a class named Cube that includes
        a. a constructor that accepts an initial value for an instance field named edge through its formal argument list.
        b. a method named display_volume that calculates and displays the volume of a cube whose edge length is edge. It is given that
        $$volume = edge^3$$
        c. a method named display_one_surface that calculates and displays the surface area of one side of a cube whose edge length is edge.
        d. a method named display_total_surface that calculates and displays the total surface area of a cube whose edge length is edge. It is given that
        $$total\ surface = 6 \times edge^2$$
    ii. Using the class cited above, write a Python program that prompts the user to enter the edge length of a cube, and then displays its volume, the surface area of one of its sides, and its total surface area.
7. In the class Cube of the previous exercise add a property named edge. It will be used to get and set the value of the private field edge. The setter must throw an error when the field is set to a negative value or zero.
8. Do the following
    i. Write a subprogram named display_menu that displays the following menu.
        1. Enter radius
        2. Display radius
        3. Display diameter
        4. Display area
        5. Display perimeter
        6. Exit

ii. Write a class named `Circle` that includes
   a. a constructor and a private field named `radius`.
   b. a property named `radius`. It will be used to get and set the value of the private field `radius`. The getter must throw an error when the field has not yet been set, and the setter must throw an error when the field is set to a negative value or zero.
   c. a method named `get_diameter` that calculates and returns the diameter of a circle whose radius is `radius`. It is given that
   $$diameter = 2 \times radius$$
   d. a method named `get_area` that calculates and returns the area of a circle whose radius is `radius`. It is given that
   $$area = 3.14 \times radius^2$$
   e. a method named `get_perimeter` that calculates and returns the perimeter of a circle whose radius is `radius`. It is given that
   $$perimeter = 2 \times 3.14 \times radius$$
iii. Using the subprogram and the class cited above, write a Python program that displays the previously mentioned menu and prompts the user to enter a choice (of 1 to 6). If choice 1 is selected, the program must prompt the user to enter a radius. If choice 2 is selected, the program must display the radius entered in choice 1. If choices 3, 4, or 5 are selected, the program must display the diameter, the area, or the perimeter correspondingly of a circle whose radius is equal to the radius entered in choice 1. The process must repeat as many times as the user wishes.

9. Assume that you work in a computer software company that is going to create a word processor application. You are assigned to write a class that will be used to provide information to the user.
   i. Write a class named `Info` that includes
      a. a constructor and a private field named `user_text`.
      b. a property named `user_text`. It will be used to get and set the value of the private field `user_text`. The setter must throw an error when the field is set to an empty value.
      c. a method named `get_spaces_count` that returns the total number of spaces that exist in property `user_text`.
      d. a method named `get_words_count` that returns the total number of words that exist in property `user_text`.
      e. a method named `get_vowels_count` that returns the total number of vowels that exist in property `user_text`.
      f. a method named `get_letters_count` that returns the total number of characters (excluding spaces) that exist in property `user_text`.
   ii. Using the class cited above, write a testing program that prompts the user to enter a text and then displays all available information. Assume that the user enters only space characters or letters (uppercase or lowercase) and the words are separated by a single space character.

   Hint: In a text of three words, there are two spaces, which means that the total number of words is one more than the total number of spaces. Count the total number of spaces, and then you can easily find the total number of words!

10. During the Cold War after World War II, messages were encrypted so that if the enemies intercepted them, they could not decrypt them without the decryption key. A very simple encryption algorithm is alphabetic rotation. The algorithm moves all letters N steps "up" in the alphabet, where N is the encryption key. For example, if the encryption key is 2, you can encrypt a message by replacing the letter A with the letter C, the letter B with the letter D, the letter C with the letter E, and so on. Do the following:

    i. Write a subprogram named `display_menu` that displays the following menu:
        1. Encryption/Decryption key
        2. Encrypt a message
        3. Decrypt a message
        4. Exit

    ii. Write a class named `EncryptDecrypt` that includes
        a. a constructor and a private field named `encr_decr_key`.
        b. a property named `encr_decr_key`. It will be used to get and set the value of the private field `encr_decr_key`. The getter must throw an error when the field has not yet been set, and the setter must throw an error when the field is not set to a value between 1 and 26.
        c. A method named `encrypt` that accepts a message through its formal argument list and then returns the encrypted message.
        d. A method named `decrypt` that accepts an encrypted message through its formal argument list and then returns the decrypted message.

    iii. Using the subprogram and the class cited above, write a Python program that displays the menu previously mentioned and then prompts the user to enter a choice (of 1 to 4).). If choice 1 is selected, the program must prompt the user to enter an encryption/decryption key. If choice 2 is selected, the program must prompt the user to enter a message and then display the encrypted message. If choice 2 is selected, the program must prompt the user to enter an encrypted message and then display the decrypted message. The process must repeat as many times as the user wishes. Assume that the user enters only lowercase letters or a space for the message.

29.11 Review Questions

Answer the following questions.

1. What is object-oriented programming?
2. What is the constructor of a class?
3. What does a decorator in Python?
4. When do you have to write a field name using dot notation?
5. What is the `self` keyword?
6. Explain the difference between a class variable and an instance variable.
7. Why a field should not be exposed in OOP?
8. What is meant by the term "class inheritance"?

Some Final Words from the Authors

We hope you really enjoyed reading this book. We made every possible effort to make it comprehensible even by people that probably have no previous experience in programming.

So if you liked this book, please visit the web store where you bought it and show us your gratitude by writing a good review and giving us as many stars as possible. By doing this, you will encourage us to continue writing and of course you'll help other readers to reach us.

And remember: Learning is a process within an endless loop structure. It begins at birth and continues throughout your lifetime!

Index

A

accumulate · 152, 193
actual argument list · 300, 301
algorithm · 33
alphanumeric · 43
and operator · 107
application software · 20
argument list · 300
arithmetic operations · 110
arithmetic operator · 56, 57, 110
assignment operator · 182

B

backslash · 257
base class · 336
Beaufort Francis · 142
Beaufort scale · 142
BMI · 84, 317
Body Mass Index · 84, 317
Boolean · 43
Boolean expression · 119, 129, 155, 182
Boolean expressions · 105, 106
bootstrap loader · 20
break out of the loop · 184, 185
bugs · 37
built-in · 291, 295, 296, 312

C

caller · 295, 299, 303
Celsius · 83
chaining · 97
character · 43
child class · 336
class · 319
class field · 326
class instance · 321
class object · 321
code · 22
code editor · 22
command · 33
commands · 19
comments · 37, 81
comparison operations · 110
comparison operator · 110
comparison operators · 105, 186
compiler · 21, 22, 25, 26, 44
compilers · 37
complex Boolean expression · 107, 110
compound assignment operators · 58, 182
computer program · 34
concatenation · 60
concatenation assignment · 60
constructor · 322
Corrado Böhm · 81

D

data input · 34, 51, 82
data processing · 34, 82
data structures · 239
debugger · 26
debugging · 37
decision structure · 81, 105, 119, 129, 278
Decision Structures · 233
declaration · 44
decorators · 331
default argument values · 304
default precedence · 110
definite · 155
definite loop · 165
definite loop structure · 151
del() · 260, 261
derived class · 336
device driver software · 20
dictionary · 256, 261, 262
division-by-zero · 169

E

Eclipse · 26, 27, 35
element · 240
elif · 136
ellipsis · 17
empty dictionary · 256
empty list · 243
end a loop · 184
endless iterations · 185
endless loop · 185
equal · 105
execute · 68, 77

exponentiation operator · 56

F

Fahrenheit · 198
find() · 96, 99
finite · 33
finite sequence · 33
flag · 277
float() · 87
floats · 43
for · 165
for structure · 165
formal argument list · 300, 301
from inner to outer · 186, 231
frozensets · 240
fsum() · 88, 250, 253
function · 295
functions · 291

G

get method · 328
Giuseppe Jacopini · 81
global · 306
global scope · 305
Grace Hopper · 37
greater than · 105
greater than or equal to · 105

H

hardware · 19
hash character · 37, 81

I

IDE · 26, 27
IDEs · 36
IDLE · 26, 35, 65
`if` Structure · 119
if-elif structure · 145, 147, 194
`if-elif` Structure · 135
if-else structure · 129, 130, 145, 147
immutable · 244, 248, 256, 258, 263
indefinite loop · 155
indefinite loop structure · 151
indentation · 120
index · 92, 240, 242
index position · 240

infinite loop · 185
instance field · 326
instantiation · 320, 321
instruction · 33
instructions · 19
int() · 85
integer · 43, 85
Integrated Development Environment · 25, 26
interpreter · 22, 25, 26, 44
interpreters · 37
iterate · 151, 165, 248
iterate forever · 185
iterates · 157, 158, 184
iteration · 155

K

Kelvin · 198
keyword · 35, 36
keyword arguments · 304

L

len() · 96, 100, 261
less than · 105
less than or equal to · 105
list · 240
list of arguments · 295, 299
local scope · 305
logic error · 36
logical operations · 110
logical operator · 107, 110
logical operators · 107
loop structure · 81, 151
lower() · 97

M

machine language · 21
main code · 299, 302, 312
math module · 88, 89
mathematical function · 85
matrices · 240
max() · 86, 261
maximum · 122, 261, 280
maximum value · 86
membership operator · 109, 110
min() · 86, 262
minimum · 122, 262, 280
minimum value · 86
modular programming · 292

module · 66, 292
multiplication table · 186
mutable · 240, 248, 326, 327

N

named argument · 305
negative index · 245
negative indexes · 92, 94
nested · 145, 147, 186, 187
nested decision structure · 145, 252
nested loop · 173
nesting · 100
not equal · 105
not operator · 109
number of characters · 96
number of elements · 261
number to string · 97

O

object-oriented programming · 319
objects · 319, 320
operating system · 20
or operator · 108

P

parent class · 336
parentheses · 57
pass value · 295, 297, 300
portion of a string · 94
precedence rule · 57, 110
private variable · 330
problem · 33
procedural programming · 292, 319
procedure · 299
procedures · 291
product · 160, 192
program · 19
programmer · 19, 34
property · 330
Python project · 71

R

random · 87
random module · 88
random word · 99
randrange() · 87, 98, 100

range · 87
range() · 87
real · 43, 87
region of interest · 112, 114
replace() · 96
reserved word · 35, 47
results output · 34, 82
runtime error · 36

S

scope of a variable · 305
selection structure · 105
sequence of integers · 87, 166
sequence structure · 81
set method · 328
sets · 240
simple Boolean expression · 105
simple Boolean expressions · 107, 108
simultaneous assignment · 56
slice · 245
slicing · 94, 245, 251, 255
sort() · 262
sorted() · 263
sorting · 262
source code · 22, 26, 27, 36, 65, 67, 71
spaghetti code · 292
sqrt() · 89
square root · 89
statements · 19, 33
str() · 97
string · 43, 48
string position · 96
string replacement · 96
strings · 91, 240
structured programming · 81
subclass · 336
subprogram · 85, 291
substring notation · 92
sum · 88, 156, 158, 191
superclass · 336
syntax error · 36
syntax errors · 69, 78
System software · 20

T

tab character · 51, 187
tab stop · 51
three main stages · 34, 82
three parties · 34
truth table · 108, 109

tuple · 244
Turtle · 203

U

ultimate rule · 182, 195, 196, 199, 314
unit · 291
upper() · 97, 196
user · 34
user-defined function · 295
user-friendly · 52
utility software · 20

V

value assignment operator · 55
variable · 41

W

wavy red line · 36, 79
while structure · 155
William Shakespeare · 115

More of our Books

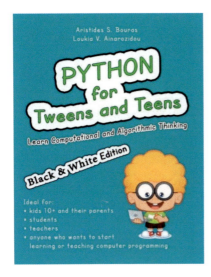

ISBN-10: 1546611215
ISBN-13: 978-1546611219

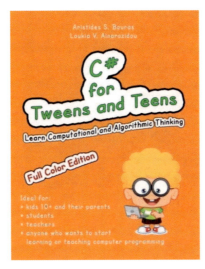

ISBN-10: 1973727684
ISBN-13: 978-1973727682

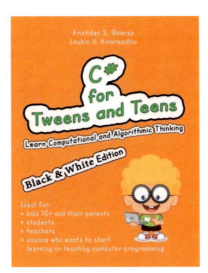

ISBN-10: 1973727765
ISBN-13: 978-1973727767

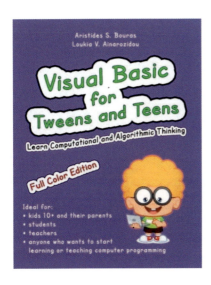

ISBN-10: 1982083670
ISBN-13: 978-1982083670

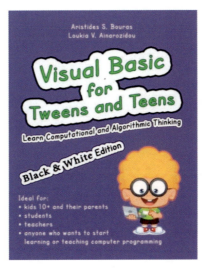

ISBN-10: 1982083697
ISBN-13: 978-1982083694

ISBN-10: 1514802163
ISBN-13: 978-1514802168

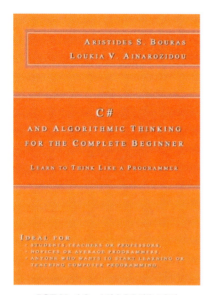

ISBN-10: 1508952485
ISBN-13: 978-1508952480

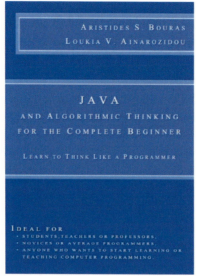

ISBN-10: 1506179398
ISBN-13: 978-1506179391

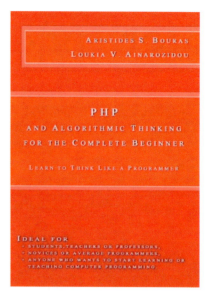

ISBN-10: 1503015912
ISBN-13: 978-1503015913

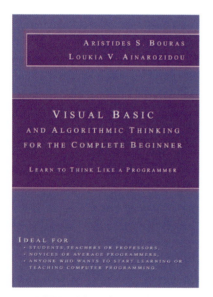

ISBN-10: 1511798963
ISBN-13: 978-1511798969

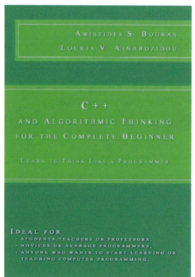

ISBN-10: 1508577552
ISBN-13: 978-1508577553

RCode: 180213

Made in the USA
Columbia, SC
06 August 2019